Making Human Capital Analytics Work

MEASURING THE ROI OF HUMAN
CAPITAL PROCESSES AND OUTCOMES

Patricia Pulliam Phillips, PhD
President and CEO, ROI Institute

Jack J. Phillips, PhD
Chairman, ROI Institute

New York   Chicago   San Francisco   Athens   London   Madrid
Mexico City   Milan   New Delhi   Singapore   Sydney   Toronto

1 2 3 4 5 6 7 8 9 0   DOC/DOC   1 2 0 9 8 7 6 5 4

ISBN   978-0-07-184020-0
MHID   0-07-184020-6

e-ISBN   978-0-07-184062-1
e-MHID   0-07-184062-1

Library of Congress Cataloging-in-Publication Data
Phillips, Patricia Pulliam.
  Making human capital analytics work : measuring the ROI of human capital processes and outcomes / Jack J. Phillips. — 1 Edition.
    pages cm
  ISBN 978-0-07-184020-0 (hardback : alk. paper) — ISBN 0-07-184020-6 1. Human capital. 2. Personnel management. I. Phillips, Jack J. II. Title.
  HD4904.7.P485 2014
  658.3'01—dc23   2014014770

McGraw-Hill Education books are available at special quantity discounts to use as premiums and sales promotions or for use in corporate training programs. To contact a representative, please visit the Contact Us pages at www.mhprofessional.com.

Dedicated to
Dr. Jac Fitz-enz

The Father of Human Capital Analytics

A professional colleague, mentor, business
partner, and personal friend

Contents

| CONTENTS

CHAPTER 11   **Report Results and Drive Improvement**   255

CHAPTER 12   **Manage and Sustain the Human Capital Analytics Practice**   273

Notes   291

Index   295

Preface

SNEAK PREVIEW

Making Human Capital Analytics Work: Measuring the ROI of Human Capital Processes and Outcomes provides useful, practical tools for HR managers and specialists to show the value of HR. Written in an easy-to-understand format, this new book shows how HR managers can apply analytics by developing relationships between variables, predicting the success of HR programs, determining the cost of intangibles that are hard to value, showing the business value of particular HR programs, and calculating and forecasting the ROI of various HR projects and programs. This comprehensive book focuses on three types of analytics: descriptive, predictive, and prescriptive. It also shows how to measure the success of various HR programs with a financial ROI.

Making Human Capital Analytics Work describes how human capital professionals can develop actionable information from data generated through their analytics practice. It will be an indispensable guide for the HR team as they show the value of what they do and their connection to the business. This book is not just about data collection and analysis, but a template to change the mind-set and influence of the team, focusing on results throughout the process. It shows how to use data to drive decisions and build support for the HR function through the use of analytics. In summary, it is a valuable addition to the library of anyone involved in and supporting the HR function and human capital programs.

STATUS OF HR

Although human capital is important to executives, the HR function is not always viewed as a viable contributor to the organization. According to *The*

Economist, the HR budget is often cut more than budgets of other functions during tough economic times. Many would argue, including us, that it should probably be increased during those times; it is those times in which a strategic focus on people can truly make a difference. HR is often the basis of jokes, Dilbert cartoons, and watercooler horror stories. Some view the HR team as a company police force, concerned more with compliance than strategy. According to Jack Welch, the most admired CEO of all time, some of his colleagues see HR as a "health and happiness slide show."

In an effort to demonstrate its importance, HR often focuses on transactional activities such as benefits administration and compliance investigations. However, the transactional parts of HR are being (or have been) automated, outsourced, or transferred to other parts of the organization. With this shift, HR becomes principally administrative, focusing on developing, revising, and administering policy. This administrative focus can cause many organizations to dismiss HR altogether. For example, J. Craig Mundy suggests that HR no longer needs to be a function in an organization but rather it should be a part of every manager's job.[1]

Although this scenario appears dismal, on the bright side, showing and proving the value of the HR function can have significant implications. Organizations cited as most admired and the best places to work reach this status, in part, because of top executive support of HR. This support occurs when HR demonstrates business value. Research continues to show that investment in HR programs often correlates with increased productivity, profitability, customer satisfaction, and even share price for publicly traded companies. So value in HR exists. The question is: How can HR demonstrate value in terms that resonate with key executives and influence their decision making?

WHAT'S NEEDED

HR executives, managers, and specialists need a set of tools to show how to connect HR to the business, how to predict the value of HR projects and programs, and how to optimize the value of human capital. On a practical basis, HR executives need to know how to place monetary value on the hard-to-value measures, such as employee engagement, job satisfaction, conflict, stress, and teamwork. In addition, it is helpful to understand relationships between different variables, taking the mystery out of what is causing low productivity, inadequate quality, delayed processes, and excessive costs. Sometimes a need to predict outcomes (e.g., which employees are most likely to stay with an organization, which ones have high potential, which ones are prone to accidents) is evident. Finally, the business value, including the financial ROI, of HR programs needs to be shown in a practical, rational way using that data to optimize the contribution of the HR function.

OUR EXPERIENCE

Making Human Capital Analytics Work is a combination of much research, study, and practice on analytics. It also represents a culmination of many other books we have written as we tackle the challenge of making analytics work in organizations. We became interested in analytics many years ago. In 1973, Jack devoted his master's thesis to a project to show the value and success of a cooperative education program at Lockheed Martin as he pursued a master's in decision science, a program in business analytics at the business school at Georgia State University. In 1987 at the University of Alabama, he devoted his PhD dissertation to develop an HR effectiveness index. In this research, he found significant correlations between the index (comprised of six HR measures) and the productivity and profitability of 72 firms. This study showed the relationship between investing in human capital and the corresponding outcomes.

Patti's master's research examined the impact of cultural differences found in U.S. and Japanese organizations based in Thailand, as she pursued her master's in public and private management in 1996. Her research included a look at the relationship between indicators of cultural differences among employees and how those differences contributed to or detracted from productive work. Her PhD dissertation in 2003 focused on the use of measurement and evaluation, including often challenging analytics processes, in government—particularly the federal government.

We are both fascinated by the study of relationships between variables and how they connect and predict outcomes. We are especially interested in how to use those relationships to make decisions within organizations.

We have approached this topic in our work. Jack served as director of learning and development for two firms and head of HR at three firms, including a Fortune 500 firm. Ultimately, he served in senior executive roles, including president and chief operating officer of a regional Federal Savings Bank. During those years, Jack sought to make connections, showing the value of HR in terms that executives could appreciate and understand. In return, his HR programs enjoyed success and received excellent funding, support, and commitment, often the by-product of an effective human capital analytics process.

Patti used analytics in various roles during her tenure at a large electric utility company. There, she and her colleagues were involved in measuring client satisfaction, conducting market research, and forecasting and modeling the impact of various rate plans.

For the past 20 years, the ROI Institute has focused directly on this issue, showing the value of different solutions and programs. Through the ROI Institute, we have been able to teach thousands of individuals how to connect the dots and make a difference with human capital analytics. Along the way, we have had the pleasure of writing more than 50 books that support analytics in some way. The good news is that this new book is a culmination of those efforts distilled in one volume, with tips on how to make it work for the organization. It depicts the fascinating journey we've experienced and still enjoy as we work with organizations in more than 60 countries.

THE AUDIENCE

The principal audience for this book includes HR managers, executives, directors, coordinators, and advisors in medium to large organizations. Target organizations include private businesses, governments, nonprofits, educational institutions, healthcare firms, and nongovernmental organizations (NGOs). For any organization with a formal HR function, this book will prove a helpful guide for HR leaders to show the value of HR.

The second audience is executives who fund and request human capital projects and programs. These "ultimate clients" want to see the business value of investing in human capital. This book will encourage them in terms of what's possible and provide tips, techniques, and strategies to create, fund, and support a productive analytics practice in the organization.

A third audience includes the analysts who often execute studies, collect data, provide the analysis, write the report, and communicate the results. For these analytics practitioners, this book will be an indispensable guide, providing tools, templates, and tips to make analytics work.

A fourth audience includes managers in support roles, not within HR. They are concerned about the HR contribution and are interested in analytics projects or studies. This book offers insight and information for those in support roles. It shows them what is possible through HR analytics and projects.

The fifth audience includes those who have an external role to support human capital/HR accountability—consultants, professors, researchers, and analysts who track the HR function, assist the HR function, or collect data and provide services around HR. This audience should find this book a helpful tool to explore what must be accomplished to show the value of this important function.

ACKNOWLEDGMENTS

No book represents the work of the authors alone, and this book is no exception. Much of what we are presenting here we have learned from working with key clients in all types of organizations. For 20 years, we have been able to assist organizations of all types, including businesses, governments, nongovernmental organizations, universities, hospitals, not-for-profit foundations, and charitable trusts. Our clients often let us experiment as we tackle problems and opportunities. We have learned much from them. Over a 20-year period, we have enjoyed more than 500 consulting assignments.

We owe much appreciation and indebtedness to Jac Fitz-enz, a friend and colleague. We consider Jac not only the father of human capital, as he has often been labeled, but the father of human capital analytics. In the 1970s as an HR manager for an iron and steel company, Jack Phillips sent his benefits manager to attend a workshop, "Quantifying Personnel's Return on Investment," sponsored by the American Society for Personnel Administration (now SHRM). Jac conducted the workshop and was well into this process of measuring HR, understanding the dynamics of the different measures and variables. Jac became a great friend and served on Jack's PhD dissertation committee in the mid-1980s. Since then, we have developed a strong partnership, including the creation of the Certified Human Capital Analytics Professional Program. We owe much to the great work of Jac.

Outside of the human capital area, we want to acknowledge the work of Tom Davenport. We credit Tom with bringing the analytics issue to the top executives. Through his work, including several publications, he convinced executives that it was time to invest heavily in this area and showed them how the investment would reap many returns. In addition to Jac and Tom, dozens, if not hundreds, of professionals have worked in the area of human capital analytics, completing projects, making progress, speaking on the subject, and writing books about it. We have learned from them as we have read their materials, listened to their work, and exchanged information along the way. Although we may be competitors in some sense, we are all working on the same issue, to make human capital analytics the fulcrum that supports human capital and the HR function as the strategic lever it can be.

Thanks also go to our team at the ROI Institute. Several individuals have played important roles as we developed this book. Special thanks to Belinda Keith, communications manager, for her efforts to develop this manuscript. Belinda managed to fit this task into a very busy schedule. Also, thanks to Rebecca Benton Henderson, publications manager, who performed her usual great job on final editing and juggling several book projects at the same time. Finally, we thank Hope Nicholas, director of publications, for putting the final touches to the manuscript. Thanks to all of you.

Jack J. Phillips, PhD, and Patti P. Phillips, PhD

CHAPTER 1

The Case for a Logical Approach to Analytics

Human capital analytics has evolved from a patchwork of various studies and processes into an important function in an organization's human capital practice. This chapter examines the challenges of human capital analytics as well as the benefits of building an effective human capital analytics practice. It describes the progress organizations are making as the practice of analytics continues to advance and mature. The chapter also demonstrates the need for a systematic, rational, and logical way to approach the analytics process so that it can efficiently and effectively satisfy all stakeholders' needs, particularly those of top executives, including the chief financial officer.

OPENING STORY

For many years, General Electric (GE) focused on quantitative methods and mathematical processes. The company even developed an important series of books on mathematical models for management in the 1960s.[1] In one project GE attempted to show how HR could affect plant productivity and profitability.[2] An analysis of variables that affect productivity and profits revealed the eight important variables that were tracked by the HR department in a particular plant. Among those variables were:

1. **Accidents** (Excessive accidents are disruptive and decrease productivity.)

2. **Employee turnover** (Excessive turnover is disruptive operationally and increases costs.)

3. **Unplanned absences** (Excessive unplanned absences are disruptive, as work days are lost.)

4. **Grievances** (Excessive grievances reduce productivity because they often affect morale of the employees. Grievances often stem from problems in the organization that block or inhibit productivity.)

5. **Initial dispensary visits** (Unnecessary first aid visits disrupt operations and increase costs.)

The HR team tracked these measures and developed a mathematical relationship between these measures and productivity. A composite score of these variables became known as the employee relations index (ERI). The indicators were combined by means of a multiple regression formula with the variables receiving different weights. Constants were added depending on the level of the variable in a plant and for the particular plant or group in question. According to its users, the ERI was intended to help managers evaluate policies and practices, track trends in employee relations, find trouble spots, perform human relations duties more effectively, and control HR costs. Index values were compared with plant profitability (ratio of net income before taxes to capital investment). Although the plants with the higher ERIs were the most profitable ones, the relationship was not statistically significant. The interesting aspect of this study is the date. It was conducted in the 1950s and published in the *Harvard Business Review* in 1955.

In today's human capital analytics terminology, this study was based on a classic predictive model where the independent variables (i.e., accidents, grievances, absenteeism, first aid visits, and turnover) predict a dependent variable of plant profitability. Perhaps, if the researchers had used gross productivity (revenue per employee) instead of plant profitability, a significant connection (and causal relationship) could have been developed. In the

1950s this project wasn't labeled *analytics*, it was simply referred to as the development of an ERI index. This study underscores the deep roots of the concept of analytics. Yet, for some people, analytics is the new big thing.

THE EXPANDED ROLE OF HUMAN CAPITAL

The press is exploding with coverage of human capital. The number of documents produced containing the term *human capital* increased from almost 700 in 1993 to more than 8,000 in 2003, and topping 25,000 in 2013. This growth in coverage emphasizes the importance of human capital in the management of organizations.

In The Conference Board 2013 CEO Challenge, 729 CEOs provided input into their most pressing issues.[3] Human capital was the number one issue from a global perspective. An earlier study conducted by IBM in 2012,[4] "Leading Through Connections: Insights from the Global Chief Executive Officer," also identified human capital as the number one issue. A total of 1,700 CEOs were involved in this study. Even though the term *human capital* is commonplace in organizations, management's role in this important resource is often unclear. This lack of clarity lends to the mystery of human capital where investment in this resource now commands much executive time and attention.

The concept of human capital is not new. Economists have used it as far back as Adam Smith in the eighteenth century. Economists who specialize in human capital theory have won Nobel Prizes; Gary Becker is perhaps the most well known. Human capital theory explores the ways individuals and society drive economic benefits from investment in people.

The management community has a broader view of human capital. For example, *The Human Resources Glossary* defines human capital as the return an organization gains from the loyalty, creativity, effort, accomplishments, and productivity of its employees.[5] It equates to, and may actually exceed, the productive capacity of machine capital and investment in research and development.

Human capital represents the relationship between what organizations invest in employees and the organization's emerging success. The *relationship* to success is the mystery. Imagine this scenario. The CEO of a $5-billion-revenue company proposes to its board of directors that the company make an investment of $1.8 billion for the coming year. When describing the investment, the CEO is optimistic that the returns will follow, although he does not know how much of a return will be realized and cannot estimate it reliably. However, he is confident that the investment is needed and that it will pay off for the company. The executive explains that this investment, which represents almost 40 percent of its revenues, is based on benchmarked data that show other firms are making similar investments. Even when the investment is made and the consequences are realized, the CEO suggests that the value of this investment may still be unknown; but nevertheless, he asks for the money.

The investment in question is the investment in human capital. As extreme as it may seem, this scenario plays out in organizations each year as they invest in their workforce. Budget approvals are granted on faith, assuming that the requested investment will pay off. Far too much mystery shrouds the connection between the investment in employees and the success that follows. Human capital analytics can make this connection.

STRUGGLES OF THE HUMAN RESOURCES FUNCTION

Despite the importance of human capital, the ambiguity surrounding investment in it, and the lack of progress in measuring it properly, the human resources function has had its share of criticism in recent years. Almost two decades ago, a major article in *Fortune* magazine essentially said the HR function was irrelevant.[6] Thomas Stewart, the respected *Fortune* editor who wrote the article, said that HR function should be eliminated and the essential transactions should be performed by other functions or outsourced altogether. As the author bluntly described the situation, "Chances are its leaders are unable to describe their contribution to value added except in trendy, unquantifiable, and wannabe terms. . . . I am describing your human resource department and have a modest proposal: Why not blow it up?" Stewart reached this conclusion, in part, because HR had failed to show its value.

Although some may argue that this view is extreme, the article served as a wake-up call for HR executives looking for a better way to show value in the organization; that is, to show the contribution of the human resource function. This book shows how evidence of value is being calculated.

As critics ask for more measurement and accountability, the HR function has been under pressure, internally, to show value. Because the investment is quite large, many top executives ask HR executives to show the contribution to avoid budget cuts. In some cases, managers must demonstrate contribution in order to increase the budget or fund specific projects. When funding occurs, executives want to see the actual return. However compassionate executives are about people and the role of people in the organization, they are also driven by the need to generate profits, enhance resource allocation, build a successful, viable organization, and survive in the long term. The philosophy of caring for employees and striving for results appears, to some, to be counterintuitive. It is not. Caring and accountability work together, as will be demonstrated many times in this book.

The typical human resource reaction to this movement toward HR accountability has been unimpressive. HR has resisted the call for additional accountability in many ways. Some argue that people are not widgets, so they cannot be counted in the same way as products. Some consider the issue of accountability inappropriate and maintain that we should not attempt to analyze the role of people with financial concepts. They argue that the issues are too "soft," and much of what is invested in human capital will have to be taken on faith; investments must be made based on the intuition, logic, and what others have invested. Still other executives simply do not know how to address this issue. They are not as familiar with the organization as they should be, lack the necessary knowledge in operations and finance, and are unprepared for this type of challenge. Their backgrounds do not include assignments in which measurement and accountability are critical to success. Some do not understand the measurement issue and what can and should be done.

The signs indicate that resistance is diminishing. The focus on human capital analytics is contributing to a paradigm shift as human capital measurement and investment take on a new life. Table 1-1 illustrates this paradigm shift from the traditional view of human capital to the present view.

These shifts are dramatic for the human resources function. They underscore how the HR function is moving from an activity-based process to a results-based process, as new data evolve to show the importance of

TABLE 1-1 Human Capital Perspectives

Traditional View	Present View
Human capital expenses are considered costs.	Human capital expenditures are viewed as a source of value.
The HR function is perceived as a support staff.	The HR function is perceived as a strategic partner.
HR is involved in setting the HR budget.	Top executives are increasingly involved in allocating HR budget.
Human capital metrics focus on cost and activities.	Human capital metrics focus on results.
Human capital metrics are created and maintained by HR alone.	Top executives are involved in the design and use of metrics.
Little effort is made to understand the return on investment in human capital.	The use of ROI has become an important tool to understand cause-and-effect relationships.
Human capital measurement focuses on data at hand.	Human capital measurement focuses on the data needed.
Human capital measurement is based on what GE and IBM are measuring.	Human capital measurement is based on what is needed in the organization.
HR programs are initiated without a business need connected to them.	HR programs are linked to specific business needs before implementation.
Overall reporting on human capital programs and projects is input focused.	Overall reporting on human capital programs and projects is output focused.

human resources and its connection with business results. Human capital analytics makes this possible.

THE CFO'S PERSPECTIVE

When investments are made, the chief financial officer (CFO) takes notice. Typically, the CFO is involved in investment decisions such as predicting them up front, auditing the success afterward, and reporting them to top executives, directors, and shareholders. However, the concept of human capital places the CFO in an awkward position. CFOs realize that companies make a heavy investment in this area. Yet, few finance or accounting executives understand it in any detail or know how the investment creates value for the business. Studies conducted by *CFO Magazine* show that less than 20 percent of companies surveyed say they have little more than a moderate understanding of the return on human capital investments.[7] In many organizations, then, traditionally accepted finance and accounting practices cannot be used for their largest investment, human capital. Despite the CFO's emerging role as the chief resource allocator who helps direct the resources to the most productive investment, human capital remains a vast area of spending where the finance function offers little insight beyond guidance on what the company can afford to spend. Here is where a human capital analytics function, sponsored or supported by the CFO, can make a difference.

THE LAST MAJOR SOURCE OF COMPETITIVE EDGE

Most executives realize the importance of human capital in some way. They understand the fact that the other sources of capital in the organization such as finance, technology, and access to markets are basically the same, regardless of the organization. One particular organization does not necessarily have a unique access to the other types of capital. The differentiator of most organizations is human capital, thus making it the last source of competitive advantage. It is the people and how the organization attracts, maintains, motivates, and retains the knowledge, skills, and creative capability of those employees that drive organizational success. Without a doubt, human capital is critical; but in today's environment, a greater understanding of it is essential in order to make the appropriate investment.

BARRIERS TO CHANGE

Several important barriers prevent organizations from treating human capital as a true investment. First is the failure to "walk the talk." In brochures, handbooks, manuals, and HR programs, executives proudly proclaim employees as their greatest asset, but they do not necessarily walk the talk. They treat employees as expenditures and investments in employees as expenses in the organization, quickly trimming employee numbers to save costs and to drive revenue.

The second barrier is ownership: Who actually owns human capital management? For many years, it has been the human resource function.

Executives have turned to HR to claim ownership for and make improvements in this important area. However, for the human capital investment to be successful, it must be owned by the entire organization and managed by the senior executives. HR managers and senior executives must take a role in assuring that proper solutions are in place, the appropriate measures are tracked, and improvement is generated. It also means that chief financial officers and operating executives all have important roles in this process to ensure that it functions properly.

The third major barrier to change is the failure to consider the dynamics of the human capital investment. A variety of programs and projects are often implemented with little or no concern about how they affect various parts of the organization. Sometimes, projects even work in conflict with each other. Too much focus has gone toward activities, programs, and projects and not enough attention given to the outcomes, integration, success, and ultimate accountability.

A fourth major barrier is the lack of appropriate measurements. Executives who are concerned about the human capital investment do not have a clear understanding of what can be measured, what should be measured, and what is being measured. More important, they fail to recognize the connection between those measures and the success of the organization; or if a particular program or project is implemented to improve a particular measure, how to develop accountability around that project or program. A fully functioning human capital analytics team can help remove these barriers.

A HISTORY OF HUMAN CAPITAL ANALYTICS

HR's need for data to influence decision making dates back to the 1920s when personnel research set the stage for the development of measures of HR's activities and performance. In the 1940s and 1950s, about the time HR became a legitimate and essential part of organizations, practitioners and researchers began to explore ways of measuring its contribution. In the years that followed, HR practitioners wrestled with measuring contribution and using data as a strategic lever. By the late 1970s, data collection and analysis became a routine part of some HR departments. Considerable advancements in measurement and evaluation took place in the 1980s. The 1990s saw more growth in this area. Since

FIGURE 1-1   HR Accountability Progress: The Evolution of Analytics

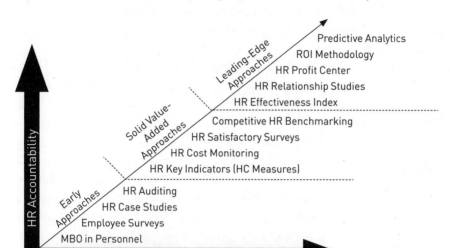

2000, much progress has been made with HR relationship studies (macro), ROI analysis (micro), and predictive analytics.

Without question, the HR function, which includes a variety of activities, does contribute to organization success; the difficulty lies in selecting the right combination of measures and the best approach to develop an adequate analytics practice. When examining the history of ways in which organizations address this issue, the approaches vary, with some clearly more effective than others. Figure 1-1 shows the progression of approaches used to demonstrate HR's influence on organization success. Each one adds to the body of work, although overlap is present in the techniques, processes, and focus of some approaches. A detailed comparison of these approaches is available in numerous other publications, including www.roiinstitute.net.

HUMAN CAPITAL ANALYTICS MATURITY

As reported in The State of Human Capital 2012 report titled, "False Summit: Why the Human Capital Function Still Has Far to Go," human capital analytics is the linchpin of human capital investments.[8] While organizations are embracing some of the tried-and-true approaches as described in the previous section, others have matured to a higher level of analytics by investing in capacity building through hiring and developing skills as well as taking advantage of technology. Also, the business questions driving the need for HR to advance with analytics are changing.

The Conference Board 2011–2012 Human Capital Analytics (HCA) Research Working Group researched how organizations progress along the analytics continuum. Using the MIT Sloan Management Review/IBM Institute for Business Value research as the foundation for their own, the HCA Research Working Group developed a maturity model that reflects how HR functions advance in their human capital analytics practice. The HCA Research Working Group found that maturity occurs as organizations identify challenges and opportunities and apply various frameworks and techniques and ultimately align key measures to business outcomes. Successful maturity requires that HR professionals have a clear strategic context and engage with their key stakeholders. Even though an organization may reach the highest level of analytics maturity, it will always experience a need for the less mature practices. Organizations can identify with any position on a maturity model with the true measure of progress defined by the human capital professional's ability to traverse the ever-changing analytics terrain.

Human capital analytics maturity includes three types of analytics. Figure 1-2 on page 13 depicts these types of analytics along a maturity continuum. Each type of analytics answers different business questions.

DESCRIPTIVE ANALYTICS

Descriptive analytics is the most fundamental level of analytics. It answers questions such as "What happened, and what is happening now?" Data from this type of analysis describe the conditions, people, and events as they were in the past or as they exist today. Descriptive analytics provides information useful in assessing the extent to which an organization is meeting its goals, as well as the extent to which employers are attracting the right candidates. An example of the use of descriptive analytics is the application of comprehensive talent assessments describing job requirements, pre-assessments, and post-assessments that give organizations information on their workforce, which they can then benchmark against others.

At a solution level, descriptive analytics help determine the value of programs as well as provide suggestions as to how to improve programs so that they can provide greater value. Descriptive data are often captured on scorecards and dashboards so that HR leaders and professionals can easily describe to stakeholders essential HR measures as well as connections to business measures that reflect the investment in human capital.

PREDICTIVE ANALYTICS

As mentioned earlier, over the past decades, efforts have been made to develop statistical relationships between key HR measures and organization performance measures. Using historical or existing data as the basis, predictive analytics moves the human capital practice further so that HR leaders can answer questions such as "What could happen, and when could it happen?" Data from predictive analytics describe conditions, people, and events as they could be in the future and when they are likely to be that way. It is useful in helping organizations determine possible outcomes of particular HR activities and influences the decisions of stakeholders.

Jac Fitz-enz's work places predictive analytics in the forefront of the human capital conversation. Since 2008, his HCM:21 model has evolved into a six-step approach that refines analysis and suggests effective actions.[9] His six steps include:

1. Assess the situation: external and internal.

2. Identify a key business opportunity.

3. Find the factors or forces that drive it.

4. Determine the scope: local or organization-wide.

5. Design an intervention or invest.

6 Evaluate, recycle, or move on.

PRESCRIPTIVE ANALYTICS

The ultimate level of maturity with human capital analytics is in prescriptive analytics. This form of analytics helps organizations answer questions such as "What is the best course of action?" Prescriptive analytics combines predictions in decision making while taking into account the impact of those decisions. It describes what is possible given particular factors and what courses of action would be optimal given all the potential combinations of options and outcomes. An example of prescriptive analytics can be found in the literature on workforce optimization. In The Conference Board's 2014 research report, "Human Capital Analytics @ Work, Volume 1," ABM, with the help of Mercer, developed a workforce optimization model that describes the optimum number of employees and activities a manager can handle and still drive profitability for ABM.[10]

Figure 1-2 depicts The Conference Board's Human Capital Analytics Maturity Model as developed by the HCA Research Working Group. This model does not suggest that one level of maturity is better or worse than another. It simply demonstrates the continuum along which organizations are moving as they advance their human capital analytics practice. This book is an effort to help organizations develop along this progression.

TYPES OF DATA

Although most organizations use some approach to placing similar types of measures together, a logical data categorization framework is needed that uses levels of data, recognizing that the next level is usually more valuable than the previous level from the perspective of the senior executive group. These levels are depicted in Figure 1-3.

Level 0 represents the Input to a solution and details the numbers of people and hours, the focus, and the cost of the solution. These data represent the activity around a human capital investment rather than the contribution of the solution. Level 0 data indicate the scope of the effort, the degree of commitment, and the support for a particular solution. For some, this information equates to value. However, commitment as defined by expenditures is not evidence that the organization is reaping value.

The next level is Reaction. It details how employees, associates, members, and other individuals connected to the organization react to a particular solution or project. These data, such as relevance, importance to success, appropriateness, usefulness, and intent to use, are important. They represent perceived value of a solution from the perspective of those involved in it in some way. These data are important, because adverse reaction is often a clear indication that nothing will come of the solution—it will serve merely as an expense rather than an investment. For example, an employee referral as a recruiting source can be successful or unsuccessful, based on the reaction of employees to that solution. If they think it is valuable and important, and it is rewarding for them to make the referral,

FIGURE 1-2 Human Capital Analytics Maturity

Analytics Maturity

Organizations mature along a continuum of three levels of analytics capability.

Business Alignment

The three key elements to achieving Descriptive, Predictive, or Prescriptive Analytics

1 CHALLENGE/OPPORTUNITY
- *Strategic Context*
- *Origin (how it was identified)*
- *Identify & Engage Stakeholders*

2 FRAMEWORKS/METRICS
- *Approach & Techniques*
- *Refine Stakeholder Management*

3 BUSINESS ALIGNMENT & OUTCOME
- *Ongoing Stakeholder Engagement*

TRANSFORMED

PRESCRIBE
(What should happen?)

PREDICT
(What could happen?)

DESCRIBE
(What happened/
What is happening)

EXPERIENCED

PREDICT
(What could happen?)

DESCRIBE
(What happened/
What is happening)

ASPIRATIONAL

DESCRIBE
(What happened/
What is happening)

Source: This graphic representation was designed by several members of the Research Working Group. The concept of the three levels of analytics capability is adopted from: Steve LaValle, Eric Lesser, Rebecca Shockley, Michael S. Hopkins, and Nina Kruschwitz, "Big Data, Analytics, and the Path from Insights to Value," *MIT Sloan Management Review 62*, no. 2 (2011) 21–32. Fitz-enz, J. Phillips, P. and Ray, R. (2012) *Human Capital Analytics: A Primer. The Conference Board.* Research Report R-1500-12-RR. p. 15. Used with permission.

FIGURE 1-3 Types and Levels of Data

Level	Measurement Focus	Typical Measures
0 Inputs	Inputs into the solution, including indicators representing scope, volumes, costs, and efficiencies	Types of topics Number of programs Number of people Hours of involvement Costs
1 Reaction	Reaction to the solution, including the perceived value of the project	Relevance Importance Usefulness Appropriateness Intent to use Motivational
2 Learning	Learning how to use the solution, including the confidence to use what was learned	Skills Knowledge Capacity Competencies Confidences Contacts
3 Application and Implementation	Use of solution and materials in the work environment, including progress with implementation	Extent of use Task completion Frequency of use Actions completed Success with use Barriers to use Enablers to use
4 Impact	Consequences of use of the solution expressed as business impact measures	Productivity Revenue Quality Time Efficiency Customer satisfaction Employee engagement
5 ROI	Comparison of monetary benefits from the solution to solution costs	Benefit-cost ratio (BCR) ROI (%) Payback period

they will do it. Otherwise, they will not. Another example is the reaction employees have to a new diversity and inclusion effort. Positive reaction that reflects commitment to it is a good indication the process will be embraced as important to organization strategy.

The next outcome level is Learning. Measures of learning ensure that the individuals involved in a solution know what they need to know or know how to do what they need to do to make a solution, system, initiative, or project successful. These data may represent knowledge, information, awareness, and critical skill sets necessary for work to be done, programs to be implemented, and processes to be completed. Without the requisite knowledge, things can go awry. For example, almost 70 percent of employees in one of the largest healthcare organizations in Canada did not receive flu shots, although senior executives had requested flu shots for all employees. As a healthcare provider, it is important for employees to avoid flu because they could be absent more frequently and they may pass the flu along to their patients. At the same time, they may be exposed to the flu more than any other occupation. Some analysis revealed that they did not pursue the flu shots because of some misunderstandings and misinformation about the shots and their effectiveness. When employees became more enlightened and the misinformation was clarified, the percentage of employees receiving flu shots increased significantly.

The next level, Application and Implementation, also referred to as behavior or implementation, is a measure of people's actions, activities, and behaviors. Measures at this level are critical. Sometimes solutions break down or do not work because people do not do what they should do to make implementation of a solution successful. Sometimes executives think that when something is not working, they want new behavior in place, suggesting that the new behavior will correct things. An example repeatedly told in the analytics literature is one describing Harrah's use of smile frequency as a predictor of customer satisfaction. This simple behavior led Harrah's to implement a program and thereby affect a key organization outcome measure.[11] Behavior, action, and implementation represent critical measures that lead toward organization performance.

The fourth level of data is Impact. This category includes measures that are in the system and represent all types of business data. In most organizations, these measures exist by the hundreds, if not thousands, and they reflect the condition of output, quality, cost, and time, which are major categories of any work in an organization. These measures usually define the problem or opportunity that initiates an analytics project. For example, an excessive number of patient accidents were the driver for an analytics project at a healthcare firm. Reduction in customer satisfaction and new customer accounts were the drivers for an analytics project for a large financial institution.

A fifth level of data is ROI, a measure that reflects ultimate accountability. It is a benefit-cost ratio (BCR), the financial ROI expressed as a percentage, or the payback period (PP) that indicates how long it will take for the investment to pay for itself. Although other measures of financial return exist (e.g., return on equity, return on assets, etc.), BCR, ROI, and PP seem to be the most common measures and are most appropriate for measuring financial output of human capital investments. These data are the output of the process and represent an important part of analytics. Ultimately, many analytics projects lead to ROI and require a comparison of the benefits to costs.

TYPES OF ANALYTICS PROJECTS

The variety of tasks, processes, and procedures involved in analytics is vast. Some analysts suggest that any type of analysis to understand, support, or improve human capital programs is an analytics project. However, it is helpful to think of projects in five different but related categories. These categories are helpful because they are common and represent typical existing studies that can easily be located, analyzed, and compared. Each category is described in more detail throughout the book.

Sometimes only one of these analytics processes is taken. For example, an organization may recognize a need to understand the financial value of a measure before investing in a solution or initiative. On the other hand, it may be important to show the ROI for a particular solution. This analysis includes demonstrating causation, converting data to money, and comparing the output to the cost of the solution. Regardless of the analytics project, these five categories should encompass whatever type of analysis is required.

Converting Data to Money (Type I)

A tremendous push to understand the value of measures is evident in most organizations, and one of the best ways to understand value is to convert it to money. If it is something that needs to increase, such as engagement, executives want to know the monetary value of it. If it is something that needs to be eliminated or prevented, such as an accident or incident, executives want to know the cost of each item to understand the magnitude of the problem. One type of analytics project is to convert data to money. Some measures are easily converted, but others are harder to value and require a more advanced analytics process. Hard-to-value data items include:

- Job Engagement
- Job Satisfaction
- Stress
- Employee Complaints
- Health Status

- Ethics
- Teamwork
- Networking
- Customer Satisfaction
- Reputation

For example, an electric utility wanted to know the monetary value of stress created as the industry became deregulated. Utility teams had to be more productive and more efficient. This push for productivity caused excessive stress among team members, and the executives were interested in having a better understanding of the monetary value of the problem.

The good news is that work has been done by organizations to convert some common hard-to-value data into money. A classic example is that of Sears, where an HCA project connected employee attitude to customer perception to revenue.[12]

Showing Relationships and Causation (Type II)

This type of analysis involves understanding the relationship (or lack thereof) between variables and involves correlation and regression analysis. For example, a question of interest may be "Does increasing employee engagement increase the likelihood that employees will work more safely, be more productive, or reduce errors?" Or the question may be one of determining any difference in performance of engaged employees versus non-engaged employees. Analysis for these types of questions not only attempts to see whether a correlation exists, but to see whether correlation indicates a causal relationship. Typical correlations that are being pursued through the use of analytics are:

- Job satisfaction versus retention
- Job satisfaction versus attraction

- Job satisfaction versus customer satisfaction
- Engagement versus productivity
- Engagement versus safety
- Engagement versus sales
- Engagement versus quality
- Organizational commitment versus productivity
- Stress versus productivity
- Conflict versus productivity
- Culture versus productivity
- Ethics versus profit

The opportunities are limitless in terms of exploring relationships inside an organization. In addition, this step looks for causation that might not be based on mathematical relationships. Sometimes other methods can be used to explore the cause of a problem or determine what will influence an opportunity. These different techniques are listed in Table 1-2. An important point of this step is that the cause of the problem reveals the solution to the opportunity that needs developed.

Applying Predictive Models (Type III)

Predictive models for projects are an extension of the relationship category. When relationships or connections are made, can they be used in

TABLE 1-2   Analysis Techniques

Diagnostic questionnaires	Statistical process control
Focus groups	Brainstorming
Probing interviews	Problem analysis
Job satisfaction surveys	Cause-and-effect diagram
Engagement surveys	Force-field analysis
Exit interviews	Mind mapping
Exit surveys	Affinity diagrams
Nominal group techniques	Simulations

a predictive way? The independent variable predicts dependent variables. Typical predictive relationships that have been established in some organizations are:

- Recruiting source predicts retention

- Selection test predicts safety performance

- Interviews predict absenteeism

- Values survey predicts early turnover

- Health risk status predicts absenteeism

- Absenteeism predicts productivity

- Benefits participation predicts retention

- Compensation predicts retention

Again, the opportunities are limitless in terms of developing these models. Sometimes the model involves a chain of measures so that one measure predicts another, and then that variable predicts another. The predictive model from Sears, mentioned earlier, connects job satisfaction to the percent of revenue growth. In this example, a movement in job satisfaction will predict improvement in customer satisfaction, which would predict a growth in revenue for the store. Results from the project show that a 5-point improvement in the total job satisfaction drives a 1.3-unit improvement on a customer satisfaction survey, which drives a 5.5 percent improvement in revenue growth. The profit margin is applied to the sales growth to develop a value-added dollar figure. By way of this model, improvements in job satisfaction become a predictor of profit in stores.

Conducting Impact and ROI Analysis (Type IV)

A dominant type of analytics project involves showing the impact and ROI of a specific human capital program. These types of studies describe the reaction, learning, application, impact, and ROI for a particular solution. Executives find it helpful to understand the value of particular solutions. Most analytics projects lead to solutions. Impact and ROI studies are usually reserved for those programs and projects that are expensive, important, and command executive attention. They can cover a variety of areas:

- Recruiting/selection
- Training/learning/development
- Leadership/coaching/mentoring
- Knowledge management
- Organization consulting/development
- Policies/procedures/processes
- Recognition/incentive/engagement
- Change management/culture
- Technology/systems/IT
- Green/sustainability projects
- Safety/health programs
- Talent retention solutions
- Project management solutions
- Quality/Six Sigma/Lean Engineering
- Meetings/events
- Marketing/advertising
- Communications/public relations
- Public policy/social programs
- Risk management/ethics/compliance
- Flexible work systems
- Wellness and fitness programs

All Roads Lead to ROI

It is helpful to understand the importance of impact and ROI in the minds of executives who fund a variety of human capital projects and programs. In discussions with these executives, the focus often shifts or evolves to the ROI issue. For example, an organization has invested a tremendous amount of money on employee engagement. Engagement is being measured with an employee engagement survey. Executives may ask this question, "What is the value of having more engaged employees?" or "If engagement scores increase, what outcomes can we expect?" These questions suggest that executives are interested in the monetary value. This is a Type I analytics project.

In order to answer the question, engagement program owners would have to connect engagement to money—typically through an easy-to-value measure. The data may show that engagement is connected to gross productivity, which can be defined as revenue per employee. If engagement has been moved from a lower level to a higher level, the gross productivity movement can be pinpointed. These data are easily converted to money. Adding the profit margin shows the actual monetary contribution of improvement in job engagement. This is a Type II analytics project. If the relationship is operationalized, after testing and validation, this is now a Type III project.

By showing the productivity improvement connection, the next question is, "So what is the ROI?" Answering this question requires comparing the monetary benefits of improvements in gross productivity connected to engagement with the fully loaded cost of the engagement solution. This ROI analysis is a Type IV human capital analytics project. Quickly, a request for Type I leads to Type II, which leads to Type III, and finally Type IV, the ROI. Sometimes executives, when facing a potential planned program for improving job engagement based on the initial assessment of the score, may ask for a value of forecasted ROI before they get started. This more detailed project would be a Type V human capital analytics project, an ROI forecast before it is implemented. Obviously, if implemented this would also require a Type IV analysis, w on a follow-up basis. When discussing almost any soluti ital analytics project with executives, they often as if we do it? What is the impact? What is the mone ROI?" All roads lead to ROI.

Forecasting ROI (Type V)

Sometimes when major projects or programs are implemented, it is helpful to understand the potential payoff for the program before it is implemented. This assessment involves forecasting the impact that will be influenced by the program, converting it to monetary value, and comparing it to the proposed cost of the solution. A challenge with forecasting is to be as accurate as possible so that the forecast can be realistic and used for decisions. Of course, if a forecast is conducted as a requirement, follow up and make sure that the forecast has been achieved. Some of the major programs that are being subjected to forecasting are:

- Wellness and fitness programs
- Flexible work systems
- New compensation arrangements
- New benefits structures
- OD projects
- Transformational projects
- Talent retention projects
- Talent management projects
- Leadership projects
- Change projects

HUMAN CAPITAL ANALYTICS MODEL

With such a variety of projects, it is sometimes difficult to address human capital analytics with systematic processes, but it is possible and necessary. As W. Edwards Deming said, "If you can't explain what you do as a process, you don't know what you are doing." Executives want to know whether consistent processes can be repeated from time to time and that the assumptions are conservative in the analysis. These qualifications are necessary so that they can believe the results, which lead us to a set of process steps that are described in greater detail in Figure 1-4, the Human Capital Analytics Model developed by the ROI Institute. It is through the use of this model that organizations can make analytics work.

Define the Problem/Opportunity

The first step is to define the problem, making sure that the business measure or measures linked to the project are clearly defined or the phenomenon is clearly described. The issue here is a problem or opportunity that must be clearly described to make the project successful. Sometimes

FIGURE 1-4 Analytics Model for Making Analytics Work

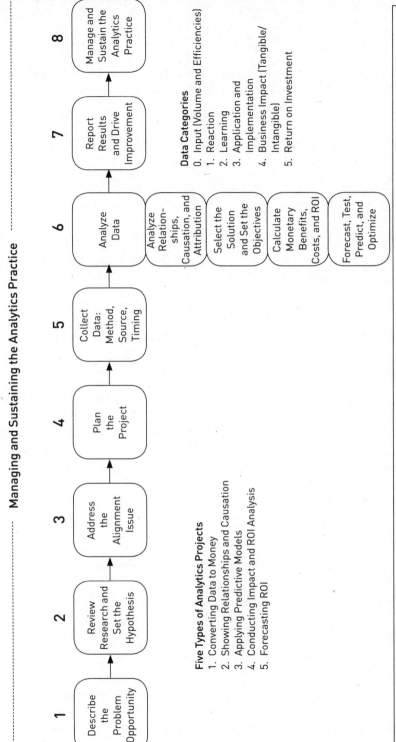

Managing and Sustaining the Analytics Practice

1	2	3	4	5	6	7	8
Describe the Problem Opportunity	Review Research and Set the Hypothesis	Address the Alignment Issue	Plan the Project	Collect Data: Method, Source, Timing	Analyze Data	Report Results and Drive Improvement	Manage and Sustain the Analytics Practice

Five Types of Analytics Projects
1. Converting Data to Money
2. Showing Relationships and Causation
3. Applying Predictive Models
4. Conducting Impact and ROI Analysis
5. Forecasting ROI

Analyze Relationships, Causation, and Attribution

Select the Solution and Set the Objectives

Calculate Monetary Benefits, Costs, and ROI

Forecast, Test, Predict, and Optimize

Data Categories
0. Input (Volume and Efficiencies)
1. Reaction
2. Learning
3. Application and Implementation
4. Business Impact (Tangible/Intangible)
5. Return on Investment

STANDARDS

initial problems or opportunities are often presented to the human capital analytics team in vague terms. The challenge of this step is to make sure that it is a problem worth solving or an opportunity worth pursuing.

Review Research and Set the Hypothesis

When the problem is clearly defined, the question is: What do we expect to occur? For example, is job satisfaction related to attraction or does job engagement relate to an increase in sales? These expectations are established as a hypothesis or, sometimes, multiple hypotheses. A hypothesis can be written mathematically but is often stated in simple terms to executives. The key is to anticipate expectations early in the process.

Address the Alignment Issue

Alignment ensures that the project is connected to important levels of data throughout the project. Chapter 4 introduces the V Model, which aligns needs with objectives and evaluation. A human capital analytics project fits into the V Model at some point, as alignment can occur in several levels. Although this issue is addressed in step one, the alignment process keeps the focus. It may require detailed analysis, whereas other times it may be a quick conclusion based on the data. Alignment is critical at the business level, where specific business measures are identified in the beginning.

Plan the Project

Any analytics project will need a plan, maybe several of them. Planning is critical to ensure all key issues in the study are addressed, including making initial assumptions of how the project will unfold. Of the four types of plans, the first is the data collection plan, describing methods of data collection, sources of data, and timing of data collection. The second plan, the analysis plan, indicates what particular types of analyses are planned and how they would be used in the project. A third plan is the communication plan, detailing how the results will be reported to a variety of audiences, and important topics with HCA projects. A fourth plan is a classic project plan that indicates the timing of the project from the beginning until the results are communicated and actions are taken. Proper investment in these four plans will make the entire project much easier.

Collect Data

Every human capital analytics study will involve collecting data. Data collection ranges from monitoring the data in the system to using questionnaires, interviews, focus groups, and observation. This step involves all the methods from the plan, which are now fully initiated and the data collected.

Analyze Relationships, Causation, and Attribution

When trying to understand a problem, it is necessary to sort out from among several factors the cause, which moves beyond correlation. This step involves quantitative methods such a hypothesis testing and experimental design or qualitative methods such as problem solving or brainstorming. When a solution is implemented and improvement in a business impact measure has occurred, the question is how much of the improvement is actually connected to the solution. This critical step of attribution isolates the effects of different processes from the solution. It is necessary for accuracy and credibility. Several methods are available to accomplish this step.

Select the Solution and Set the Objectives

This analysis can come at different times, but at some point a solution is needed. It could come early, after using descriptive statistics, or it can come after detailed analysis points to what exactly caused the problem. The solution is implemented to improve one or more impact measures. A variety of tools and processes will be used to ensure that this is the proper solution to address the problem or opportunity in the most economical way. An important part of this step is to set the objectives at different levels.

Calculate Monetary Benefits, Costs, and ROI

Sometimes a project involves converting data to money. From a client perspective, the best way to understand a problem or an opportunity is to convert it to money, based on additional profits, reduced costs, or avoided costs. There are a variety of techniques available for converting data to money. This step is necessary if the project includes ROI analysis. When a solution is implemented, it is helpful to understand the impact of the solution in monetary terms, converting data to money at a later step in the process through a variety of techniques.

Sometimes it is necessary to develop the full cost of a particular human capital solution. Executives need an understanding for the investment in particular area. For example, executives may ask for the total cost of wellness and fitness in terms of coordination, administration, equipment, facilities, programs, and even time for those who are involved in this process. These costs are necessary for an ROI calculation when the monetary benefits of the program are compared to all of the cost—the definition for the financial ROI. In either case, all cost must be included, both direct and indirect costs.

FORECAST, TEST, PREDICT, AND OPTIMIZE

Sometimes the ROI forecast for a particular solution is needed, or the forecast of success from a predictive model may be needed. In today's climate, executives want to know whether a solution will work before it is implemented. This step also involves a predictive model at the impact level, testing the model for feasibility and accuracy, optimizing it, and exploring what can be done to maximize the impact and ROI.

REPORT RESULTS AND DRIVE IMPROVEMENT

Any human capital analytics project involves many stakeholders. The challenge is to make sure that all stakeholders have the data and results, understand their role in achieving them, and know how to make improvements or adjustments. Some audiences need detailed information; others need brief snapshots. The key is to identify the appropriate audience, select the appropriate methods, and deliver a message that helps them achieve and understand the results. This final step includes driving improvements using results from the analytics project. These results are used to make a decision. The key is to use the data to drive the improvement or the change desired and follow through to make sure that has happened.

MANAGE AND SUSTAIN THE ANALYTICS PRACTICE

A variety of issues and events will influence the successful implementation of human capital analytics. Specific topics or actions may include:

- A policy statement concerning human capital analytics development

- Guidelines for different elements and techniques of the human capital analytics process

- Meetings and formal sessions to develop staff skills with human capital analytics

- Strategies to improve management commitment and support for human capital analytics

- Mechanisms to provide technical support

- Specific techniques to place more attention on results

Human capital analytics can fail or succeed based on these implementation issues.

FOLLOW HUMAN CAPITAL ANALYTICS STANDARDS

Standards serve as the foundation to implementing the Human Capital Analytics Model. To ensure consistency and replication of studies, the operating standards have been developed and tested in practice. The results of a human capital analytics project must stand alone and should not vary based on the individual who is conducting the study. The operating standards detail how each major step and issue of the process should be addressed. The following standards presented and detailed in this book are referred to as:

1. Align projects to business measures.

2. Use the simplest statistics in the human capital analytics project.

3. When collecting and analyzing data, use only the most credible sources.

4. When analyzing data, select the most conservative alternative for calculations.

5. If no improvement data are available for a population or from a specific source, assume that little or no improvement has occurred.

6. Omit extreme data items and unsupported claims in the analysis.

7. Address causation in problem-solving analysis.

8. Use at least one method to isolate the effects of the solution.

9. Adjust estimates of improvement for the potential error of the estimate.

10. When a higher-level evaluation is conducted, collect data at lower levels.

11. When an evaluation is planned for a higher level, refrain from being too comprehensive at the lower levels.

12. Use only the first year of benefits (annual) in the ROI analysis for short-term solutions.

13. Use fully loaded costs for human capital analytics projects.

14. Define intangible measures as measures that are not converted to monetary values.

15. Communicate results of human capital analytics projects to all key stakeholders.

16. Use results of human capital projects to drive improvements.

These specific standards not only serve as a way to consistently address each step, but also provide a much-needed conservative approach to the analysis. A conservative approach will build credibility with the executive audience.

THE DEVELOPMENT OF THE HUMAN CAPITAL ANALYTICS MODEL

Although much progress has been made, human capital analytics is not without its share of problems and issues. The mere presence of the process creates a dilemma for many organizations. When an organization embraces the concept and implements a human capital analytics practice, the management team is usually anxiously awaiting results, only to be disappointed when they are not readily available. For the process to be useful, it must balance many issues such as feasibility, simplicity, credibility, and soundness. More specifically, three major audiences must be pleased with the practice to accept and use it:

- Team members who design, develop, and conduct the projects need a simple, user-friendly process.

- Senior managers, sponsors, and clients who fund, initiate, and support projects need a credible outcome based on a conservative process.

- Researchers, professors, and critics who must support the analysis need a proven process that is logical, reliable, and valid.

To satisfy the needs of these three critical groups, the process must meet ten essential criteria for an effective human capital analytics model:

1. The process must be **simple**, void of complex formulas, lengthy equations, and complicated methodologies. Most attempts have failed with this requirement. In an attempt to obtain statistical perfection and make use of too many theories, some analytics models have become too complex to understand and use. Consequently, they have not been used routinely.

2. The process must be **economical** and must be implemented easily. The process should become a routine part of human capital analytics without requiring significant additional resources. Sampling for projects and early planning for projects are often necessary to make progress without adding new staff.

3. The assumptions, methodology, and techniques must be **credible**. A practical approach for the process that includes logical, conservative, and methodical steps is necessary to earn the respect of practitioners, senior managers, and researchers.

4. From a research perspective, the process must be **theoretically sound** and based on generally accepted practices. Unfortunately, this requirement can lead to an extensive, complicated process. Ideally, the process must strike a balance between maintaining a practical and sensible approach *and* a sound and theoretical basis for the process. This challenge is perhaps one of the greatest among those who have developed models for the process.

5. The process must **account for other factors** that have influenced output variables. In problem solving, the cause of the program

must be pinpointed. One of the most often overlooked issues, this criterion is necessary to build credibility and accuracy within the process. The process should pinpoint the contribution of the solution when compared to the other influences.

6. The process must have the **flexibility** to be applied to a wide range of situations. Some models apply to only a small number of programs such as recruiting or learning. Ideally, the process must be applicable to all types of other human capital issues and programs. Ideally, the process should be able to adjust to a range of potential time frames, including a forecast.

7. The process must be **applicable with all types of data,** including hard data, which are typically represented as output, quality, costs, and time; *and* soft data, which include job satisfaction, customer satisfaction, absenteeism, turnover, grievances, and complaints.

8. The process must **include the costs of the solution, when costs are needed**. The ultimate level of outcome is to compare the benefits with costs. Although the term *ROI* has been loosely used to express any benefit, an accurate ROI formula accounts for costs. Omitting or underestimating costs will only destroy the credibility of the ROI values.

9. The actual calculation must use an **acceptable ROI formula**. The benefit-cost ratio (BCR) or the ROI calculation, expressed as a percent, are common measures. These formulas compare the actual expenditure for the solution with the monetary benefits driven from the solution. Although other financial terms can be substituted, it is important to use a standard financial calculation in the human capital analytics process.

10. Finally, the human capital analytics process must have a successful **track record** in a variety of applications. In far too many situations, models are created but never successfully applied. An effective HCA process should withstand the wear and tear of implementation and should get the results expected.

Because these criteria are considered essential, a human capital analytics process should meet the vast majority, if not all criteria. The bad news is that many processes do not meet these criteria. The good news is that the human capital analytics model and process presented in this book meets all of the criteria.

BENEFITS OF HUMAN CAPITAL ANALYTICS

Although the benefits of adopting an HCA practice may appear to be obvious, several distinct and important benefits can be derived from the implementation of HCA in an organization. These key benefits, inherent with almost any type of improvement process, make HCA an attractive challenge for the human resource function.

SOLVE PROBLEMS, FIND SOLUTIONS

Human capital analytics will allow all types of problems to be solved, which ultimately point to a solution. This area is perhaps one of the most important because problems surface at different times with specific business impact measures, excessive cost, and other operational issues. Knowing what caused it is critical.

UNCOVER MYSTERIES AND RELATIONSHIPS

Mysteries often surround particular measures and variables in the organization. Some relationships are perceived to exist; others are unexpected but began to surface with human capital analytics. Human capital analytics sometimes offers an opportunity to explore misconceptions and misunderstandings from the management team and false assumptions from operating executives.

MEASURE CONTRIBUTION

The analytics model in this book is the most accurate, credible, and widely used process to show the impact of HR. The analytics team will know the specific contribution from a select number of solutions. The ROI will determine whether the benefits of the program, expressed in monetary values, outweigh the costs. It will determine whether the program made a contribution to the organization and whether it was, indeed, a good investment.

Set Priorities

Conducting human capital analytics projects in different areas will determine which programs contribute the most to the organization, allowing priorities to be established for high impact solutions. Successful solutions can be expanded into other areas, if the same need exists, ahead of other programs. Inefficient solutions can be redesigned and redeployed. Ineffective programs may be discontinued.

Focus on Results

The Human Capital Analytics model is a results-based process that brings a focus on results with all projects even for those not targeted for implementation. The process requires the project team, clients, participants, and support groups to concentrate on measurable objectives: what the solution is attempting to accomplish. Thus, this process has the added benefit of improving the effectiveness of solutions.

Earn Respect of Senior Executives and Sponsors

Conducting projects is one of the best ways to earn the respect of the senior management team and the sponsor (the person who really cares about the project). Senior executives have a never-ending desire to see the value. They will appreciate the efforts to connect HR to business impact and show the actual monetary value. It makes them feel comfortable with the process and makes their decisions much easier. Sponsors who often support, approve, or initiate solutions see HCA as a breath of fresh air. They actually see the value of HR, building confidence about the initial decision to go with the process.

Alter Management Perceptions of Human Resources

The human capital analytics process, when applied consistently and comprehensively, can convince the management group that human capital is an investment and not an expense. Managers will see human capital as making a viable contribution to their objectives, thus increasing the respect for the human capital function. This step is important in building a partnership with management and increasing management support for human capital.

FINAL THOUGHTS

The use of human capital analytics is expanding, and the payoff is huge. The process is not difficult. The approaches, strategies, and techniques are not overly complex and can be useful in a variety of settings. The combined and persistent efforts of practitioners and researchers will continue to refine the techniques and create successful applications. This chapter presented a variety of issues that must be addressed in the human capital practice and outlined a model for making analytics work. The process takes a potentially complicated issue and breaks it into simple, manageable tasks and steps. The building blocks for the process were examined to show how the model has been developed. With thorough planning and consideration for all potential strategies and techniques, the process becomes manageable and achievable. The remaining chapters focus on the major elements of this model and ways to implement it to work in real settings.

CHAPTER 2

Define the Problem or Opportunity

This chapter explores the first step in the human capital analytics model—defining the problem or opportunity. Although this step seems obvious, sometimes it is missed, improperly addressed, or not particularly precise in definition. Defining the problem takes into account the cost of the problem or value of an opportunity, at least on a conceptual basis. This brief chapter discusses this issue with examples of how to fully define the problem and frame it for a potential analytics study.

OPENING STORY

Government Security Agency (GSA) faced an annual turnover rate of employees that was perceived to be quite high in the category of communication specialist. These individuals were engaged in a variety of telecommunications services and activities that required a college degree, often in computer science, information science, or electrical engineering. The first step of the analysis was to clearly understand the definition of *turnover*. Technically, any employee leaving is considered turnover. Even if that person is involved in a traffic accident, it is recorded as a turnover.

Most managers think of turnover as voluntary turnover, counting those people who leave the organization voluntarily. Others prefer the definition of *avoidable turnover*, suggesting that it's not just those who leave of their own volition, but also those who were forced to leave but could have been retained with proper counseling or with a better match of the individual and the organization. Still others prefer the definition of *regrettable turnover*, which suggests that some lesser-performing employees leave voluntarily but their departures don't pose a problem. At the more costly end of the scale is the departure of high-potential employees; turnover for this particular group is regrettable.

At GSA, the discussion led to defining turnover as the departure of high potentials (which was regrettable turnover). Further analysis of exit interview data indicated that the turnover of high potentials was occurring during the first five years of employment. The rate of departure of these high-potential employees was 29 percent. So the specific definition of the problem for GSA was a 29 percent rate of turnover of high-potential employees during the first five years of employment. Further analysis found that the cost of this turnover was twice the annual salary for each turnover statistic. Based on initial analysis describing the situation, it was obvious GSA had a problem worth solving.

SOURCE OF PROBLEM OR OPPORTUNITY

A problem or an opportunity evolves, appears, is presented, or requested in a number of ways. It is important to understand clearly where the issue originates. Proactive use of analytics will help seek out the specifics among the eight common sources of information that present problems and opportunities for the organization.

EXECUTIVE REQUEST

Perhaps the most important and sometimes frequent source of problems or opportunities is an executive request. Executives may see a problem and want to try to understand the cause. They might have a perceived solution to solve a problem, or they see a tremendous cost resulting from a problem. They might also have a potentially heavy investment in a solution and want to know its connection to the business. Early in an analytics practice, executive request might be the principal source for projects. After all, they fund the analytics function because they want to see answers to their problems or issues from their perspective. For example, executives may see an opportunity to have a great place to work, after seeing references to it in *Fortune* magazine. They see some companies promote their great workplaces, and they naturally assume this is a good thing to do. They have some perceptions of what might be involved in the value added, but they want to know more, so they request an analysis about a great workplace. Sometimes they just request that it be implemented. Either way, some analysis should indicate the value in pursuing it.

OPERATIONAL ISSUES

Sometimes an operational problem or a persistent unresolved issue creates an opportunity worth solving. In this case, the analytics team must tune in to the operational measures, scorecards, and/or dashboards. In one organization, the human capital analytics team examined an excessive number of accidents. Some had accepted the number of accidents as a part of the industry; others felt that the organization should be able to prevent accidents. Some even suggested that multiple solutions were available. Still others suggested that the individuals being hired are accident prone. Either way, the issue remained, and the analytics team explored the causes of the high accident rate, looking for links between certain factors and characteristics.

SUCCESS STORIES

We have all seen it before: Company X implements a wonderful program and experiences tremendous success. These success stories lace the pages of magazines and newspapers, are bountiful on the Internet, and dominate conference agendas. People like to talk about success and what caused it, sometimes sparking interest in duplicating the success story in the organization. For example, a success story may show a company that implements employee engagement and finds a relationship between engagement and safety. This correlation implies that improving engagement will improve safety. The success story prompts a request for the program to be replicated elsewhere in the organization.

PREVIOUS RESEARCH

A casual review of research results in many types of projects. The workplace and workforce dynamics are constantly under scrutiny and review.

With the cost of people being an organization's largest single expenditure, much research focuses on human capital practices and how they affect organizations. Subscribing to research digests, examining research success stories, or constantly perusing publications such as *Human Resource Management* provide an excellent backdrop for exploring possibilities within an organization.

BENCHMARKING

Most organizations participate in benchmarking, even in the HR arena. Sometimes benchmarking reveals data that present a challenge. For example, benchmarking call centers reveal a low rate of unexpected absences, less than 3 percent. If the organization is experiencing 5.8 percent, those involved will recognize the need to understand the difference in absenteeism rates.

STRATEGIC OBJECTIVES

One of the most important areas is the connection to a strategic objective. Each year the company sets new strategies or readjusts current strategies. These new strategies often relate directly to analytics opportunities. If one strategy is to use a diverse workforce to drive business results, then the challenge arises to show the connection between diversity and business performance—an excellent analytics project.

EXPERIENCE

The experience of others on the team and inside the organization spurs potentially helpful projects. For example, in one organization a member of the human capital analytics team remembered an experience in which the organization placed a monetary value on near misses—accidents that nearly happened but did not actually occur. Although the near misses did not cause damage or injury, the threat of damage was evident. This organization actually took some time to sample the near misses, placing monetary value on each one and indicating the impact of avoiding a near miss. This analysis translated directly into a project that would aid the operations team as they tracked near misses with a goal to reduce them. Knowing the monetary value provides some comfort that it is a good investment.

CURIOSITY

Sometimes people are just curious. The curiosity around the connection to the business drives a project. In an organization with a reputation as having a strong culture, the group wondered about the effects of its culture on performance. They were curious as to whether it really makes a difference and whether it really drives business performance. These questions led to an analytics project.

In summary, problems and opportunities are identified in many ways. The analytics team must be proactive and not wait for a request but take the lead and bring the projects to the organization before they are asked to do so.

THE PAYOFF

The first step in the process is to explore the potential payoff if the problem is solved or the opportunity is pursued. The highest level of value delivered, a positive return on investment, comes from an analysis.

- Is this project worth doing?

- Does the project address an issue worth pursuing?

- Does it represent an opportunity?

- Is it a feasible program?

- What is the likelihood of a positive ROI?

The answers to these questions are obvious for proposed projects that address significant problems or opportunities with potentially high rewards. The questions might take longer to answer for lower-profile projects or those for which the possible payoff is less apparent. In any case, they are legitimate questions, and the analysis can be simple or comprehensive. The potential payoff in monetary terms is simple: A project's payoff comes in the form of either profit increases or cost savings (derived from cost reduction or cost avoidance).

Profit increases are generated by projects that improve sales, increase market share, introduce new products, open new markets, enhance customer service, or increase customer loyalty. These activities should pay off with increases in sales revenue. Other revenue-generating measures include increasing memberships, increasing donations, obtaining grants, and generating tuition from new and returning students—all of which, after taking out the cost of doing business, yield a profit.

However, most projects pay off with cost savings generated through cost reduction or cost avoidance. For example, projects that improve quality, reduce cycle time, lower downtime, decrease complaints, prevent employee turnover, and minimize delays are all examples of cost savings. When the goal is solving a problem, monetary value is often based on cost reduction.

Cost-avoidance programs aim to reduce risks, avoid problems, or prevent unwanted events. Some may view cost avoidance as an inappropriate measure for developing monetary benefits and calculating ROI. However, if the assumptions are correct, an avoided cost (e.g., compliance fines) can yield a higher reward than an actual cost reduction. Preventing a problem is more cost-effective than waiting for it to occur and then having to resolve it.

Determining potential payoff goes hand in hand with determining the specific business measures, because the potential payoff is often based on improvements or changes in business measures. Determining the payoff involves two factors: (1) the potential monetary value derived from the business measure's improvement, and (2) the approximate cost of the program or project. Developing these monetary values in detail usually yields a more credible forecast of the defined solution. However, this step may be omitted in situations where the business need must be resolved regardless of the program cost, or when resolution of the business need has an obviously high payoff. For example, if the problem involves a safety concern, a regulatory compliance issue, or a critical customer issue, then a detailed analysis of the payoff is unnecessary.

IDENTIFYING THE NEED

A needs analysis should begin with several questions. Table 2-1 presents some questions to ask about a proposed project. The answers to these questions might make the case for proceeding without analysis, or they may indicate the need for additional analysis. The answers could show that the project is not needed. Understanding the implications of moving forward (or not) can confirm the legitimacy of the proposed program.

The good news is, for many potential projects, answers to these questions are readily available. The need may have already been realized and the consequences validated. For example, many organizations with an employee retention problem within a critical talent group have calculated the cost of employee turnover. This cost is either developed from existing

TABLE 2-1   Key Questions to Ask About the Proposed Project

• What is the issue?	• Are multiple solutions available?
• Who will support the project?	• What happens if we do nothing?
• Who will not support the project?	• How much will the solution(s)
• What intangible benefits are	cost?
important?	• Is a forecast needed?
• How can we fund the project?	• What is the potential payoff
• Is this issue critical?	(positive ROI)?
• Is it possible to correct it?	• Is this issue linked to strategy?
• How much is it costing the	• Is it feasible to improve it?
organization?	• Can we find a solution?

data or secured from similar studies. With this cost in hand, the economic impact of the problem is known. The proposed program's cost can be compared to the problem's cost (in this case, excessive turnover) to get a sense of potential added value. The cost of the program can usually be estimated if a solution has been tentatively identified.

OBVIOUS PAYOFF OPPORTUNITIES

The potential payoff is obvious for some projects but not so obvious for others. Here are some opportunities with obvious payoffs:

- Excessive turnover of critical talent: 35 percent above benchmark data

- Low market share in a market with few players

- Inadequate customer service: 3.89 on a 10-point customer satisfaction scale

- Operating costs 47 percent higher than industry average

Each item is a serious problem that needs attention from executives, administrators, or politicians. To begin with a series of questions about the severity of the problem might insult the intelligence of the requestor or client. For these situations, it would be safe to move ahead to the business measure rather than invest too much time and resources in analysis of the payoff. After the solution is defined, a forecast may be appropriate.

NOT-SO-OBVIOUS PAYOFF OPPORTUNITIES

In other proposed projects, however, the issues might be unclear or arise from political motives or biases. Some opportunities for which the payoff is not as obvious are:

- Recruit new candidates to fit our culture

- Improve employee engagement

- Create an empowered workforce

- Create a wellness and fitness center

The opportunities that are not so obvious call for more detail. Some requests are common, coming from executives and administrators who suggest a process change. The requests appear to have the program identified, but without a clear reason as to why. These types of requests could deliver substantial value, but only if they are focused and clearly defined at the start. In our work at the ROI Institute, we have seen many vague requests turn into worthy programs. Sometimes overlooking the vague is a mistake; these requests can lead to critical analysis that ensures an appropriate focus on development and results in valuable contributions.

THE COST OF A PROBLEM

Problems are sometimes expensive. To determine the cost of a problem, its potential consequences must be examined and converted to monetary values. Here is a list of potentially costly problems:

- Inventory shortages

- Employee withdrawal

- Delays

- Equipment damage

Most can easily be converted to a monetary valuation, and some already are. If a problem cannot be converted to money within the resources and time constraints of the project request, the problem is intangible. *Intangible* is not synonymous with *immeasurable*. Intangible measures are measurable; they merely do not reflect a monetary value in their current state. For example, excessive carbon emissions from operating facilities is a serious problem, but it may not be one that can be easily converted to money for the organization. Time can easily be converted into money by calculating the fully loaded cost of the individual's time spent performing unproductive tasks. Employee turnover can be converted to money, based on the cost to replace the departing employee. Productivity problems, equipment damage, and equipment underuse are other examples of problems that have an apparent cost associated with them.

Examining costs means examining *all* the costs and their implications. For example, the full costs of accidents include not only the cost of lost workdays and medical expenses, but also their effect on insurance premiums, the time required for investigations, damages to equipment, and the time of all employees who address the accident. The cost of a customer complaint includes the cost of the time to resolve the complaint, as well as the value of the item, fee, or service that is adjusted because of the complaint. The most important cost is the loss of future business and goodwill from the complaining customer, plus potential customers who become aware of the issue.

The Value of Opportunity

Just as the cost of a problem can be tabulated in most situations, the value of an opportunity can also be determined. Examples of opportunities include:

- Implementing a new recruiting process
- Installing a new performance system
- Creating a talent retention program
- Implementing a flexible work system

In these situations, a problem may not exist, but a tremendous opportunity is available to move ahead of the competition if immediate action is taken. Properly placing a value on this opportunity requires considering possible consequences if the project or program is not pursued, and taking into account the windfall that might be realized by seizing the opportunity. The monetary value is derived by following the different scenarios to convert specific business impact measures to money. The challenge lies in ensuring a credible analysis. Forecasting the value of an opportunity involves many assumptions, whereas calculating the value of a known outcome is often grounded in a more credible analysis, described in later chapters.

DEFINE THE SPECIFIC BUSINESS MEASURES

If a problem is not defined clearly and early in the process, a flawed project can result, creating inefficiencies and other issues. This process is closely linked to the previous step of developing the payoff. To determine the problem, specific measures must be pinpointed so the business situation is clearly assessed. The term *business* is a broad term and is used in governments, nonprofits, educational institutions, and private sector organizations. Projects in all types of organizations can show business contribution by improving productivity, quality, and efficiency, as well as by saving time and reducing costs.

Sometimes a behavior issue is identified:

1. Our managers are not operating as leaders.

2. Our employees are not actively involved in meeting their goals.

3. The construction team is not practicing safe operating procedures.

4. The associates are not taking steps to be fit and healthy.

The challenge is to push the behavior (or action) to impact by asking "what if" or "so what" questions to move the issue to a business measure.

BUSINESS MEASURES—HARD AND SOFT DATA

A problem should be represented by a business measure. Any process, item, or perception can be measured, and the measurement is critical to this level of analysis. If the project focuses on solving a problem, a clear understanding of that problem and the measures that define it is necessary. The measures might also be obvious if the project prevents a problem. If the project takes advantage of a potential opportunity, the measures are usually there as well. If not, a clear, detailed description of the opportunity will help clarify the measure. The key is that business measures are already in the system, ready to be captured for this level of analysis. The challenge is to define and find them economically and swiftly.

BUSINESS MEASURES REPRESENTED BY HARD DATA

Business measures are sometimes categorized by hard data and soft data. Distinguishing between the two types of data helps in the process of defining specific business measures. Hard data are primary measures of improvement presented in rational, undisputed facts that are usually accumulated. They are the most desired type of data because they are easy to measure and quantify and relatively easy to convert to monetary values. The ultimate criteria for measuring the effectiveness of an organization are hard data such as revenue, productivity, profitability, cost control, and quality assurance.

Hard data are objectively based and represent common, credible measures of performance. They are typically divided into four categories, as shown in Table 2-2. These categories—output, quality, costs, and time—are typical performance measures in organizations, including private sector firms, government agencies, nongovernmental agencies, nonprofits, and educational institutions.

BUSINESS MEASURES REPRESENTED BY SOFT DATA

Hard data might lag behind changes and conditions in human performance within an organization by months; therefore, it is useful to supplement hard data with soft data such as attitude, motivation, and satisfaction. Often more difficult to collect and analyze, soft data are used when hard data are unavailable, or to supplement hard data. Soft data are also more difficult to convert to monetary values and often are based on subjective input. They are less credible as a performance measurement and tend to be behavior oriented, but they represent important measures just the same. Table 2-3 shows common examples of soft data.

TANGIBLE VERSUS INTANGIBLE MEASURES: A BETTER APPROACH

A challenge with regard to soft versus hard data is converting soft measures to monetary values. The key to this problem is to remember that all roads lead to hard data. Although creativity may be categorized as a form of soft data, a creative workplace can develop new products or new patents, which leads to greater revenue—clearly a hard data measure. Although it is possible to convert the measures to money, it is often more realistic and practical to leave them in nonmonetary form. This decision is based on considerations of credibility and the cost of the conversion.

TABLE 2-2 Examples of Hard Data

OUTPUT	QUALITY	COSTS	TIME
• Completion rate	• Failure rates	• Shelter costs	• Cycle time
• Units produced	• Dropout rates	• Treatment costs	• Equipment downtime
• Tons manufactured	• Scrap	• Budget variances	• Overtime
• Items assembled	• Waste	• Unit costs	• On-time shipments
• Money collected	• Rejects	• Cost by account	• Time to project completion
• Items sold	• Error rates	• Variable costs	• Processing time
• New accounts generated	• Rework	• Fixed costs	• Set-up time
• Forms processed	• Shortages	• Overhead costs	• Time to proficiency
• Loans approved	• Product defects	• Operating costs	• Learning time
• Inventory turnover	• Deviation from standard	• Program cost savings	• Meeting schedules
• Patients visited	• Product failures	• Accident costs	• Repair time
• Applications processed	• Inventory adjustments	• Program costs	• Efficiency
• Students graduated	• Time card corrections	• Sales expense	• Work stoppages
• Tasks completed	• Incidents	• Participant costs	• Order response
• Output per hour	• Compliance discrepancies		• Late reporting
• Productivity	• Agency fees		• Lost time days
• Work backlog			
• Incentive bonus			

TABLE 2-3   Examples of Soft Data

Work Habits	Customer Service
• Tardiness	• Customer complaints
• Visits to the dispensary	• Customer dissatisfaction
• Violations of safety rules	• Customer impressions
• Communication breakdowns	• Customer loyalty
• Excessive breaks	• Customer retention
	• Customer value
	• Lost customers
Work Climate/Satisfaction	**Employee Development/ Advancement**
• Grievances	• Promotions
• Discrimination charges	• Capability
• Employee complaints	• Intellectual capital
• Job satisfaction	• Programs completed
• Organization commitment	• Requests for transfer
• Employee engagement	• Performance appraisal ratings
• Employee loyalty	• Readiness
• Intent to leave	• Networking
• Stress	

According to the HCA standards, an intangible measure is a measure that is intentionally not converted to money. If a soft data measure can be converted to a monetary amount credibly using minimal resources, it is considered tangible, reported as a monetary value, and incorporated in the ROI calculation. If a data item cannot be converted to money credibly with minimal resources, it is reported as an intangible measure. Therefore, when defining business needs, the key difference between measures is not whether they represent hard or soft data, but whether they are tangible or intangible. In either case, they are important contributions toward the desired payoff and important business impact data.

ISSUES ABOUT IMPACT MEASURES

When assessing business impact measures, several issues must be considered. The impact data must first be collected in order to be assessed. In many situations, the impact data are in place, but a method of collecting them from the source must be determined. Collateral measures must be considered. These measures are unintentionally positively or negatively influenced by the program. Finally, successive impact measures must be considered: What other measures will be subsequently affected as a direct result of the program's implementation?

Sources of Impact Data

Sources of impact data, whether hard or soft, are plentiful. They come from routine reporting systems within the organization. In many situations, these items have led to the need for the program or project. Table 2-4 shows a sampling of the vast array of documents, systems, databases, and reports that can be used to select the specific measure or measures to monitor throughout the program.

Some program planners and team members believe corporate data sources are scarce because the data are not readily available to them, near their workplace, or within easy reach through database systems. With a little determination and searching, however, the data can usually be identified. In our experience, more than 90 percent of the impact measures that matter to an organization have already been developed and are readily available in databases or systems. Rarely do new data collection systems or processes have to be developed.

TABLE 2-4 Sources of Data

• Department records	• Safety and health reports
• Work unit reports	• Benchmarking data
• Human capital databases	• Industry/trade association data
• Payroll records	• R&D status reports
• Quality reports	• Suggestion system data
• Design documents	• Customer satisfaction data
• Manufacturing reports	• Project management data
• Test data	• Cost data statements
• Compliance reports	• Financial records
• Marketing data	• Scorecards
• Sales records	• Dashboards
• Service records	• Productivity records
• Annual reports	• Strategic plans

COLLATERAL MEASURES

When searching for the proper measures to connect to the program and pinpoint business needs, it is helpful to consider all the possible measures that could be influenced. Sometimes, collateral measures move in harmony with the program. For example, efforts to improve safety might also improve productivity and increase job satisfaction. Thinking about the adverse impact on certain measures also helps. For example, when cycle times are reduced, quality could suffer; or when sales increase, customer satisfaction could deteriorate. Program team members must prepare for these unintended consequences and capture them as relevant data items.

SUCCESSIVE IMPACT MEASURES

A potentially confusing issue is the fact that some impact measures have a successive chain of impact. The difficulty lies in deciding whether one measure is appropriate or if all measures are appropriate. For example, Figure 2-1 details five possible consequences of sexual harassment in the workplace. The victim of the harassment suffers stress; the victim's job satisfaction drops; internal complaints of sexual harassment increase; the victim is increasingly absent from work; and employee turnover rises as the victim seeks employment elsewhere. The difficulty lies in determining which measures (if not all) are influenced by a sexual harassment prevention program. Most of these issues are sorted out in the upfront needs assessment to ensure that the particular program can indeed influence all these measures. Even if the principal focus of the project is to reduce complaints, it is important to determine whether the other measures are connected. If they are, they also could become objectives for the project.

When considering complaints, impact measures occur in a successive series. A formal internal complaint, if not resolved, could convert to an external charge with the Equal Employment Opportunity Commission. If that charge is not resolved to the victim's satisfaction, he or she has a right to sue the employer, creating a litigated complaint. Litigation leads to legal fees and expenses and also to settlements. Ultimately, all of this activity (from prevention to investigation to defense), represents a significant cost.

A project could actually have objectives for each of these aspects. Although they should all improve in relative proportion, this result might not be the case. Under U.S. law, employees have a right to sue an employer, even before an external charge is actually resolved or if it is resolved in favor of the

FIGURE 2-1 Successive Impact Measures

Consequences of sexual harassment in the workplace can be successive.

Source: Adapted from P. P. Phillips and J. J. Phillips, "Preventing Sexual Harassment—Healthcare Inc.," Chapter 1, *Proving the Value of HR: ROI Case Studies*, 2nd ed. (Birmingham, AL: ROI Institute, 2010).

victim. For those reasons, the focus might be on reducing the number of litigated complaints. The confusion comes when the monetary value of this program is calculated. Converting data to monetary value is critical when an ROI calculation is pursued. Using all six impact measures represents a tremendous amount of duplication. It would be best to take one measure and use it in the conversion process. Still, all of these objectives can be influenced by the sexual harassment prevention project. This series of successive impact measures can usually be uncovered when asking a series of "what if" questions. What if this measure happens? Does it lead to something else?

STAKEHOLDERS

Human capital analytics projects involve many stakeholders. Some are more critical than others, but they all need attention. One important group consists of those funding the project. If funding is already factored into the budget, senior executives are the funders the project. Other projects might be funded by a department, division, or individual in an effort to solve a problem or pursue an opportunity. In this case, stakeholders are particularly critical.

A second type of stakeholder is the champion, or supporter, of the project. He or she is the person who is counting on a certain outcome. This stakeholder will benefit most by the kind of analysis we provide.

A third type of stakeholder is the individual who actually must make the process work—the person often involved in the project's success. An example is a predictive analytics project in which employee performance and retention are linked to particular selection characteristics and selection assessments. The recruiting and selection team must make the process work to collect the right kind of data and use it properly.

Finally, managers of employees implementing the project have a stake in its outcome. Often these managers have some of the measures in their key performance indicators or their team members spend time on a particular project. They need to see the value of these types of projects, so the outcome clearly needs to be communicated to them.

The point is to identify stakeholders and understand their role in the project. Table 2-5 represents the full array of possible stakeholders.

STAKEHOLDER ANALYSIS

It is helpful to learn about the stakeholders identified in order to understand how to work with them.

NEEDS

Each stakeholder has specific needs. It is important to understand what they need to see and what they need out of this particular project. Their needs can vary significantly, as some need information, some need attention, some need the results, and most all of them do not need surprises.

INTEREST

The interest in the project needs to be gauged. For example, if a project involves a clear connection between engagement and the quality of the products produced, the quality manager has a high degree of interest in the project.

ISSUES AND CONCERNS

Along with interest come issues and concerns about the project. If a stakeholder did not initiate the program, that person may be skeptical about

TABLE 2-5 Stakeholders for Typical Projects and Programs

Stakeholder	Description
Stakeholder	Any individual or group interested in or involved in the project. Stakeholders may include the functional manager where the project is located, the participants, the organizer, the project leader, facilitators, and key clients, among others.
The Organization	The entity within which the particular project or program is analyzed. Organizations may be companies (either privately held or publicly held); government organizations at the local, state, federal, and international levels; nonprofits; or non-governmental organizations. They may also include educational institutions, associations, networks, and other loosely organized bodies of individuals.
Analyst	These individuals collect the data to determine whether the project is needed. They are also involved in analyzing various parts of the project. Analysts are usually more important in the beginning, but may provide helpful data throughout the project.
Bystanders	The individuals who observe the project, sometimes at a distance. They are not as actively involved as stakeholders, but are concerned about the outcomes, including the money. These bystanders are important because they can become cheerleaders or critics of the project.
CEO/ Managing Director/ Agency Executive	The top executive in an organization. The top executive could be a plant manager, division manager, regional executive, administrator, or agency head. The CEO is the top administrator or executive in the operating entity where the project is implemented.
Evaluator	This person is responsible for measurement and evaluation, following all the processes outlined in this book. If this person is a member of the project team, extreme measures must be taken to ensure he or she remains objective. It may also be a person who is completely independent of the project. This individual performs these duties full or part time.

Stakeholder	Description
Finance and Accounting Staff	These individuals are concerned about the cost and impact of the project from a financial perspective. They provide valuable support. Their approval of processes, assumptions, and methodologies is important. Sometimes, they are involved in the project evaluation; at other times, they review the results. During major projects, this group could include the organization finance director or chief financial officer.
Immediate Managers	The individuals who are one level above the participant(s) involved in the program or project. For some projects, this person is the team leader for other employees. Often they are middle managers, but most important, these people have supervisory authority over the participants in the project.
Participants	The individuals who are directly involved in the project. The terms *employee*, *associate*, *user*, or *stakeholder* may represent these individuals. For most projects, the term participant appropriately reflects this group.
Designer/ Developer	The individuals who design and develop the project solution and create the parameters for an effective and efficient project. The developers determine the content needed for success.
Project Manager	The individual(s) responsible for the project, program, initiative, or process. This individual manages the project and is interested in showing the value of the project before it is implemented, during its implementation, and after it is implemented.
Project Team	The individuals involved in the project, helping to implement it, are the individual team members who may work full or part time on this particular project. On larger-scale projects, these individuals are often assigned full time, on a temporary basis, or sometimes on a permanent basis. Small projects may require only part-time duties.
Sponsor/ Clients	The individuals who fund, initiate, request, or support a particular project or program. Sometimes referred to as the sponsor, this key group, usually at the senior management level cares about the project's success and is in a position to discontinue or expand the project.

it. He or she might not understand the analysis or the connections to the business and may not believe them. The key is to recognize these stakeholders' perspectives and concerns about these kinds of projects and address them throughout implementation.

INFLUENCE

Some stakeholders have tremendous influence. It is helpful to assess how particular stakeholders can influence the project and its outcomes, as well as the implementation of the results. If they are influential (many are), it is important to work diplomatically with them to ensure that their influence is maximized in the right direction.

EXPECTATIONS

Finally, the expectations of stakeholders need to be detailed. What specifically are stakeholders expecting from the project, and what are they expected to do for the project? Particular roles and responsibilities need to be clearly outlined. Sometimes the expectation is just to listen and observe, but many times it is to be actively involved.

WORKING WITH THE STAKEHOLDERS

In summary, stakeholders need a lot of attention and constant communication. Not only should the proper stakeholder be identified and analyzed, but he or she should be kept informed routinely. It is better to overcommunicate than undercommunicate. Surprises are never a good thing, even if they are pleasant. Communication about a negative outcome needs to be planned carefully. This planning will be discussed in a later chapter on communicating results.

FINAL THOUGHTS

This chapter focuses on identifying the problem or opportunity. This identification is the starting point in the analytics model and is an important early step. If the project is not identified properly, the outcomes of the project will be plagued with issues. Project definition and stakeholder analysis will be time well spent in the overall structure of the project. The next chapter focuses on a second step, the hypothesis and review of the literature.

3

Review the Research and Set the Hypothesis

This chapter focuses on reviewing the research and defining the hypothesis. A hypothesis is the proposed explanation of an issue or the relationship between variables. Several hypotheses can apply to a given problem. In developing a hypothesis, one must first review the work of others in relation to the problem. A human capital analyst forms a hypothesis using existing studies, benchmarking data, literature searches, external databases, and informal methods to review information pertinent to the organization in question.

OPENING STORY

Lockheed Martin had been using the cooperative education program for many years. Designed primarily for engineering students, the co-op program allowed college students to alternate semesters of work and school, usually resulting in a five-year degree. The assumption was that the students learned practical information, became more valuable to the company, chose to remain with the company, and progressed more rapidly than those outside the program. Lockheed Martin perceived the co-op program as an effective recruiting tool, often generating better employees who understood the organization because they had worked in many different areas during their co-op experience.

Concerned about program cost, executives asked for a review of the program's value. Initial research included informal benchmarking with co-op directors at the universities; a literature search, including a review of *The Journal of Cooperative Education*; and interviews with engineering managers and former co-op students. When the research was complete, analysts established several hypotheses, listed here:

1. *Co-op students are more likely to join the organization when they graduate.*

Effective recruiting was one of the basic reasons for initiating the program. Recognizing the value of the participants' experience, a second hypothesis was set:

2. *Co-op students are more likely to progress in the organization at a greater rate than non-co-op students, as measured in promotions and salary increases.*

The literature suggested that:

3. *Co-op students joining the organization have longer tenures.*

4. *Co-op students show higher retention rates than non-co-op students.*

Because Lockheed Martin had largely selected students with higher grade point averages, another hypothesis emerged:

5. *Higher grade point averages result in more success on the job.*

These hypotheses establish what was perceived as a relationship to be validated in the analysis. The study was conducted; the first four hypotheses were accepted, and the last was rejected.[1]

THE HYPOTHESIS

A hypothesis is a proposed explanation of the relationship between two or more variables, such as engagement and productivity. An example is the statement, "Productivity will improve as a result of increased engagement." The statement is either rejected or not rejected based on the statistical analysis. (Some individuals prefer to use the terminology "fail to reject" or "not rejected" rather than "accept." The rationale is that in some situations, failing to reject the hypothesis on the basis of a single test may not be sufficient to accept the hypothesis.)

Hypotheses differ from a problem statement or objective in that they provide tentative answers to problems (i.e., engagement leads to improved productivity). Remember that when a hypothesis is used, statistical analysis is necessary. Common types of statistical analyses used in hypothesis testing are found in the HCA technical papers at www.roiinstitute.net.

Hypotheses are often presented as null hypotheses. A null hypothesis would state that no improvement in productivity is a result of increased engagement. If the analysis proves otherwise, then the null hypothesis is rejected. The conclusion: Improvement is caused by something other than chance, likely the improvement in engagement. This conclusion is based on a specified confidence level, which is discussed later. This null hypothesis may not be formally stated, but it is assumed and is the basis for the statistical analysis.

Human capital analytics hypotheses vary. Table 3-1 presents examples of testable hypotheses. Using appropriate statistical analysis, an analyst can test each of the 26 items. The good news is that many of them, if not all, have already been tested, indicating the scope of possibility for these types of analyses.

LOCATING EXISTING PUBLISHED STUDIES

A review of published studies aids in researching proposed explanations of the relationship between variables. Table 3-2 represents a summary of typical business impact and ROI studies for specific types of solutions. The measures are quite broad for some programs. For example, leadership development may pay off in a variety of measures, such as improved productivity, enhanced sales and revenues, improved quality, cycle-time reduction, direct cost savings, and employee job satisfaction. In other solutions, the influenced measures are quite narrow. For example, labor-management cooperation solutions typically influence grievances, stoppages, and employee satisfaction. Orientation solutions typically influence measures of early employee turnover, initial job performance, and productivity. Influence on these measures depends on the objectives and design of the solution. The

TABLE 3-1   Examples of Testable Hypotheses

1. A recruiting source will improve retention.
2. A recruiting source will improve employee performance.
3. A selection tool can predict ethics violations.
4. A selection tool can predict safe work behavior.
5. A selection tool can predict early turnovers.
6. A selection tool can predict unplanned absences.
7. Years of education predict performance ratings for knowledge workers.
8. Onboarding programs can improve time to proficiency.
9. Job skills training drives productivity and quality.
10. Supervisor training drives work unit performance.
11. Leadership development drives job engagement.
12. Job engagement drives productivity, safety, and quality.
13. Job engagement drives retention.
14. Job engagement drives customer satisfaction.
15. A performance management system improves business performance.
16. A career enhancement program improves retention.
17. Job satisfaction drives customer satisfaction.
18. Excessive stress increases medical costs.
19. Excessive conflicts decrease productivity.
20. Employee assistance plan use decreases absenteeism.
21. Health risk assessments predict productivity and healthcare costs.
22. Participation in a fitness program improves productivity.
23. An inclusive workforce drives innovation.
24. A flexible work system improves retention, stress, and satisfaction.
25. Recognition drives productivity, quality, and cost.
26. Participation in employee benefits can predict retention.

table also illustrates the immense number of measures that can be driven or influenced.

A word of caution: Presenting specific measures linked to a typical solution may give the impression that these are the only measures influenced. In practice, a solution can have many outcomes. Table 3-2 shows the most likely measures arising from studies reviewed by ROI Institute. In the course of two decades, we have been involved in more than 4,000 studies, and common threads exist among particular solutions.

TABLE 3-2 Typical Impact Measures for Projects and Programs

Program	Key Impact Measurements
Absenteeism control/reduction	Absenteeism, customer satisfaction, delays, job satisfaction, productivity, stress
Advertising	Revenue, market share, loyalty, new customers, satisfaction, brand awareness
Association meetings	Absenteeism, costs, customer service, job satisfaction, productivity, quality, sales, time, turnover
Branding projects	Brand awareness, image, loyalty, new customers, market share
Business coaching	Costs, customer satisfaction, efficiency, employee satisfaction, productivity/output, quality, time savings
Business development	Revenue, customer loyalty, new customer satisfaction
Career development/ Career management	Job satisfaction, promotions, recruiting expenses, turnover
Cloud computing	Costs, response time, downtime, reliability
Communications programs	Conflicts, errors, job satisfaction, productivity, stress
Compensation plans	Costs, job satisfaction, productivity, quality
Compliance	Charges, losses, penalties/fines, settlements
Diversity/Inclusion	Absenteeism, charges, complaints, losses, settlements, turnover, innovation, productivity
E-learning/Mobile learning	Cost savings, cycle time, error reductions, job satisfaction, productivity improvement, quality improvement, compliance discrepancies
Employee benefits projects	Costs, time savings, job satisfaction
Employee relations	Complaints, turnover, absenteeism, job satisfaction, engagement, grievances
Employee retention programs	Engagement, job satisfaction, promotions, turnover
Engagement initiatives	Safety, productivity, quality, turnover, absenteeism, cycle time, customer satisfaction

(continued)

TABLE 3-2   Typical Impact Measures for Projects and Programs (*continued*)

Program	Key Impact Measurements
Engineering/ Technical conferences	Costs, customer satisfaction, cycle time, downtime, job satisfaction, process time, productivity/output, quality, waste
Ethics programs	Fines, fraud, incidents, penalties, theft
Executive education	Absenteeism, costs, customer service, job satisfaction, productivity, quality, sales, cycle time, turnover
Flexible work systems	Productivity, turnover, office space costs, sick leave, absenteeism
Franchise/Dealer meetings	Cost of sales, customer loyalty, market share, quality, efficiency, sales
Gain-sharing plans	Operating costs, productivity, turnover
Golfing events	Customer loyalty, market share, new accounts, sales, upselling
Job satisfaction projects	Turnover, absenteeism, stress, complaints
Labor-management cooperation programs	Absenteeism, grievances, job satisfaction, work stoppages
Leadership	Costs, time savings, sales efficiency, employee satisfaction, engagement, productivity/output, quality
Lean programs	Cost savings, productivity improvement, quality improvement, cycle time, error reductions, job satisfaction, response times, rework, and waste
Management development	Absenteeism, costs, customer service, job satisfaction, productivity, quality, sales, time, turnover
Marketing programs	Brand awareness, churn rate, cross selling, customer loyalty, customer satisfaction, market share, new accounts, sales, upselling
Medical meetings/ Events	Compliance, efficiency, medical costs, patient satisfaction, quality

Program	Key Impact Measurements
Medical procedures	Medical errors, patient safety, patient outcomes, wait times, cycle time, operating costs, efficiency, patient satisfaction, patient complaints, legal claims
Motivational programs	Sales, safety, customer satisfaction, revenues, productivity, quality, cycle time, costs
Orientation, onboarding	Early turnover, performance, productivity, quality of work, training time, time, proficiency
Outsourcing initiatives	Operating costs, productivity, quality, cycle time, revenue
Personal productivity/Time management	Job satisfaction, productivity, stress reduction, time savings
Physician engagement	Operating costs, patient outcomes, quality, productivity, cycle time, wait times, patient satisfaction
Procurement solutions	Operating costs, time savings, quality, stability, schedule
Project management	Budgets, quality improvement, time savings
Public policy projects	Productivity, patient outcomes, safety, time savings, cost savings, quality, satisfaction, and image
Public relations	Image, brand awareness, customer satisfaction, new customers, share price, investor satisfaction, reputation
Quality programs	Costs, cycle time, defects, response times, rework
Recruiting source (new)	Costs, yield, early turnover, job satisfaction
Retention management	Engagement, job satisfaction, turnover
Rewards systems	Job engagement, safety, patient satisfaction, productivity, revenue, cycle time, costs
Risk management	Fines, penalties, legal claims, losses, downtime, stress
Safety programs	Accident frequency rates, severity rates, first aid visits, medical treatment cases, property damages

(continued)

TABLE 3-2 Typical Impact Measures for Projects and Programs (*continued*)

Program	Key Impact Measurements
Sales meetings	Customer loyalty, market share, new accounts, sales
Selection process	Early turnover, training time, productivity, job satisfaction
Self-directed teams	Absenteeism, customer satisfaction, job satisfaction productivity/output, quality, turnover
Sexual harassment prevention	Absenteeism, complaints, employee satisfaction, turnover
Six Sigma	Costs, errors, defects, response times, rework, waste
Skill-based pay	Labor costs, productivity, turnover, absenteeism, job engagement
Software projects	Absenteeism, costs, customer service, job satisfaction, productivity, quality, sales, time, and turnover
Strategy/Policy	Revenue, productivity, output, market share, patient outcomes, safety, quality/service levels, cycle time, operating costs, job satisfaction, patient satisfaction
Stress management	Absenteeism, job satisfaction, medical costs, turnover
Supervisor/team leader	Absenteeism, complaints, costs, job satisfaction, productivity, programs, quality, sales, time, turnover
Talent management	Job engagement, productivity, output, safety, quality, efficiency, cost/time savings, employee satisfaction
Team building	Absenteeism, costs, customer service, job satisfaction, productivity, quality, sales, time, turnover
Technical training	Productivity, errors, quality, times savings, operating costs, safety, patient quality, patient satisfaction
Technology implementation	Process times, cycle time, response rates, error rates, productivity, efficiency, job satisfaction
Wellness/fitness programs	Absenteeism, accidents, medical costs, turnover
Workforce management systems	Staffing levels, costs, overtime, job satisfaction, turnover, absenteeism, quality

The good news is that most solutions drive business measures. The measures are based on improvements in the various business units, divisions, regions, and individual workplaces. These measures matter to senior executives. The difficulty often comes in ensuring that the connection to the solution exists. A connection is established through a variety of techniques to isolate the effects of the solution on particular business measures and will be discussed in a later chapter.

More than 300 studies showing connections between human capital investments and business outcomes are described in a variety of books published by major publishers. These case study books were developed by the ROI Institute in partnership with publishers and are listed on the ROI Institute website, www.roiinstitute.net. Additional studies beyond these books are published in journals and trade publications made available through publishers and research repositories such as EBSCOhost and LexisNexis, to name two.

USING BENCHMARKING TO IDENTIFY STUDIES AND RELATIONSHIPS

Benchmarking studies are a potential resource for research describing relationships between variables. Benchmarking has experienced phenomenal growth in the past three decades. Virtually every function of an organization has been involved in some type of benchmarking to evaluate activities, practices, structure, and results. In many cases, the benchmarking process develops standards of excellence from organizations that are considered to have best practices. In these cases, information derived from benchmarking can serve as the basis for developing hypotheses.

Two approaches to benchmarking are (1) develop and implement a benchmarking project, or (2) participate in appropriate national benchmarking. With the proper focus and effort, an organization can develop its own benchmarking study, the results of which can be rewarding.

Developing a Customized Project

Originally focused on improving quality in organizations, benchmarking quickly spread to other functions and has become an indispensable management tool for continuous improvement. Benchmarking is a continuous process of collecting best-practice information from organizations and using it to improve another organization. It involves learning from others but is not a process of duplicating what others have done. It represents a pragmatic search for ideas. The process is usually time consuming and requires much discipline to make it effective and successful. It is not a quick fix, but a continuous, ongoing process.

Benchmarking satisfies a variety of needs and serves several purposes. It identifies trends and critical issues of human capital analytics. Measures from benchmarking can become the standards of excellence for an activity, function, system, practice, solution, or specific results. In this sense, it has become an important solution-evaluation tool. Benchmarking also allows the organization to compare certain solution features, such as the features of the employee benefits package. For these and other reasons, benchmarking is an important tool for the HR function.

Although several approaches are available, here are seven phases of benchmarking:

1. Determine what to benchmark

2. Build the benchmarking team

3. Identify benchmarking partners

4. Collect benchmarking data

5. Analyze the data

6. Distribute information to benchmarking partners

7. Initiate improvement from benchmarking

These phases appear to address the human capital analytics needs. This step-by-step process is not described here but is included in other references.[2] These steps can be substantial but will be worth the effort to find out how other firms in the same area are approaching analytics.

PARTICIPATING IN EXISTING BENCHMARKING PROJECTS

It is sometimes helpful to join or become part of existing benchmarking projects. These initiatives are often available within a professional HR society. For example, the Corporate Executive Board (CEB) conducts significant benchmarking and/or identifies best practices in HR.

The Society for Human Resource Management (SHRM) conducts ongoing HR benchmarking, as do other professional HR societies. Also, the HR section of participating organizations within business or industry trade groups develops benchmarking projects for its members. Such existing networks offer excellent opportunities to tap in to valuable information.

Tying into an existing project holds several advantages. First, it is usually inexpensive. Participating members who usually represent a large database share the cost of the entire project. In some cases, the trade group or professional society underwrites part of the cost of the project. Second, it is less time consuming, because data collection instruments are already designed and the process has been streamlined for efficient input. Others have done most of the work. Third, most projects represent a large database, thus making the data more significant and meaningful for comparative purposes. The fourth advantage is the exposure that often comes from participating in the benchmarking process. Most organizations are drawn to these projects seeking best practices and are sometimes labeled as having best practices themselves, whether or not the label is accurate, just by association with a benchmarking group.

Participating in benchmarking may have several disadvantages as well. First, the participants may not represent those with the best practices. Often a screening process for new participants is absent. Any organization with a predetermined size and willingness to pay the fee can participate. The second disadvantage is that an existing group may not consist of similar organizations. For example, a financial institution may want to compare its successes with a large database of other financial institutions, but the existing database isn't appropriate. A trade group database usually alleviates this concern. A third disadvantage is that joining an existing project allows few ways to influence what measures are taken and the ways in which the process actually works. Others have made these decisions, and the data may not contain the desired items.

A proactive approach to benchmarking is a comprehensive one that ties into existing projects, while at the same time developing a custom-designed effort for the given organization. This approach can save time and costs and provide a variety of information on key variables that may need to be improved.

SEARCHING/LOCATING DATABASES

Databases contain the work and research of others. Fortunately, many databases include studies on human capital analytics projects, and most are accessible through the Internet. Studies are available on retention, absenteeism, engagement, grievances, accidents, and even job satisfaction. The difficulty is in finding a database with studies or research appropriate to current projects. Ideally, data should come from a similar setting in the same industry, but such sources are not always possible to access. Sometimes data on all industries or organizations are sufficient, perhaps with some adjustments to suit the program at hand.

For some, the web holds the most promise for finding studies not readily available. Tremendous progress has been made and continues to be made in web searches. General web directories and portals may be particularly helpful. The key to successful use of web directories is discerning relevant and credible information. Search engines, such as Google, Google Scholar, Bing, Yahoo!, and others offer vast coverage. They stand out in three ways:

1. They are large and contain billions instead of millions of records.

2. Virtually no human selectivity is involved in determining which web pages are included in the search engine's database.

3. They are designed for searching (i.e., responding to a user's specific query) rather than browsing and therefore provide much more substantial searching capabilities than directories.

Groups, mailing lists, and other interactive forums create a class of Internet resources that too few researchers take advantage of but that is useful for a broad range of applications, including finding the value of data.

A range of news resources is also available on the Internet, including news services, news wires, newspapers, news consolidation services, and more. Because some studies around particular values are newsworthy, these studies may prove excellent sources for capturing the value of data.

A typical concern about web searches is the quality of the content. But in fact, high-quality content does exist with careful assessment. The following guidelines can help in finding quality content.

1. **Consider the source.** From what organization does the content originate? Look for the organization to be identified both on the web page itself and in the URL. Is the content identified as coming from known sources, such as a news organization, government, an academic journal, a professional association, or a major investment firm? The URL will identify the owner, and the owner may be revealing in terms of quality.

2. **Consider the motivation.** What is the purpose of this site—academic, consumer protection, sales, entertainment, or political? The motivation can be helpful in assessing the degree of objectivity.

3. **Look for the quality of the writing.** Content that contains spelling and grammatical errors can indicate content quality problems as well.

4. **Look at the quality of the source documentation.** First, remember that even in academic circles, the number of footnotes is not a true measure of quality. On the other hand, if facts are cited, does the page identify the origin of the facts? Look at some of the cited sources to see whether the facts were actually quoted correctly.

5. **Is the site, and its content, as current as it should be?** If a society is reporting on current events, the need for currency and the answer to the question of currency will be apparent.

6. **Verify the facts using multiple sources, or choose the most authoritative source.** Unfortunately, many facts given on web pages are simply wrong due to carelessness, exaggeration, guessing, or other reasons. Often they are wrong because the person creating the page content did not check the facts.

Remember that quality content is critical when identifying and reporting on a particular measure.

CONDUCTING LITERATURE REVIEWS

Literature reviews can be an overlooked, valuable resource. Although they might sound somewhat academic and time consuming, they can identify appropriate studies and relationships needed in a human capital analytics project. They can also disclose gaps in the literature, providing an opportunity to add information that will close that gap. A literature review may begin with a broad topic (e.g., *"Our employees have too much stress. Find out what is causing it and what it is costing us."*), and then progressively narrow to the point at which you identify the specific issues you intend to address. Here are some tips to conduct a literature review.

COLLECT BACKGROUND INFORMATION

Start gathering background information on your topic. It is helpful to consider how others define the issues in the analytics project. This step may include the use of dictionaries, textbooks, or searches using your favorite search engine. This step helps frame the definitions and vocabulary associated with the topic.

MAP ISSUES TO SOURCES

Next, start mapping specific sources of information for the issues associated with the topic. For example, if your topic is employee stress, one specific issue of interest may be the cause of stress. Databases housing peer-reviewed research provide information on this issue. A search of databases such as EBSCOhost or LexisNexis may locate relevant articles. Google Scholar is another good source of research articles, abstracts, and journals such as *California Management Review, HR Management, People and Strategy, Journal of Applied Psychology, Strategic HR Review, International Journal of Human Resource Management*, and more. And don't forget books. Information on issues related to your topic may be available in the business press. Use Amazon.com or other online booksellers as search engines to find books providing relevant information. The point of this step is to start organizing your information and the relevant sources.

READ WITH A CRITICAL EYE

Reading interactively versus passively offers the greatest opportunity to differentiate relevant from irrelevant literature. This approach means that when reading a research article, case study, or book, you should have a clear sense of your topic. As you read, consider the following questions:

- What is the fundamental premise or problem that this piece of information addresses?

- What do the authors say; what do they not say?

- If you are reading results of a research report, are the results telling the entire story?

- In what context are the results developed?

- What approaches or methods were used?

- How credible are the sources of information?

When reviewing existing research, look for key indications of viability of the study:

- Research questions guide the literature review conducted for the study.

- Literature review and statements of the problem inform the research objectives.

- Objectives set up the research design.

- Research objectives, design, and type of data dictate the method of data analysis.

- Analysis of the data influences the kinds of conclusions, inferences, and generalizations made by the research.

By focusing on these issues and by keeping a statement describing the need for your project in front of you, you can more quickly eliminate sources that provide only cursory information.

Summarize Findings

As you read, use a variety of tools to make notes of key findings from the literature, including stick-on notes, mind mapping, and pocket dictators. Bring notes together into a summary of findings. Content analysis is helpful here, but not necessary. Review your notes and seek common themes and issues. Although challenging for major projects, this synthesis of information demonstrates your complete understanding of the issue and ensures that you target the right measures for your analytics project. As you summarize your findings, be sure to cite your sources. Sources of information provide a foundation for findings and a premise for your underlying assumptions.

A literature review adds clarity to what you already know and brings new information. Through this process you will have greater awareness of meanings, methods, and measures associated with your topic.

INFORMAL RESEARCH METHODS

In addition to the more formal approaches of searching databases, previous studies, benchmarking, and literature reviews, less formal information-gathering approaches can be taken that are powerful and just as revealing.

EXPERIENCE OF OTHERS IN THE ORGANIZATION

One of the first steps is to contact others who are knowledgeable and experienced in the organization and who may understand a particular issue or project. They also may know of existing studies or have previous experience with relevant studies. These colleagues might be able to offer valuable insight.

VISITS WITH EXPERTS

A face-to-face visit with a topic expert within the organization may be helpful to understand connections or disconnects. Even with an assumed connection to an issue, you must obtain verification and validation before pursuing the project. Others may be able to press, slant, twist to redefine a particular impact measure, or suggest other measures that may be related to the project.

PROFESSIONAL GROUPS

Professional organizations, now in the human capital analytics area, might provide colleagues with the same or similar studies. For example, at ROI Institute, the Human Capital Analytics Research Alliance is comprised of HCA practitioners. Other examples are The Conference Board's Human Capital Analytics Council and i4cp's Workforce Analytics Exchange.

Conferences

Conferences focusing on human capital analytics can serve as a source of input, and their number is growing. Short of attending the conference, reviewing the conference proceedings or even speaking with a conference participant can uncover areas where the same or similar studies could have been conducted.

Human Capital Analytics Books

Numerous books on analytics, human capital analytics, and business analytics have been and are being published. These books often have many examples, studies, and scenarios that might connect to the question at hand. It is certainly worth a try.

FINAL THOUGHTS

This chapter focuses on reviewing the research and setting the hypothesis. The hypothesis is the proposed explanation of the issue or relationship between two or more variables. To accept the hypothesis, research has to be conducted. Some research includes formal methods of locating other studies, using benchmarking, using external databases, and reviewing literature. Informal methods can be just as effective. After the research is complete, one or more hypotheses are established; the research provides a basis for analysis to test the hypothesis.

CHAPTER 4

Achieve Business Alignment

Ideally, every analytics project should be aligned to business measures. Unfortunately, many are not. Alignment occurs at different levels and should occur at the conception of the problem, which often helps lead to a solution. Next, alignment occurs throughout implementation of the solution when stakeholders focus on specific business measures. Finally, to show executives that the project was worthwhile, alignment must be demonstrated through follow-up, which means tracking the business data, isolating the effects of the solution, and validating that business alignment did occur. This chapter explores the alignment process and introduces a V Model concept created by the ROI Institute, making connection between human capital analytics projects and business needs.

OPENING STORY

A few years ago, San Diego–based Scripps Health set a goal to become a "great place to work." To move forward with this initiative, the project team set out to answer the following alignment questions:

1. Is this issue a problem worth solving or an opportunity worth pursuing?

2. What are the specific business measures we need to address in this project?

3. What should the organization do (or stop doing) to improve the business measures?

4. What do we need to know or learn to make this project successful?

5. What should the perception of this project be from key stakeholders?

Recognizing that a "great place to work" organization should drive several business measures, Scripps examined those measures first. The literature quickly revealed voluntary employee turnover would decrease, recruiting attractiveness would improve, the quality of new employees would improve in the future, and engagement of employees should be examined as they become an important part of the organization. A review of the current data in these categories (attractiveness, retention, quality, and engagement) indicated that Scripps had an opportunity for improvement. They decided to pursue "great place to work" status in an effort to improve these numbers. They recognized that if they achieved this goal, they should contribute to an increase in revenue for the hospital, possibly an improvement in the quality of healthcare, a reduction in operating costs from improvements in retention and recruiting, and other important measures. With these primary business needs, the literature revealed some of the cost of the current levels of turnover, the cost to achieve the same level of quality and quantity of applicants that could be derived through a "great place to work" organization, and the cost of disengaged employees. The engagement piece was a little fuzzy because it was difficult to convert it to money at that particular time. But the research demonstrated that engagement is a problem worth pursuing.

In summary, Scripps found that the "great place to work" brand was an opportunity that would pay off in terms of attracting improved quality and quantity of applicants and lowering turnover of key talent. These findings provided the initial phase of alignment. With a need for payoff identified and specific business measures identified, attention turned to what must be accomplished to achieve the business measure. The project included three goals: (1) managers must get the employees more involved, (2) the jobs need to be adjusted to include greater levels of engagement, and (3) employees need to be rewarded for their engagement efforts. Learning objectives focused on what must be learned by key stakeholders. In general, managers must learn how to keep their employees engaged, the employees must learn how to change their mind-set to become more engaged, and the employees must realize the importance of engagement as the basis of special work initiative.

Finally, the ways in which the various stakeholders will perceive the project had to be determined. Employees must see this project as necessary and important to the success of the organization. Managers must see the project as relevant to their work and their needs. Everyone should see this as an excellent opportunity to improve the image and branding of Scripps. Based on the upfront analysis, the specific project objectives were:

1. Employees will perceive the "great place to work" as important to their own success.

2. Employees and managers will see that a "great place to work" is important to the image and branding for Scripps.

3. Managers will see a "great place to work" as relevant to their particular issues and needs.

4. Employees will learn new aspects of the job to become more engaged in the processes.

5. Employees will learn what is important to be recognized properly for an engagement.

6. Managers will learn how to get employees more engaged.

7. Managers will work with employees to enhance engagement.

8. Jobs will be redesigned to reflect engagement aspects.

9. A recognition system will be implemented to reward appropriate engagement.

10. Turnover or talent will be reduced by 30 percent.

11. Recruiting efficiency will improve by 15 percent.

12. The quality of the employees will improve.

13. Job candidates and qualifications will increase.

14. Employee engagement scores will be enhanced.

15. The ROI of this project will be 25 percent.

These objectives became part of the solution going forward to make sure that the alignment was always evident throughout the project.

This case study shows the power of an upfront analysis to clearly understand the problem and to work toward a particular solution. Having the alignment at five levels enables objectives to be set for the solution and sets up the process for potential evaluation all the way through those same five levels. The project was a success. The objectives were met. Ultimately, this project gained recognition in a variety of magazines, including *Fortune* in its list of 100 best workplaces.

IMPORTANCE OF BUSINESS ALIGNMENT

It is difficult to have a conversation about a project without discussing the subject of business alignment. Some classic questions that are often asked about business projects are:

- How will this project help our business?

- Is this project aligned with our goals?

- What is the business contribution?

- How is this project helping my key performance indicators?

- What is the business value of this initiative?

- Will the results of this project appear on my quarterly report?

These and similar questions focus on the issue of aligning projects to the business. Solutions must be aligned to the business early in the process and throughout the implementation. The business alignment must be validated after the program has been fully implemented and operational.

For this book we define business alignment as ensuring that a new project, solution, or process is connected directly to business impact measures, usually expressed in terms such as output, quality, cost, or time. It is important for alignment to be verified in the beginning of the project, during the life of the project, and in follow-up, confirming that the project contributed to improvements in one or more important business measures. When a project is properly aligned to the business, the organization will see a difference. When it is not aligned, the results can be disappointing and sometimes disastrous.

VALUE OF THE PROJECT

Sometimes the value of the project is reflected in the extent of the business alignment. Projects should be connected to the organization in terms of key business measures. When this alignment is achieved, the value of the project increases, particularly for those who fund and support it.

IMAGE OF THE PROJECT

Projects that are not connected to business often suffer from an image problem, while projects that are clearly connected often have a more positive image. A properly aligned project brings respect and enhances the reputation of those who organize, control, implement, and even own the project.

INVESTING IN THE PROJECT

Sometimes business alignment can determine whether a project is funded. Investment or funding decisions are usually made before a project is implemented. Also, investment decisions are made during a project to provide needed resources to keep the project going. After a project is completed, a decision is often made to invest in the same or similar projects in the future based on the success of the project. In today's economy, lack of business alignment often results in lack of investment.

SUPPORTING THE PROJECT

Projects must have management's support in order to succeed. Support comes in a variety of forms, such as allocating resources for the projects, encouraging people to be involved in them, allowing time to make them successful, and verbally endorsing the projects. Managers and administrators will support projects they view as important, and aligning projects to the business increases the perceived importance of a project. If the projects are not aligned, importance and support will diminish quickly.

PROJECT APPROVAL

Some organizations implement projects only if they are properly aligned to the business; otherwise the projects are not approved. Additionally, in these organizations, projects will not be continued unless the alignment is maintained. The alignment is a critical part of projected success.

Collectively, these issues make alignment a critical topic that cannot be ignored, regardless of the particular function in the organization.

THE V MODEL: A BUSINESS ALIGNMENT TOOL

The V Model is the tool with which business alignment becomes a visible process. Figure 4-1 shows the connection between evaluation and needs assessment for projects and programs. It shows the important link between the initial problem or opportunity and the evaluation of the solution. It also shows the three points where business alignment occurs: at the beginning of the project (A), during the project (B), and during the follow-up evaluation (C).

The concept of levels, on which the V Model is based, has been used for centuries to express increased value at a higher level. For example, when something is said to be moved to "the next level," it is suggested that the new level is more valuable than its predecessor. It is best to think of the V Model in terms of the evaluation side first. Evaluation of a particular solution moves through different levels of measuring:

- **Reaction** to the solution (Level 1)
- **Learning** skills and knowledge to make the solution successful (Level 2)
- **Application** of skills and knowledge in the workplace (Level 3)
- **Impact** measures linked to the solution (Level 4)
- **ROI**, a comparison of monetary benefits to the cost of the solution (Level 5)

FIGURE 4-1 The V Model

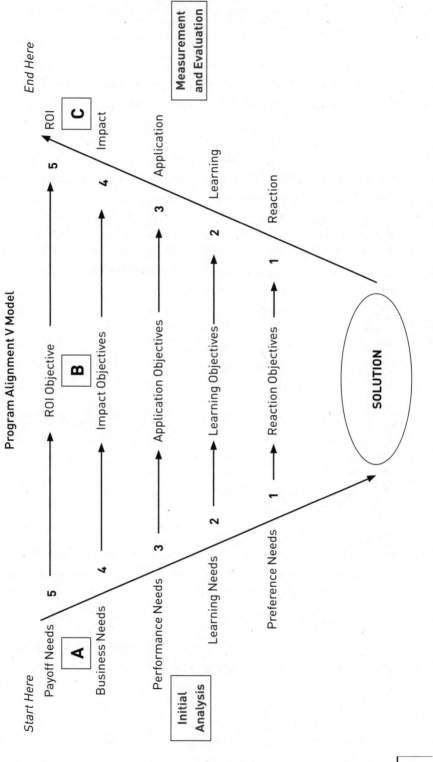

Program Alignment V Model

Start Here

End Here

Initial
Analysis

Measurement
and Evaluation

Payoff Needs **A** 5 ROI Objective **B** 5 ROI **C**

Business Needs 4 Impact Objectives 4 Impact

Performance Needs 3 Application Objectives 3 Application

Learning Needs 2 Learning Objectives 2 Learning

Preference Needs 1 Reaction Objectives 1 Reaction

SOLUTION

79

From the viewpoint of a program's key stakeholders, the clients or sponsors, for example, moving evaluation to the next level represents increased value; and most clients want to see the business contribution (Level 4) and even sometimes ROI (Level 5). In terms of evaluation of the solution, it is at Level 4 that the effect of the solution will be isolated on the data to indicate specifically how much improvement is connected to this particular solution. When this connection is established, the business alignment for the solution is validated.

The measures that are captured at each level are defined in the objectives. The five corresponding levels of objectives are illustrated in Figure 4-1. The impact objective is the business alignment through the solution. With an impact objective, all the stakeholders are focused on the ultimate goal of the solution in terms of business contribution. The focus is there for the organizers, designers, developers, facilitators, participants, managers of participants, and others who have an interest in the solution. The objectives increase in value as the levels progress, with Levels 4 and 5 being the most valuable from a client's perspective. These objectives are developed during the needs assessment. The needs assessment defines particular needs at each level. Here, the highest and most important level is the potential payoff of the solution, followed by business needs, performance needs, learning needs, and preference needs. Much of this chapter is devoted to these needs.

How the V Model Works with Human Capital Analytics

At Level 5, the potential payoff needs for a particular solution or initiative are addressed. This step examines the possibility for a return on investment before the solution is pursued. At Level 4, the specific business measures that need improvement to take advantage of the payoff opportunity are examined. At Level 3, the specific performance that must change, or action that must be taken to address the business needs, is defined. At Level 2, the specific information, knowledge, or skills that are required to address the performance needs are identified. Finally, the preferences for the program define the Level 1 needs. This connection is important for understanding all elements that make up a successful program or project.

All five types of human capital analytics projects described in Chapter 1 appear at some point on the V Model. In the first type, converting data to money can occur either on the left side or the right side of the V Model. Sometimes a request to convert data to money is a result of a measure that is improved based on a variety of different initiatives, solutions, and projects. Executives want to know about the money, which occurs at the right side of the business impact level. Sometimes a particular measure that is not converted to money may be deteriorating. For example, when stress is increasing within groups, the challenge is to understand the monetary impact of having excessive stress. As shown in Table 4-1, this issue occurs on the left side of the model when examining whether it is a problem worth solving or an opportunity worth pursuing.

The second type of human capital analytics projects addresses relationships between measures and causation. This issue occurs on both sides of the model. For example, some analysis must be conducted to understand the cause of a problem, which may include examining relationships of other variables through causal analysis. On the right side of the model, a concern about the attribution of this particular solution when it is implemented is addressed at the business impact level. Also, when moving toward ROI analysis and attempting to convert data to money, a method often used links hard-to-value measures to easy-to-value measures. This examination of relationships assumes a causal connection. The third type of analytics project involving predictive modeling occurs on the left side as the particular business measures are identified and predictions made for future outcomes on the right side of the model. Various scenarios are run to see how well the model actually predicts the impact measure.

The fourth type of human capital analytics project involves measuring the impact and ROI of a particular solution. This process is accomplished by using the right side of the V Model as the project is evaluated at reaction, learning, application, and impact levels. The impact data connected to the program are converted to money to compare the cost to calculate the ROI.

Finally, for projects involving ROI forecasting, the left side of the V Model becomes operational. The data that are developed working through the various levels of needs are then used to develop the forecast. Business impact measures are converted to money, and the cost of the solution is estimated. Using these data, analysts can forecast the ROI for a human capital initiative.

TABLE 4-1   Project Type and Occurrence on V Model

	Project Type	Occurrence	Purpose
I	Converting Data to Money	Both Sides	• To define monetary value of key measures • Determine if initiative is worth pursuing
II	Relationships and Causation	Both Sides	• Understand cause of a problem • Identify critical measures • Attribute improvement in business measures to initiative • Convert soft measures to money
III	Predictive Modeling	Left Side	• Identify critical measures • Identify future outcomes • Conduct scenario planning • Identify and address risks
IV	Impact and ROI Analysis	Right Side	• Evaluate project success at various levels • Determine change in critical measures • Connect project to business • Compare benefits to costs
V	Forecasting ROI	Left Side	• Project improvement in business measures • Estimate project cost • Forecast ROI

USING THE V MODEL

The V Model provides an effective way to examine any project or solution. It shows the points of alignment and demonstrates for the client and sponsor how the entire project framework is developed. It represents an extremely useful way to illustrate the connection between the upfront analysis and evaluation of the follow-up. The objectives provide the transition between the two. Other books contain several examples of V Models to show how they can be implemented for a variety of projects and programs.[1]

In some cases, it is obvious when serious problems affect the organization's operations and strategy. For example, at a hospital, an annual turnover of critical talent at 35 percent is an obvious issue and has potential payoff written all over it. In another organization, new account growth is flat and customer loyalty is low based on industry standards. These types of payoff opportunities make it clear that these problems need to be solved or an opportunity with a clearly identified business need should be pursued. This topic was covered in Chapter 2.

BUSINESS NEEDS: THE FIRST POINT OF ALIGNMENT

At Level 4, business data are examined to determine which measures need to improve. This review includes organizational records and reports, examining all types of hard and soft data. The performance of one of the data items usually triggers the consulting project. For example, when market share is not what it should be (operating costs are excessive, product quality is deteriorating, or productivity is low), the business measure is easily pinpointed. These key issues come directly from the data in the organization and are often found in the operating reports or records. This issue was explored earlier.

PERFORMANCE NEEDS

Level 3 analysis involves determining performance needs. The task is to determine the cause of the problem (or what is creating the opportunity) identified at Level 4 (e.g., what is causing the business to perform below the desired level). Something in the system is not performing as it should and may include, among other things, the following:

- Inappropriate behavior
- Dysfunctional behavior
- Ineffective systems
- Improper process flow
- Ineffective procedures
- Unsupported processes

- Inappropriate technology

- Inaction of stakeholders

The analysis usually reveals that a group of people are not performing as they should. The reason for this inadequate performance is the basis for the solution, the project. For example, if employee healthcare costs are increasing more than they should and sick leave usage is increasing, the cause may be unhealthy habits of employees. A wellness and fitness program may be needed.

Performance needs must be uncovered using a variety of problem-solving or analysis techniques. One approach may involve the use of data collection techniques discussed in this book, such as surveys, questionnaires, focus groups, or interviews. Another may involve a variety of problem-solving or analytical techniques such as root-cause analysis, fishbone diagrams, and other analysis techniques. Whatever is used, the key is to determine all causes of the problem so that solutions can be developed. Often, multiple solutions are appropriate.

LEARNING NEEDS

The analysis at Level 3 usually uncovers specific learning needs for project participants. The analysis may reveal deficiencies in knowledge and skills that can contribute to the problem—if they are not the major cause of it. In other situations, the solution will need a learning component as participants learn how to implement a new process, procedure, or technology. Learning typically involves acquisition of knowledge or the development of skills necessary to improve performance. In some cases, perceptions or attitudes may need to be altered to make the process successful in the future. The extent of learning required will determine whether formalized training is needed or if more informal, on-the-job methods can be utilized to build the necessary skills and knowledge.

PREFERENCE NEEDS

The final consideration, the preference for the project solution, involves determining the preferred way in which those involved in the process will need or want it to be implemented. A fundamental issue at this level is the perceived value of the project. Typical questions that surface are, "Is this important?" "Is this necessary?" and "Is it relevant to me?" Preference needs may involve implementation issues, including decisions such as when learning is expected and in what amounts, how it is presented, and the overall time frame. Implementation issues may involve timing, support, expectations, and other key factors. The important issue is to try to determine the specific preferences to the extent possible so that the complete profile of the solution can be developed based on all relevant needs.

OBJECTIVES

It is easy to see that the detailed needs analysis at the different levels yields program objectives. Objectives may be written as statements or hypotheses. Projects involving major resources and those of significant importance to the organization require a thorough needs assessment, and corresponding objectives should be developed at all levels. Perhaps the ROI objective can be omitted, but impact and application objectives are critical. Application objectives detail what individuals should do to make the project successful. Impact objectives are the consequence of those skills and represent the specific business measures identified in the upfront analysis. They provide a focus on business during the project, ensuring that alignment is a top priority for all of those involved, particularly the participants and the facilitators in a formal learning setting. Objectives are developed to be specific, often with accuracy, quality, and time specifications. More detail on objectives is provided later.

LEVELS OF EVALUATION

The levels of evaluation, as previously described, provide the framework for data collection to measure the success of the project. The levels of evaluation build on objectives. Objectives define precisely what is measured and often include the definition of success for that measure. These classic levels apply for all types of projects and programs. These levels date back to John Quincy Adams, as he developed levels of leadership effectiveness. Adams suggested that leaders cause others to dream more (Level 1), learn more (Level 2), do more (Level 3), and become more (Level 4). Additional information on levels of evaluation can be found in later chapters.

FINAL THOUGHTS

Business alignment is critical and essential. This introduction outlines why it should be undertaken and where to begin. The V Model clearly shows the steps that ensure alignment at the beginning of the project, as it is connected to business need. It also ensures that appropriate impact objectives are developed to keep the project focused and connected to a business measure throughout its implementation. Finally, on the follow-up when postprogram data are collected, the business measure is monitored as part of the evaluation at Level 4, impact evaluation. When the impact of the program is isolated, the resulting business contribution is clearly defined, showing the proof that the program or project made a difference. Every type of human capital analytics project occurs at some point on the V Model. As a process, business alignment cannot be ignored, and the V Model is a tool to keep alignment on track.

CHAPTER 5

Plan the Project

t is difficult to imagine pursuing any type of analytics project without proper planning. Unfortunately, planning is not always as thorough, accurate, or complete as it should be to make the project successful. All too often, analysts suggest that information will evolve as data are manipulated, which consequently leads to analytics with no purpose and an approach that cannot be replicated. Proper planning with the right individuals, using the right tools, takes additional time, but it makes the project more effective and helps it deliver better results. This chapter explores a rationale for proper planning, as well as the tools to make it happen. Four planning documents are introduced: a data collection plan, an analysis plan, a communication plan, and a project plan. Collectively, the documents address the complete array of key issues we need to think through prior to moving forward with any type of human capital analytics project. In addition to using planning documents, planning meetings with key stakeholders will help clarify the need for and approach to the analytics project. It is also an opportunity to secure critical buy-in and commitment for the approach. Both completion of the planning documents and a meeting with stakeholders can deliver a powerful human capital analytics project.

OPENING STORY

A large U.S.-based hotel company with operations in 78 countries has maintained steady growth to include more than 540 hotels. The company enjoys one of the most recognized names in the global hospitality industry with 98 percent brand awareness worldwide and excellent overall guest satisfaction.

The hospitality industry is competitive, cyclical, and subject to economic swings. Room rentals are price sensitive, and customer satisfaction is extremely important to the company. Profits are squeezed if operating costs get out of hand. Top executives constantly seek ways to improve operational efficiency, customer satisfaction, revenue growth, and retention of high-performing employees. Executives, particularly those in charge of individual properties, are under constant pressure to show improvement in these key measures.

To help the executives meet these goals, HR provided a variety of support services and teams, personal planning and execution tools, and customized learning processes including individual coaching sessions. Most of the executives indicated that they would like to work with a qualified coach to assist them through a variety of challenges and issues. The executives believed coaching to be an efficient way to learn, apply, and achieve results. Consequently, the company developed a formal coaching program—Coaching for Business Impact (CBI)—and offered it to executives at the vice president level and above.

From the start, the senior executive team became interested in showing the value of the coaching project. Although they supported coaching as a method to improve executive performance, they wanted to see the actual return on investment. The goal was to evaluate the coaching process for 25 executives, randomly selected (if possible) from participants in the CBI program.

The human capital analytics team began the planning process, which required them to review the objectives of the solution. Intentionally, the objectives were not clearly defined; the first challenge was to develop objectives at all five levels of outcomes from the solution. Then the data collection plan was detailed, which showed how the data would be captured at each level. It showed specific data items to be captured, the method of data collection, the timing for the collection, and the source of the data. Next, the data analysis plan detailed how the impact data would be analyzed. The data categories were included on the plan, along with how effects of the solution were to be isolated from other factors, the method of converting data to money, the cost of the solution, and the intangibles expected from the process. The team then developed a plan to communicate the results of the project. In this particular solution, six groups were targeted for the results. The method of communication ranged from a face-to-face briefing to a complete study. Finally, a project plan was developed, detailing the various steps during analytics project implementation. Actions were then taken as a result of the project.

During the planning process, the analytics team made adjustments to the project. A second session was added to elevate the coaching engagement from behavior to impact, the result desired by executives. Another session was conducted to gain commitment to provide the data necessary to show the value of the program. Finally, an action plan, a built-in data collection tool, showed participants the impact of the program. In essence, the planning changed the design of the solution to focus more clearly on results.

This opening story illustrates the importance of project or program planning. In this case, the project involves showing the financial ROI of a business coaching solution. The planning not only provided the details to make the project successful and the process more efficient, but it also enhanced the results along the way.

THE IMPORTANCE OF PLANNING

Human capital analytics is no exception when it comes to the importance of planning. This chapter presents four planning tools that should be considered first. More details should be provided whenever possible. In planning, too much detail is not the problem, but rather the lack of detail. We have never heard of a project going astray due to excessive planning. It is helpful to review what makes the planning so important.

Although It Takes Time, It Saves Time

Completing the planning documents may take several hours—at most a full day for a major project. Even though this amount of valuable time may not seem readily available, the time investment will pay off in the future. A detailed plan shows exactly what will be accomplished and by which methods. It takes the mystery out of the project and makes it mechanical going forward, not haphazard and randomly developed.

ADDRESSES THE KEY ISSUES AND QUESTIONS

Collectively, the planning process addresses 15 to 20 key issues about the project that include describing intended techniques, methods, and approaches. This process takes much of the later decision making away, particularly decisions made by others. Decisions are preliminarily made by key stakeholders in the planning meeting, ensuring buy-in into the approach.

KEY STAKEHOLDERS AGREE ON APPROACH

When the planning documents are developed, various stakeholders agree on them. The key client actually signs off on the process. Stakeholders become committed to the plan because they are part of it and they help make decisions about it. This initial agreement creates a cohesive team going forward.

FOCUS ON RESULTS

An advantage to planning is that it facilitates adjustments to the approach to achieve necessary results. One of the most obvious processes is the development of objectives. Whether the objectives are written as statements, hypotheses, or research questions, achieving clarity on the objectives and their relevant indicators is imperative before moving forward with an analytics project. Objectives communicate to project implementers, as well as other stakeholders, what you plan to measure and your expectations for results.

IMPROVES EFFECTIVENESS AND EFFICIENCY OF PROJECT

Because planning requires making decisions early, execution is much more efficient because it directs more focus on results. It is more efficient because the scheduling and sequencing, coordination, and timing are all settled. Planning helps save time, money, and stress and ensures buy-in of the approach.

DATA COLLECTION PLAN

Develop the data collection plan first. This plan specifies objectives and relevant measures, data collection methods, data sources, and timing of data collection. It also outlines who is responsible for data collection.

OBJECTIVES

The data collection plan begins with objectives. Each objective represents the measures you plan to take. If your project is an ROI study, you will develop objectives for reaction, learning, application, impact, and even ROI. Figure 5-1 includes objectives for the coaching project described at the beginning of this chapter.

An effective analytics project flows from the objectives. For coaching, it is important to clearly indicate the objectives at different levels as shown in the figure. The detailed objectives associated with this project reflect the four classic levels of evaluation plus a fifth level for ROI. Some of the levels, however, have been adjusted for the coaching environment. With these objectives in mind, it becomes a relatively easy task to measure progress on these objectives.

SOLUTION-FOCUSED PROJECTS

Figure 5-2 shows the completed data collection plan for the coaching project. The plan captures the following techniques and strategies used to collect data:

1. **Objectives.** The objectives are listed as shown in Figure 5-1 and are repeated only in general terms.

2. **Measures.** Additional definition is sometimes needed beyond the specific objectives. The measures used to gauge progress on the objective are defined.

3. **Methods.** This column indicates the specific method used for collecting data at different levels. In this case, action plans and questionnaires are the primary methods.

4. **Sources.** For each data group, sources are identified. For coaches, sources are usually limited to the executive, coach, manager of the executive, and the individual/team reporting to the executive. Although the actual data provided by executives will usually come from the records of the organization, the executive will include the data in the action plan document. Thus, the executive becomes a source of the data to the analytics team.

FIGURE 5-1   Objectives of Business Impact Coaching

Level 1: Reaction Objectives
The executive will:
1. Perceive coaching to be relevant to the job
2. Perceive coaching to be important to job performance at the present time
3. Perceive coaching to be value added in terms of time and funds invested
4. Rate the coach as effective
5. Recommend this program to other executives

Level 2: Learning Objectives
After completing this coaching solution, the executives should improve their understanding of or skills for each of the following:
1. Uncovering individual strengths and weaknesses
2. Translating feedback into action plans
3. Involving team members in projects and goals
4. Communicating effectively
5. Collaborating with colleagues
6. Improving personal effectiveness
7. Enhancing leadership skills

Level 3: Application Objectives
Six months after completing this coaching solution, executives should:
1. Complete the action plan
2. Adjust the plan accordingly for changes in the environment
3. Show improvements on the following items:
   a. Uncovering individual strengths and weaknesses
   b. Translating feedback into action plans
   c. Involving team members in projects and goals
   d. Communicating effectively
   e. Collaborating with colleagues
   f. Improving personal effectiveness
   g. Enhancing leadership skills
4. Identify barriers and enablers

Level 4: Impact Objectives
After completing this coaching solution, executives should improve at least three specific measures in the following areas:
1. Sales growth
2. Productivity/operational efficiency
3. Direct cost reduction
4. Retention of key staff members
5. Customer satisfaction

Level 5: ROI Objective
The ROI value should be 25%.

5. **Timing.** The timing refers to the time for collecting specific data items from the beginning of the coaching engagement.

6. **Responsibility.** The responsibility refers to the individual(s) who will actually collect the data.

OTHER SOLUTIONS

This example illustrates the data collection plan for the implementation of a solution. For other types of analytics projects, such as converting data to money, finding relationships between variables, and the cause of a problem, this slightly modified plan is recommended. Most solutions will probably just involve Level 4 data, but sometimes they may involve Level 3 data and on rare occasions even learning and perception data at Levels 2 and 1.

ANALYSIS PLAN

The second planning document is the data analysis plan, which details how the data will be analyzed, along with several different dimensions. These plans usually involve attribution, causation, and statistical methods as well.

SOLUTION-FOCUSED PROJECTS

For solution-focused projects, the data analysis plan focuses on how the solution will be evaluated all the way through to impact and ROI analysis. Figure 5-3 shows the completed plan for data analysis for the coaching project. This document addresses the key issues needed for a credible analysis of the data and includes the following:

1. **Data items.** The plan shows when business measures will be collected from one of the five priority areas.

2. **Isolating the effects of coaching.** The method of isolating the effects of coaching on the data is an estimation, where the executives actually allocate the proportion of the improvement to the coaching process (more on the consequences of this activity later). Some of the more credible methods, such as control groups and trend analysis, are not appropriate for this situation. Although the estimates are subjective, they are developed by those who should know them best (the executives), and the results are adjusted for the error of the estimate.

FIGURE 5-2 Completed Data Collection Plan

Solution: Coaching for Business Impact   **Responsibility:** _____   **Date:** _____

Level	Objective(s)	Measures/ Data	Data Collection Method	Data Sources	Timing	Responsi- bilities
1	**Reaction**	• 4 out of 5 on a 1 to 5 rating scale	• Questionnaire	• Executives	• 6 months after engagement	• HR Staff
	• Relevance to job					
	• Importance to job success					
	• Value add					
	• Coach's effectiveness					
	• Recommendation to others					
2	**Learning**	• 4 out of 5 on a 1 to 5 rating scale	• Questionnaire	• Executives	• 6 months after engagement	• HR Staff
	• Uncovering strengths/ weaknesses			• Coach		
	• Translating feedback into action					
	• Involving team members					
	• Communicating effectively					
	• Collaborating with colleagues					
	• Improving personal effectiveness					

#	Objective	Measures	Targets	Data Sources	Timing	Responsibilities
	• Enhancing leadership skills					
3	**Application/ Implementation** • Complete and adjust action plan • Show improvements in skills • Identify barriers and enablers	• Checklist for action plan • Questionnaire	• 4 out of 5 on a 1 to 5 rating scale	• Executives • Coach	• 6 months after engagement	• HR Staff
4	**Business Impact (3 of 5)** 1. Sales growth 2. Productivity/efficiency 3. Direct cost reduction 4. Retention of key staff members 5. Customer satisfaction	• Action Plan	1. Monthly revenue 2. Varies with location 3. Direct monetary savings 4. Voluntary turnover 5. Customer satisfaction index	• Executives	• 6 months after engagement	• HR Staff
5	ROI • 25 percent					

Comments: *Executives are committed to providing data. They fully understand all the data collection issues prior to engaging into the coaching assignment.*

FIGURE 5-3 The ROI Analysis Plan for Coaching for Business Impact

Solution: Coaching for Business Impact **Responsibility:** **Date:**

Data Items (Usually Level 4)	Methods for Isolating the Effects of the Solution	Methods of Converting Data to Monetary Values	Cost Categories	Intangible Benefits	Communication Targets for Final Report	Other Influences/ Issues During Application	Comments
• Sales growth • Productivity/operational efficiency • Direct cost reduction • Retention of key staff members • Customer satisfaction	Estimates for executive [Method is the same for all data items]	• Standard value • Expert input • Executive estimate [Method is the same for all data items]	• Needs assessment • Coaching fees • Travel costs • Executive's time • Administrative support • Administrative overhead • Communication expenses • Facilities • Evaluation	• Increased commitment • Reduced stress • Increased job satisfaction • Improved customer service • Enhanced recruiting image • Improved teamwork • Improved communication	• Executives • Senior Executives • Sponsors • NHLO staff • Learning & Development Council • Prospective participants for CBI	A variety of other initiatives will influence the impact measure, including our Six Sima process, service excellence program, and our efforts to become a great place to work.	It is extremely important to secure commitment from executives to provide accurate data in a timely manner.

3. **Converting data to monetary values.** Data are converted by use of a variety of methods. For most data items, standard values are available. When standard values are not available, the input of an in-house expert is pursued. This expert is typically an individual who collects, assimilates, and reports the data. If neither of these approaches are feasible, the executive estimates the value.

4. **Cost categories.** The standard cost categories included are the typical costs for a coaching assignment.

5. **Communication targets.** Several audiences are included for coaching results, representing the key stakeholder groups: the executive, the executive's immediate manager, the sponsor of the program, and the HR staff. Other influences and issues are also detailed in this plan.

OTHER PROJECTS

For the non-solution-focused projects, a different analysis plan is recommended. Non-solution-focused projects involve converting data to money, defining relationships between variables, and determining the cause of a particular relationship or problem. In those cases, a modified plan would be appropriate for analysis planning. This normal flexible planning details not only the types of data, the causation, and converting data to money if needed, but also the particular statistical techniques and processes planned in the analysis. Together these plans should provide the tools to do analysis for the project.

COMMUNICATION PLAN

Although communicating the results of an analytics project is often the most neglected step, it is the most important. A golden rule of evaluation: If you ask for the data, do something with them. In order to do something constructive, the right people must know the results.

The plan goes from describing target audiences to purpose, communication timeline, distribution channel, and responsibility. The plan also includes a place for communication status. Figure 5-4 shows the communication plan for the business coaching project.

FIGURE 5-4 Communication Plan

Target Audience	Purpose/Objectives of Communication	Communication Timeline	Distribution Channel	Responsibility	Status
Senior Executives	1. Present results 2. Gain support	End of project	Live briefing	Project Leader	
Executives involved in the project	1. Highlight their success 2. Reinforce the process used in the project	One week from final report is generated	Brief summary	Project Leader	
Analytics Team	1. Underscore the importance of measuring results 2. Explain the techniques used to measure results	Three weeks from end of project	Meeting with complete report	Project Leader	
HR Team	1. Demonstrate accountability for expenditures 2. Show the complete results of the project	Within three weeks of the project	Meeting with complete study	Project Leader	
Perspective Participants	1. Create a desire to be involved in the project 2. Market future projects	Prior to the announcement of new coaching opportunities	Brief summary	Project Leader	

PROJECT PLAN

The final planning document is the project plan, which maps each step of the evaluation process. Figure 5-5 shows an example. This plan is a culmination of the previously described plans, plus the detailed steps. The project plan begins with project approval and ends with communication and follow-up activities. As you complete each chapter in the book, the steps in the project plan will become clear. The first step is the project go-ahead, followed by problem definition, business alignment, and setting the hypothesis. The project plan includes these steps, as well as steps to design the data collection instruments and to administer the data collection process. The final section of the project plan includes any follow-up activity after you have communicated results.

The project plan helps track resources. Accounting for resources expended while implementing the project is a plus. It will save you time as you go. There are a variety of useful tools available to help plan a comprehensive analytics project. They allow you automatically to account for the costs of people involved in the evaluation, as well as the cost of other resources. However, spreadsheet tools such as Microsoft Excel work just

FIGURE 5-5 Project Plan

	F	M	A	M	J	J	A	S
Decide to Conduct Analytics Project	■							
Define/Align the Problem/Opportunity	■							
Set Hypotheses	■							
Design Data Collection		■						
Collect Data (L1–L2)			■					
Collect Data (L3–L4)					■			
Complete Preliminary Data Analysis					■			
Complete Data Analysis						■		
Write Report						■		
Print Report							■	
Communicate Results							■	
Initiate Improvements							■	
Complete Implementation								■

fine, or your organization may have an internal project planning tool. Microsoft Word is even a sufficient tool to develop a project plan, although it does lack some of the calculation capabilities. Nevertheless, the plan should represent an operational tool. Develop it by using the best tool for you and your team. It will save you time, money, and frustration!

ANALYTICS PROJECT PLANNING

The project plans are developed, completed, and finalized in a project planning meeting (although some of the input will be known and developed before this meeting). This crucial meeting brings together the various stakeholders. Four important issues must be addressed:

1. Who should be involved in the planning meeting?
2. What are the success factors (credible sources, access to data, etc.)
3. What is the agenda?
4. Who will approve the project plan?

Planning Participants

Participants of the planning meeting vary according to project. It is essential for the project owner, who may be the project leader as well, to participate. This person will drive the project. Next is the analytics project designer. And third is a project analyst, who will actually collect and analyze the data. The project analyst(s) could be a team or one senior leader. In the coaching example, it would be the person who manages the coaching process inside the organization. The business unit partner, who would represent the interests of the particular business unit, would also be involved. In the case of the hotel company, it would be someone familiar with the various units. It may be a property manager. A subject matter expert who understands the coaching process should participate, as well as another who understands the dynamics of the property manager's job. Finally, the solution user could be involved in some cases.

Success Factors

To make the planning meeting successful, several issues have to be addressed or be in place. This meeting must involve people with credible sources of information. Sometimes for a planning session like this, substitutes are sent who are not necessarily the best and most credible people, which is critical. Access to the data is another issue. When business impact is in use, it should be readily available to the team, or at least the capture process should be known to the group. Also, the group must cover all the issues, so no key participants can be missing. In terms of duration, this meeting can last anywhere from an hour for small projects to four hours for more involved projects. The key is to move swiftly and have the data prepared ahead of time if possible. It is important to consider the output to be a draft at this point, which could be adjusted by a different group when additional information is known.

Agenda

The meeting agenda is straightforward. The purpose of the meeting must first be explained. Next on the agenda are the objectives of the program. The project description itself can be detailed, as are the objectives for the particular elements of the project. For a solution-focused project, such as the coaching example, the objectives need to be detailed. Objectives should be developed ahead of time. Then a step-by-step description of the data collection plan, the analysis plan, the communication plan, and the project plan are presented. In each case, it is helpful to have much of the documents completed before the meeting, so that the team is merely filling in the gaps. After the planning documents are complete, a quick review of the next steps would be in order.

Approval

Now that the plans are complete, the adjustments are made based on any other feedback. The key is to seek commitment from key stakeholders so that they understand what their role will be and the role of those whom they represent. Their commitment is critical. Then, perhaps one of the most important points is to get the client to sign off on the project. Signoff can be a simple process, just present the plan of action and obtain agreement. It is helpful in this discussion to point out those things that might be considered weaknesses in the project, controversies around the project, or the difficult parts of the project. Finally, if budgets need to be secured (many times they do), they need to be secured at this time. The project planning meeting often yields an estimate of project cost.

So there you have it, one of the most important meetings related to a particular project.

FINAL THOUGHTS

Planning an analytics project is critical to its success. Thoughtful time and effort spent on planning will pay off in multiple ways throughout the project. Also, it is one of the most effective ways to enhance the focus on results throughout the project. This planning process contains four central documents. When these documents are completed and finalized in a planning meeting, the project is ready to go, most of the decisions have been made, and the road map has been developed. The next challenge is to collect the data.

6

Collect Data

Every human capital analytics project requires data collection, with some techniques comprising more types of data than others. This chapter explores various data collection methods, including classic processes such as surveys, questionnaires, tests, interviews, focus groups, observation, and performance monitoring.

OPENING STORY

Some of the most ambitious human capital analytics projects occurred at Sears Roebuck & Company. Faced with serious difficulties due to poor financial performance, Sears underwent a transformational project that changed the culture of the company. Led by the CEO with 100 top-level executives at Sears, the organization developed a business model that tracked the success of management behavior through employee attitudes, customer satisfaction, and financial performance.[1] This connection was made evident through multiple linkages and was referred to as the Employee-Customer-Profit Chain. In this model, employee attitudes were directly correlated with customer satisfaction. For example: 10 questions from their 70-question employee survey correlated with a 1.3-point improvement in customer satisfaction measured on a 10-point scale. The survey demonstrated that job satisfaction drives customer satisfaction. The 1.3-point improvement in customer satisfaction was shown to drive a 0.5 percent increase in revenue growth. Applying the store-level profit margin to this revenue growth showed the profits achieved from investing in employee attitudes.

At the heart of this project were five task forces collecting a massive amount of data:

- A customer task force reviewed customer surveys for several years and conducted 80 videotaped customer focus groups in the United States so every member of the task force could watch.

- An employee task force conducted 26 employee focus groups and studied all the data on employee attitudes and behavior, including a 70-item opinion survey given to employees every other year.

- The values task force collected 80,000 employee surveys and identified six core values that Sears employees thought strongly about.

- The innovation task force conducted external benchmarking, undertook a research project on the nature of change, and suggested an effort to generate 1 million ideas from employees.

- A financial task force built a model for the drivers of a total shareholder return over a 20-year period and drew emphasis about what Sears would have to do to be in the top quartile of Fortune 500 companies. A large quantity of data involved a variety of sources, and when combined with the appropriate analysis, developed the model described earlier.

The human capital analytics project was the cornerstone of the transformation that dramatically improved the financial results at Sears, turning around a loss of $3.9 billion.

Although every human capital analytics project involves data collection, the Sears project was one of the most extensive. This case underscores the point that data must be collected from a variety of sources, using a variety of techniques, sometimes at different time frames. These methods become an important part of the overall planning for data collection described in the previous chapter.

DATA COLLECTION ISSUES

Data collection comes in a variety of forms and is usually grouped into questionnaires, surveys, tests, interviews, focus groups, observations, and organizational performance data. Before presenting these techniques, it is helpful to review data collection issues and general design considerations. Each technique is presented with specific applications and a few specific design considerations.

It is also helpful to distinguish between external and internal research. The material presented in this chapter focuses on internal research. Internal research includes data collected within the organization such as employee perceptions and behaviors or indicators of organizational performance. External research may involve the use of a literature search, case studies, benchmarking, and other methods to collect data described in Chapter 3.

Types of Data

The type of data sometimes dictates the type of data collection. A comprehensive human capital analytics project usually includes a combination of impact data (hard and soft data) and application (behavior) data. For example, in a project to measure the success of an employee assistance program (EAP), five sets of data are needed:

- A reduction in healthcare costs associated with the EAP

- Improvement in EAP use

- Changes in job satisfaction

- Reduction in absenteeism

- Improvement in turnover

These changes include both hard data (turnover, absenteeism, and healthcare costs), soft data (job satisfaction), and application data (EAP use).

Preliminary Questions

Before developing data collection techniques, several issues should be addressed. The following questions help determine the optimum design for data collection:

- **How will the data be used?** Prior to selecting the technique, the basic purpose(s) of evaluation must be reviewed. Will the data be used to calculate ROI? Will it be used to solve a problem? Will it be used to measure the relationships between variables? The answers can have an impact on the type of data collection technique needed.

- **How will the data be analyzed?** Data are collected to be analyzed, summarized, and reported to others. The types of analyses, including statistical comparisons, should be considered before designing the appropriate technique.

- **Who will use the information?** Another important consideration is the target audience for communicating results. Who will review the information, and will the data be in a raw state or in a summarized form? Answers to these questions can lead to specific data items.

- **What type of data is needed?** An analytics project requires soft and hard data. Which ones are best for the project? Even though costs, output, time, and quality are usually desired; attitudes, reactions, or observations may also be needed.

- **Should the instrument be tested?** It may be appropriate to test a data collection instrument before using it, particularly in projects representing a significant investment. Testing provides an opportunity to analyze the data to find design problems.

- **Is a standard instrument available?** In some cases, standard instruments can prove effective for data collection with less cost than custom-designed instruments. In these cases, content and objectives must be consistent with the areas covered in the project. The measurement of broad-based issues, such as job engagement, job satisfaction, and culture may be appropriate for standard instruments.

- **What are the consequences of wrong answers or biased responses?** An often-overlooked issue is biased information supplied by participants. Data are sometimes supplied on a voluntary or anonymous basis, and biases may enter into the analysis. When opinions are sought, reliability is always in question. Purposeful wrong answers can influence outcomes.

Validity

The most important characteristic of a data collection instrument is its validity. A valid instrument measures what the individual using the instrument intends to measure. The degree to which it performs this function satisfactorily is usually called the relative validity. The analytics team should be concerned with validity when the appropriateness of a particular instrument is questioned. The economics of design may dictate that little time is spent on the subject, whereas an elaborate project demands more attention to validity. Four basic approaches are used to determine whether an instrument is valid. Adopted by the American Psychological Association, these approaches include (1) content validity, (2) construct validity, (3) concurrent validity, and (4) predictive validity.[2] Taking action to make the instrument valid is usually referred to as "defending" the validity of the instrument. Other resources are available to discuss validity in more detail.[3] No magic formulas ensure that an instrument is valid when it is designed. However, a few simple guidelines may help improve validity:

- **Include an ample number of appropriate items.** Too few items on an instrument can hamper its validity, while too many can be cumbersome and time-consuming. A proper balance improves validity.

- **Reduce response bias.** Participants responding to questions on an instrument may tend to say what they think administrators want them to say. This desire to please can render an instrument invalid. Participants should be encouraged to provide candid responses.

- **Involve subject matter experts regularly.** One of the best ways to improve validity, particularly content validity, is to have subject-matter experts review the materials, processes, steps, and procedures. Experts on the topic can help ensure that efforts are appropriate and materials are an accurate reflection of the real situation.

- **Ensure accuracy, completeness, and thoroughness.** Every step of the process should undergo scrutiny to ensure that the instructions are followed and the data analysis is accurate. The collection is rigorous and thorough.

- **Ensure objective instrument administration.** In some cases, the staff administering the instrument may be biased in the expected outcomes. For example, if one group is expected to outperform another, the administrator can sometimes influence the results.

RELIABILITY

Reliability is another important characteristic of a data collection instrument. A reliable instrument is one that is consistent enough that subsequent measurements of an item produce approximately the same results. For example, an engagement survey is administered to an employee. The same survey is administered to the same employee two days later. The results should be the same, assuming that nothing has occurred in the interim period to influence the perception of engagement. A reliable instrument will have consistent results. If results differ significantly each time the instrument is used, then the instrument is unreliable.

The causes of potential fluctuation of results is called error, and a number of sources of errors can affect the reliability of instruments. They include:

- Fluctuations in the mental alertness of participants

- Variations in conditions under which the instrument is administered

- Differences in interpreting the results from the instrument

- Random effects caused by the personal motivation of the participants

- The length of the instrument (with a longer instrument, more data are collected, but reliability may be increased at the expense of other factors)

Pre- and postmeasurements, where data are collected from participants before and after an intervention, require the use of reliable instruments; otherwise, the changes in responses cannot be attributed to the intervention. Several procedures are available to determine whether an instrument is reliable: test/retest, alternate form, split half, and inter-item correlations.[4]

IMPROVING RESPONSE RATES

Response rates are important in survey and questionnaire design and analysis. Low response rates always raise concerns. If the response rates are too low, usable information will be negligible. Table 6-1 lists the techniques to achieve a better response rate.

TABLE 6-1   Techniques to Increase Response Rates

1. Provide advance communication.	☐
2. Communicate the purpose.	☐
3. Identify who will see the results.	☐
4. Describe the data integration process.	☐
5. Let the target audience know that they are part of a sample.	☐
6. Add emotional appeal.	☐
7. Design for simplicity.	☐
8. Make it look professional and attractive.	☐
9. Use local manager support.	☐
10. Build on earlier data.	☐
11. Pilot test the questionnaire.	☐
12. Recognize the expertise of participants.	☐
13. Consider the use of incentives.	☐
14. Have an executive sign the introductory letter.	☐
15. Send a copy of the results to the participants.	☐
16. Report the use of results.	☐
17. Provide an update to create pressure to respond.	☐
18. Present previous responses.	☐
19. Introduce the questionnaire during the program.	☐
20. Use follow-up reminders.	☐
21. Consider a captive audience.	☐
22. Consider the appropriate medium for easy response.	☐
23. Estimate the necessary time to complete the questionnaire.	☐
24. Show the timing of the planned steps.	☐
25. Personalize the process.	☐
26. Collect data anonymously or confidentially.	☐

ADMINISTRATIVE ISSUES

Data collection instruments should be easy to administer and should not be burdensome or difficult for the participant or the analytics team member. Directions and instructions should be simple and straightforward, increasing the likelihood that the instrument will be administered consistently with different groups. Written instructions to participants (as well as verbal explanations) will help to ensure consistent application.

Other characteristics of an effective instrument are simplicity and brevity. Readability levels should be appropriate for the target audience's knowledge, ability, and background. Whenever possible, short, objective responses should be sought. Lengthy essay responses detract from the simplistic approach. The lowest number of questions necessary to cover a topic is recommended. Evaluators tend to oversurvey (ask more questions than necessary), which can frustrate participants.

As in every other HR initiative, economics must be considered in the design and/or selection of an instrument. An effective instrument is economical for its planned use. Costs must be considered in designing, developing, or purchasing an instrument. The time to administer an instrument, as well as the time to analyze the data and present them in a meaningful format, is another cost consideration.

QUESTIONNAIRES

Probably the most common data collection technique is the questionnaire. Ranging from short reaction forms to detailed follow-up instruments, questionnaires come in all sizes. They can be used to obtain subjective information about participant reactions as well as to document measurable results for use in an economic analysis. While versatile and popular, it is important that questionnaires be designed properly to satisfy their intended purposes. Improperly worded questionnaires are a major cause of problems in research methods.

TYPES OF QUESTIONS

Five basic types of questions are typically used. A questionnaire may contain any or all of these types of questions:

- **Open-ended question** asks for an unlimited answer. The question is followed by ample blank space for the response.

- **Checklist** presents a list of items. A participant is asked to check those items that apply to the situation.

- **Dichotomous question** asks for alternate responses, a yes/no, or other possibilities.

- **Multiple-choice question** presents several choices. The participant is asked to select the most correct one.

- **Ranking scales** require the participant to rank a list of items.

QUESTIONNAIRE DESIGN ISSUES

Questionnaire design can be a simple and logical process. A flawed design or an improperly worded questionnaire will be confusing, frustrating, and potentially embarrassing. The following steps ensure a valid, reliable, and effective questionnaire:

- **Determine the information needed.** Itemize the topics that are in some way related to the project. Questions can be developed later. It might be appropriate to develop this information in outline form so that related questions can be grouped.

- **Select the type(s) of questions.** Using the five types of questions described earlier, select the type(s) that best fit the intended purpose, taking into consideration the planned data analysis and variety of data to be collected.

- **Develop the questions.** Develop the questions based on the type of question(s) planned and the information needed. Questions should be simple and straightforward to avoid confusion or lead the participant to a desired response. Avoid terms or expressions unfamiliar to the participant. Develop the appropriate number and variety of questions, taking into consideration validity and reliability issues.

- **Test the questions.** After the questions are developed, test them for understanding. Ideally, questions should be tested on participants in a pilot group. If this approach is not feasible, questions should be tested on a group of employees at approximately the same job level and working environment as the potential participants. Critical input is helpful to revise and improve questions.

- **Format the questions into a neatly arranged questionnaire with proper instructions.** Format the questionnaire so the questions flow, following some kind of logical order. Position the questions so respondents can easily read, interpret, and respond.

- **Plan for data tabulation and summary.** A final step is to plan for data tabulation and summary. Even though technology makes data tabulation easy, it does not hurt to develop a code book or spreadsheet that will support data entry and tabulation, particularly if multiple people are involved. Also developing tables for data summary ahead of time makes report development go smoothly.

After completing these steps, the questionnaire is ready for use.

QUESTIONNAIRE APPLICATIONS

Questionnaires have a place in the evaluation of almost every type of HR program. They are used to:

- Uncover specific problems
- Collect reactions/perceptions from participants (Level 1)
- Measure capability to perform a task (Level 2)
- Report success, use, and behavior (Level 3)
- Identify barriers to success (Levels 1–4)
- Collect impact data for individuals and teams (Level 4)
- Suggest who should be involved in future solutions (Level 0)
- Solicit recommendations for improvement (Levels 1–4)

Questionnaires can be administered at different times. They represent one of the most versatile and effective methods of obtaining important information about design, effectiveness, and weaknesses. A few examples of specific human capital analytics applications are:

- Measure reaction to a new reward system.
- Obtain input on the cause of accidents.

- Gain input and suggestions for a new benefits program from a sample of employees.

- Survey sales representatives on the success of a new incentive program.

- Obtain feedback from employees and their supervisors on a new creativity solution.

- Gain input on features and concerns from participants in a new wellness program.

The applications vary, making questionnaires one of the most versatile data collection techniques. For additional information on questionnaire design, see our resource list located at www.roiinstitute.net.

SURVEYS

Surveys represent a specific type of questionnaire with several applications for human capital analytics. An analytics project may be designed to capture employee attitudes toward the job, policies, procedures, benefits, pay, the organization, and/or the immediate supervisor. Periodic measurements show changes in attitudes that have an impact on a work group, department, division, or entire organization.

Sometimes an organization will conduct a survey to measure employee engagement. Then, based on the feedback, HR solutions are undertaken to change engagement in areas where improvement is needed. Sometimes referred to as attitude surveys, opinion surveys, feedback surveys, or employee surveys, this data collection technique can help evaluate HR in a variety of ways. Surveys can be used to:

- Provide feedback to managers on how well they balance various managerial and leadership responsibilities.

- Build a database to inform the organization of the content and processes of selecting, developing, training, and retaining employees.

- Assist in the design and modification of policies, management systems, and decision-making processes, thereby improving overall organizational effectiveness.

- Provide a way to assess progress during periods of change.

- Assess the organization's internal climate and monitor the trends.

Measuring attitudes and perceptions is a complex task. Attitudes cannot be precisely measured, because information collected may not represent the participant's true feelings or actions. Also, the behavior, beliefs, and feelings of an individual will not always correlate. Attitudes tend to change with time, and a number of factors form an individual's attitude. Even with these shortcomings, it is possible to get a reasonable measure of employee attitudes and perceptions.

SURVEY DESIGN ISSUES

The principles of survey construction are similar to questionnaire design discussed earlier. However, a few guidelines are unique to the design or purchase of an attitude survey:

- **Limit statements to areas in which employees are capable of responding.** Employees should be capable of expressing an attitude or opinion on the subject. For example, suppose employees are asked about their attitudes toward a job-posting system in the company. If the system has just been initiated and little information has been provided, it will be difficult for employees to respond accurately.

- **Involve appropriate management.** Executives and administrators involved with this process must be committed to take action when survey results indicate that action is necessary. Management concerns, issues, and suggestions should be addressed early in the process, before the survey is conducted.

- **Keep survey statements as simple as possible.** Participants need to understand the meaning of a statement or question. Statements should be precise, straightforward, and easy to understand. Ambiguous statements must be avoided.

- **Try to keep participant responses anonymous.** If possible, participants should feel free to respond openly to statements or questions without fear of retaliation. Confidentiality is of utmost importance. Research indicates a link between survey anonymity and accuracy. If data are collected that can identify a respondent, then a neutral third party should collect and process the data.

- **Communicate the purpose of the survey.** Participants will usually cooperate in an activity when they understand the rationale for it. When a survey is administered, participants should be provided an appropriate explanation of its purpose and be told what will be done with the information. Also, they should be encouraged to provide correct and proper statements or answers.

- **Communicate survey results in comparison to a baseline or benchmark.** Attitude measures by themselves are virtually meaningless. They must be compared to attitudes over time or compared to other groups or organizations. The attitudes of a group of employees may be compared to all employees, a division, or a department. For purchased surveys, information may be available from similar industries in the form of normal data. Specific comparisons should be planned before designing and administering the survey.

- **Design for easy tabulation.** In an attitude survey, yes/no responses or varying degrees of agreement and disagreement are the usual formats.

Supplier-Produced Surveys

Many organizations purchase existing surveys to use in evaluations. These surveys have several advantages. They can save time in development and pilot testing. Most of the reputable companies producing and marketing surveys designed them to be reliable and valid for specific applications. Often these firms can easily tabulate the results, thereby saving time and expense. Also, externally developed surveys make it easy to compare results with others. For example, a company conducted a survey to determine what employees thought about an employee empowerment program. Based on the results, the company planned a communications program to reinforce the major elements where needed. They conducted a survey before and after the communications program and compared the results with other organizations within the same or similar industries.

Survey Applications

Surveys have a significant place in human capital analytics projects. In some organizations, surveys are the primary means to evaluate the HR function (e.g., satisfaction, engagement, culture). A typical approach is to conduct surveys annually, communicate the results to employees, outline specific action plans, correct problem areas or deficiencies, and measure progress the next year.

In addition to overall measures, surveys can be used to measure reaction toward a specific function of HR or an individual solution. For example, employees may be asked to provide responses about compensation, benefits, or the affirmative action program. As with overall survey results, this information can provide feedback necessary to make changes, implement new programs, or discontinue old programs.

Specific programs can easily be evaluated based on attitude surveys. For example, when a company implements a new Lean Six Sigma program, it can solicit employee attitudes to identify major problems, concerns, or successes connected with the program. Because surveys are a type of questionnaire, their use is almost as widespread as questionnaires, making them an integral part of the data collection process.

TESTS

Tests measure learning in human capital analytics projects. For example, an assessment test may predict performance on the job. A test administered during a sales enablement process predicts sales. An applicant score on a standardized test can predict the success of on-the-job training. Consequently, measuring what people know or what they can do is an important issue in the collection process and generates Level 2, learning data.

Types of Tests

Written tests (or automatic input with keyboard or mobile device) are the most common tests used in HR processes and represent a quick method for assessing knowledge. Most written tests are inexpensive to administer and to score for large groups.

Performance tests are usually more costly to develop and administer than written examinations. Performance testing allows the participant to exhibit skills, knowledge, or attitudes. The skill can be manual, verbal, or analytical, or a combination of the three. Performance testing is used frequently in job-related training to allow participants to demonstrate what they have learned. In supervisory and management training, performance testing comes in the form of skill practices or role play.

The one way to classify tests is by purpose and content. This classification divides tests into aptitude tests or achievement tests. Aptitude tests measure basic skills or acquired capacity to learn. An achievement test assesses a person's knowledge or competence in a particular subject. It measures the end result of education and training.

Another way to classify tests is by test design. The most common designs are oral examinations, essay tests, objective tests, and performance tests. Oral examinations and essay tests have limited use in human capital analytics projects. They are probably more useful in academic settings. Objective tests call for specific and precise answers, based on program objectives. Attitudes, feelings, creativity, problem-solving processes, and other intangible skills and abilities cannot be measured accurately with objective tests. Performance testing is useful in training, selection, and promotion.

Test Design Issues

The following design and administration elements are necessary to achieve an effective test.

- The test should reflect a representative sample of the target audience. It should allow the participant to demonstrate as many skills as possible related to the program. This inclusiveness increases the validity of the test and makes it more meaningful to the participant.

- The test should be thoroughly planned. Every phase of test administration should be planned, including timing, participant preparation, collection of necessary materials and tools, and evaluation of results.

- Thorough and consistent instructions are necessary. As with other instruments, the quality of the instructions can influence test results. All participants should be provided with the same instructions, which should be clear and concise. Charts, diagrams, blueprints, and other aids should be provided if they are normally provided in the work setting.

- Procedures for objective assessment should be developed. Acceptable standards must be developed for the test. Standards are sometimes difficult to develop due to varying degrees of speed, skill, and quality associated with test outcomes. Predetermined standards allow employees to know in advance what has to be accomplished for satisfactory and acceptable test completion.

- Information that will lead participants astray or that is irrelevant to the specific knowledge area being assessed should be omitted. The HR program is designed to assess particular skills. Participants should not be distracted or tricked into obvious wrong answers unless they face the same obstacles in the real-world environment.

Following these general guidelines, tests can be effective tools for project evaluation.

TEST APPLICATIONS

Testing is appropriate in any situation where employees need to demonstrate skills or knowledge. Primary applications are in the areas of training and development and employment functions. The following is a sample of applications of testing in HR:

- A large waste treatment company selects supervisors through a combination of an assessment process and a variety of tests. The assessment process uses exercises that allow supervisor candidates to demonstrate the skills and abilities needed to function in a supervisor job. Each exercise is validated through the content validity process. The tests are related to specific job dimensions and are validated in other settings for similar jobs. The candidate's performance on the assessment exercises and tests provides an overall rating to determine whether he or she should be part of the supervisory pool. A human capital analytics project involves predicting the on-the-job success from the overall rating.

- A large financial services company began a continuous process-improvement program with its employees. Using a variety of processes, including training sessions, team meetings, newsletters, posters, payroll stuffers, and other media, employees are taught fundamentals of continuous process improvement. The company administers tests at six-month intervals to measure the general level of knowledge among employees concerning different processes, terms, techniques, and principles. This process provides a measure of progress from which program planners and coordinators could make changes.

- An engineering company requires candidates for the job of industrial engineer to demonstrate time study skills. Participants are asked to conduct a time study on an actual job in a plant. An expert observes the participants and performs the same study and compares his results with those of participants. These comparisons provide an adequate reflection of the skills needed in the job. This realistic job preview is intended to reduce turnover in the first six months, and the analytics project is designed to test this hypothesis.

- As part of a management development program, managers at one company are trained to motivate average performers. Part of the evaluation requires managers to write a skill practice session in an actual situation involving an average performer in the department. Participants are then asked to conduct the skill practice (performance test) with another member of the group using the real situation and applying the principles and steps taught in the program. The facilitator observes the skill practice and provides a written critique at the end of the practice. These critiques provide part of the evaluation of the program.

- Potential aircraft assemblers participate in a pre-employment program on the basics of aircraft production assembly techniques. At the end of the program, participants are required to complete a special job-related project. They are provided a blueprint and a list of materials and are asked to build the item according to the specifications outlined on the blueprint. The time for completion, quality of work, and accuracy of the completed project are translated into an overall rating. A successful rating is necessary for the candidate to be selected for the permanent job of an aircraft assembler. A human capital analytics project involves predicting the on-the-job success of the candidates using the rating as a predictor.

These testing applications are only a few that are available to measure current levels of skills and abilities. Applications of testing are enormous because so many HR programs involve learning.

INTERVIEWS

One of the most useful data collection techniques is the interview. Because of their flexibility, interviews can be conducted by the analytics team or a third party. Interviews can secure data unavailable in performance records, or data difficult to obtain through written responses or observations. Also, interviews can uncover success stories that can be useful in a program's overall evaluation. Participants may feel reluctant to fully describe the results of a program in a questionnaire but will volunteer information to a skillful interviewer who uses probing techniques. The interview process will help secure reactions, uncover changes in job-related behavior, and determine program results. A major disadvantage of the interview is that it is time-consuming. The interviewer must prepare to ensure that the process is reliable and is conducted effectively.

Types of Interviews

Interviews usually fall into two basic types: structured and unstructured. A structured interview is much like a questionnaire in that specific questions are asked with little room to deviate. The primary advantages of the structured interview over the questionnaire are that the interview process can ensure that all questions have been covered and the interviewer understands the responses supplied by the participant. When compared to the unstructured interview, the structured interview is more efficient and accurate for collecting factual information.

The unstructured interview allows probing for more information and provides the most in-depth information for complex or elusive issues. This type of interview employs a few general questions that can lead to more detailed information as data are uncovered. The interviewer who conducts an unstructured interview should be skilled in the probing process and use typical probing questions such as the following:

- Can you explain your response in more detail?

- Would you give me an example of what you are saying?

- Could you explain the difficulty that you say you encountered?

- What other factors influenced this situation?

- Can you explain this process in more detail?

By using probing questions, the interviewer can delve more deeply into the information needed from the participant and still follow a free-flow format. The interviewer may also acknowledge what has been said with a follow-up question for more information or can restate the previous comment and thus obligate the interviewee to respond with more information.

INTERVIEW DESIGN ISSUES

Although the same principles involved in designing questions for a questionnaire can also apply to interview questions, here are a few specific steps in the development of an interview that can lead to a more effective instrument:

- **List basic questions to be asked.** After a decision has been made about the type of interview, itemize specific questions. Each question should be brief, precise, and designed for easy response.

- **Try out the questions.** Interview questions should be tested on several participants, and their responses should be analyzed. If possible, the interviews should be conducted as part of the trial run of the HR program.

- **Train the interviewers.** The interviewer should receive training in probing, collecting information, and summarizing it in a meaningful form.

- **Provide clear instructions to the interviewee.** The person being interviewed should understand the purpose of the interview and know what will be done with the responses. Expectations, conditions, and rules of the interview should be thoroughly discussed. Confidentiality considerations should be clearly communicated.

- **Administer the interviews according to a plan.** As with the other evaluation instruments, interviews should follow a predetermined plan. Timing, people involved, and location are all relevant issues in developing an interview plan. With a large number of participants, a sampling plan saves time and reduces the cost of the evaluation.

INTERVIEW APPLICATIONS

As with questionnaires, the interview represents another versatile data collection technique. A few specific applications of the interview reveal the varied uses of this technique.

- Many organizations conduct exit interviews with employees who are voluntarily leaving. These interviews provide important information for decreasing employee turnover, improving efficiencies, and so on.

- A technology firm uses telephone interviews to collect data from employment applicants who are not offered a job. The purpose is to ensure that they were treated in a professional way and that the correct procedures and policies were followed. Although these employees are not pleased with the outcome of the process, they will usually provide helpful information on the entire employment process.

- Some organizations use field interviews to follow up on management development solutions to ensure that managers used the content and achieved results. The interview uncovers specific actions taken, the successes achieved, and the barriers to implementing the content.

- An electric utility conducts random interviews with employees who recently used a new preferred provider organization (PPO). The interview is part of an evaluation of the effectiveness of the

PPO. Interviewees relate their experiences with the new PPO and any problems encountered.

- A large bank conducts interviews with a sample of employees to collect information on the effectiveness of the compensation plan. Because the program involves several elements, from job descriptions to performance reviews, it is important for the bank to obtain information on how all of these elements are functioning. The information provides feedback to program planners for possible improvements to the program. Often, the success of a compensation plan hinges on users' perceptions of the program.

- A multi-industry firm interviews a randomly selected group of participants from a productivity improvement effort. Employees are asked to detail their actions to improve productivity and the results they achieved from their efforts. If no results were achieved, participants are asked to explain what prevented improvements. Probing allows the interviewer to detail specifics.

This sample of applications illustrates the many ways in which interviews can be used to collect information for analytics projects.

FOCUS GROUPS

Focus groups are particularly useful in providing in-depth feedback for human capital analytics projects. For some professionals, the focus group process is becoming the evaluation instrument of choice. Focus groups are small group discussions conducted by experienced facilitators. They solicit qualitative judgments on a particular topic or issue following a planned agenda. Individual input builds on group input. With this process, individuals build on the ideas and comments of others to provide an in-depth view not attainable from questioning people individually. Unexpected comments and new perspectives can be easily explored.

For years, the HR profession has largely ignored the focus group potential for evaluation. In other types of research, particularly marketing, the focus group has long generated quality information on which to base decisions. Marketing researchers use the focus group to test new products, assess marketing campaigns, and evaluate advertising. The process is also used to secure input for changes in company policies, provide feedback on problems within an organization, and collect information for needs analyses. Analytics teams are now seeing the benefits of using focus groups.

The basic premise for using focus groups is that when quality judgments are subjective, several individual judgments are better than one. When compared with questionnaires, surveys, tests, or interviews, the focus group process has several advantages:

- A focus group is inexpensive and can be quickly planned and conducted.

- Participants often motivate one another, which generates new ideas and hypotheses.

- The format is flexible to allow for in-depth probing and confirmation.

- Its flexibility makes it possible to explore a solution's unexpected possible outcomes or applications.

In summary, the focus group is an effective and quick way to collect data on a project. However, for complete results, focus group information should be combined with data from other instruments.

Focus Group Design Issues

Although no standards specifically guide how to use focus groups for measurement and evaluation, the following guidelines should be helpful:

- **Plan topics, questions, and strategy carefully.** As with any evaluation instrument, planning is critical. The specific topics, discussion questions, and issues to be discussed must be carefully planned and sequenced. This planning enhances the reliability of the process when results are combined from more than one group. Also, it ensures that the group process is productive and stays on track.

- **Secure management buy-in.** Because focus groups are a relatively new process for HR, they might be unknown to some management groups. Managers should be informed about focus groups and their advantages in order to raise confidence levels for the information obtained from group sessions.

- **Keep the group size small.** The group size should be appropriate to provide opportunity for one participant to build on another's comments. Although no precise group size is mandated, a range of 8 to 12 seems appropriate for most focus group applications. A group has to be large enough to collect different points of view, but small enough to provide each participant a chance to discuss issues freely and exchange comments.

- **Select an appropriate number of groups.** It is important that enough focus groups are assembled to provide the quality information that can be used to reach conclusions. Although it is dangerous to suggest a percentage, a range of 5 to 20 percent of the target population may be appropriate for most focus group applications. This number depends on many factors such as the size of the target group, the importance of having complete group representation of the target population, and the cost involved in conducting additional focus groups.

- **Use a representative sample of the target population.** Groups should be stratified appropriately so that participants represent the target population. The group should be homogeneous in experience, job level, and influence in the organization.

- **Prepare facilitators.** Unlike some instruments, the success of a focus group rests with the facilitator. The rapport that the facilitator builds with the group can encourage participants to fully express their feelings. The facilitator must be trained in the focus group process and have an opportunity to practice it before using it to collect evaluation data. Facilitators must understand group dynamics, know how to filter opinions from vocal members of the group, be able to moderate those who want to dominate the group, and be able to create an environment in which participants feel comfortable in offering comments. Because of these strict requirements, some organizations use external facilitators.

Focus Group Applications

The focus group is particularly helpful when information is needed about the quality of an HR program or to assess behavior change resulting from the program. For example, the focus group process has been used in the following evaluation situations:

- To find the cause of a problem

- To evaluate the solution design and implementation in a pilot test solution

- To assess specific solution elements, features, or components

- To judge the overall effectiveness of the solution as perceived by participants immediately following a program's implementation

- To determine the solution's impact in a follow-up evaluation after the solution has been completed or implemented

Essentially, the process is helpful when evaluation information is needed that cannot be collected adequately with other methods. Some specific applications of the focus group are:

- A large utility company undertook a human capital analytics project to change the culture of the organization from bureaucratic and inefficient to creative and entrepreneurial. As part of the project, groups of randomly selected employees were assembled in focus groups to discuss the changes needed.

- A large bank was interested in the perception of the employee benefits package. A sample of employees were invited in focus groups to secure information about the perceived adequacy of the benefits package, problems with specific benefits, and specific concerns over the direction of employee benefit planning.

- A government agency conducted a diversity management program. As part of the evaluation of a pilot program, all participants reported on changes in attitudes and perceptions in focus groups. Also, in addition to the evaluation information, participants outlined specific steps needed to continue with the implementation of the program.

- An international technology service firm implemented a quality of work life program. In focus groups, evaluators determined reactions, successes, and failures of the program.

Essentially any application using the interview may be appropriate for the focus group. Its use is growing and the results are impressive.

OBSERVATION

Another useful data collection technique involves observing participants to record changes in on-the-job behavior. This technique is appropriate for measuring the success of programs such as organizational change, safety, or total quality. Sometimes observation is used to uncover problems or confirm assumptions about behaviors or current actions. The observer may be a member of the analytics team (most common), a member of a peer group, or an outside party. Observation is an excellent method of evaluating behavioral change, because actual behavior is measured. Also, participants' interactions with others, both verbal and nonverbal, can be evaluated.

OBSERVATION DESIGN ISSUES

The effectiveness of the observation process can be improved with the following guidelines for their design and use.

- **Observers must be fully prepared.** Observers must fully understand what information is sought. They must be trained for the assignment and offered a chance to practice observation skills.

- **The observations should be systematic.** The process must be planned so that the observation is executed effectively without surprises. In some cases, participants being observed may be informed in advance about the observation and the reasons they are being observed. The timing of observations should be planned. If an observer must observe a participant when times are not normal (i.e., in a crisis), the data collected may be unreliable.

- **The observers should know how to interpret and report what they see.** The observation process involves judgmental decisions. Observers must analyze behaviors as they are being displayed, including the range of actions taken by the participants. Observers should know how to summarize findings and report results in a meaningful manner.

- **The observer's influence should be minimized.** Even though it is impossible to completely isolate the effect of an observer, the presence of the observer and the significance of the activity should be minimized. Otherwise, participants being observed may display the behavior they think is appropriate, and they will usually be at their best. Observers should dress in a similar manner to the participant being observed and should stand at a discrete distance, if possible. Also, the longer the observation period, the less the disruptive effect of the observer.

OBSERVATION METHODS

Five methods of observation are available: behavior checklist, coded behavior record, delayed report, audio monitoring, and video recording. The method should be selected according to the type of information needed.

- A **behavior checklist** can be useful for recording the presence, absence, frequency, or duration of a participant's behavior as it occurs. To make observation more effective, only a small number of behaviors should be listed in the checklist and they should be listed in a logical sequence if they normally occur in sequence. Also, behaviors expected to be used more frequently should be placed first so they can be easily checked. A checklist has some disadvantages. It will not usually provide information on the quality, intensity, or possibly the circumstances surrounding the behavior observed. Measuring the duration of a behavior is difficult and may require a stopwatch and a section on the form to record the time interval.

- A **coded behavior record** is more time-consuming than a checklist. Codes are entered to identify a specific behavior. This approach is useful when it is essential to document, as much as possible, what actually happened or when too many behaviors exist for a checklist. Also, coding can often be compiled on a computer. Disadvantages of this approach are that the data are difficult to summarize and interpret, and the observer must remember special codes or devise codes as the observation is taking place.

- In the **delayed report method** the observer does not use forms or written materials during the observation, but rather, information is either recorded after the observation is completed or at particular time intervals during an observation. The observer tries to reconstruct behavior during the observation period. An important advantage of this approach is that the observer is not as noticeable, because no forms are completed or no notes are taken during the observation. The observer can be a part of the situation and less distracting to the participants. A disadvantage is that the delayed information may not be as accurate and reliable as the information collected at the time the behavior occurred.

- **Video/audio monitoring of employees** may stir some controversy. It is, however, an effective way to determine whether skills are being applied consistently and effectively. For it to work smoothly, it must be fully explained and the rules clearly communicated. It may be awkward and cumbersome to provide for videotaping of the behavior. When compared to direct observation, the participants may be unnecessarily nervous or self-conscious when they are being videotaped. If the camera is concealed, the privacy of the participant may be invaded.

- **Recording the behavior or action** captures exactly what happened in detail either electronically, by checklists, or procedures. Several disadvantages inhibit its use. With more software in use and procedures in place, this approach is common.

OBSERVATION APPLICATIONS

Although not as versatile as other data collection techniques, the observation process does have some important applications. Whenever a specific skill or analytics projects application needs to be verified, direct observation may be the most effective approach. Some specific examples of observations are as follows:

- In a telecommunications company, all customer-contact employees are expected to respond to customer requests in a helpful and productive way, using a specific step-by-step procedure. To determine whether employees respond properly, supervisors monitor telephone conversations on a selected, and sometimes random, basis.

- In a sales training solution for a retail firm, new sales representatives learn a specific process to generate sales, using a series of steps. After the solution is implemented, a "planted" potential customer observes the sales reps. The use of specific skills is recorded through the delayed report method.

- After the implementation of a corrective discipline solution in an electric utility company, supervisors conduct disciplinary performance discussions following the specific steps for applying corrective discipline. The department manager always sits in on these meetings and is asked to observe. The department uses a behavior checklist to determine whether the supervisor followed the process, steps, and actions when discussing the disciplinary problem. The supervisor was not aware that the department manager was "observing" the process.

- A claims processing center for an insurance company was experiencing a tardiness problem. Employees logged in to the computer when they arrived at work and the system recorded when the first claim was processed. Management was concerned about the late arrivals. The company implemented a tardiness reduction program and stressed to employees that they must be on time and process claims when the customers are available. The number of employees arriving in the department late past the normal work period was observed and recorded before and after to measure the change. The electronic monitoring provided an adequate measure of the changes in tardiness.

These examples show the various applications of observation as a data collection method. It can be an important tool in analytics projects.

ORGANIZATIONAL PERFORMANCE DATA

Data are available in every organization to measure organizational performance. Although it may appear awkward to refer to performance records as a data collection technique or analytics instrument, in the context of human capital analytics projects, they serve the same purpose as focus groups or attitude surveys. They enable the human capital analytics team to measure performance in areas such as output, quality, costs, and time, and are necessary for an accurate evaluation system. Table 6.2 lists common performance records or measurements for employees.

Existing data should be considered first. In most organizations, these data will be available. If not, additional record-keeping systems will have to be developed for analysis and measurement. At this stage, as with many other stages in the process, the question of economics must be considered. Is it economical to develop the record-keeping system to complete an analytics project? If the costs are greater than the expected return for the entire program, then it is meaningless to develop one.

Using Existing Data

If existing records are available, specific guidelines are recommended to ensure that the measurement system is easily developed.

- **Identify appropriate records.** The performance records of the organization should be thoroughly researched to identify those that are related to the proposed objectives of the human capital analytics project. Frequently, an organization has several performance measures related to the same item. For example, the efficiency of a production unit can be measured in a variety of ways:

  ○ Number of units produced per hour

  ○ Number of on-schedule production units

- Percent utilization of the equipment
- Percent of equipment downtime
- Labor cost per unit of production
- Overtime required per unit of production
- Total unit cost

Each of these, in its own way, measures the efficiency of the production of a work unit. All related records should be reviewed to identify those that are most relevant to the project.

TABLE 6-2   Examples of Performance Records

Absenteeism	Output
Accident costs	Overtime
Accident rates	Percent of quota achieved
Budget variances	Processing time
Complaints, employee and customer	Production schedules
Cost reduction	Productivity
Costs, overhead	Products returned
Costs, unit	Project schedule variations
Cycle time	Rejects, scrap
Delivery time	Reports completed
Design time	Sales (revenue)
Downtime	Sick leave costs
Efficiency	Tardiness
Employees promoted	Terminations, employee
Equipment utilization	Transactions completed
Errors	Turnover, employee
Grievances	Waste
Inventory adjustments	Work backlog
New accounts	Work stoppages
On-time shipments	

- **Determine whether a sampling plan is necessary.** When a large number of participants are involved in a project or when total numbers are not available, a sampling of records may be adequate to supply the information needed. The sampling plan should be structured to provide an adequate sample size based on random selection, if possible.

- **Convert current records to usable ones.** Occasionally, existing performance records are integrated with other data and are difficult to isolate from unrelated data. In this situation, all existing related data records to be used in the measurement should be extracted and retabulated to be more appropriate for comparison in the evaluation. Conversion factors may be necessary. For example, the average number of new sales orders per month may be reported regularly in the performance measures for the sales department. In addition, another performance record may report the sales costs per sales representative. However, the average cost per new sale is needed for the project. The two existing performance records are combined to supply the data necessary for comparison.

Developing New Data

In some cases, performance records are not available for the information needed for the human capital analytics project. The analytics team must guide the development of these record-keeping systems, if they are economically feasible.

For example, one hotel implemented a new selection tool designed to have a better value fit with the candidate and the hotel. The impact measure is the turnover in the first six months. This "early turnover" is the percentage of employees who leave the company in the first six months of their employment. The hypothesis is that the "test" should influence this turnover figure. At the time of the implementation, early turnover data was not available. The hotel began collecting early turnover figures for comparison when it implemented the program, thus providing a basis for evaluating the hypothesis.

When creating new performance records, several questions are relevant:

- Which department will develop the record-keeping system?
- Who will record and monitor the data?
- Where will it be recorded?
- Will forms be used?
- Who will bear the costs?

These questions will usually involve other departments or a management decision extending beyond the scope of the analytics team. Possibly the administration division, finance department, or industrial engineering section will be instrumental in determining whether new records are needed and how they should be collected.

SAMPLING

Many human capital analytics projects will involve sampling a group of people. Although big data applications suggest that we use all the data, many projects, if not most, will have to rely on a sample. The effort to make large data sets usable is greater than choosing a small sample. Also, sometimes it is more accurate to have a small sample clearly selected to compare with another group. Sampling has to be a part of the process and is covered in more detail in other resources. An HCA technical paper on sampling is available at www.roiinstitute.net.

FINAL THOUGHTS

Table 6-3 summarizes the features of data collection instruments presented in this chapter. Use this table as a quick reference to compare the various types of instruments. It is adapted in part from an aid developed by the U.S. Office of Personnel Management. It is important to remember that a variety of instruments are often appropriate in an analytics project.

This chapter explored the seven basic types of data collection instruments. These are classic instruments that have been in use for many years. Each has advantages and disadvantages and is best used in specific ways in human capital analytics projects. Table 6-3 shows some advantages and disadvantages that help to make a selection decision. Also, the table shows which instruments are appropriate for the level of data being collected. The next chapter is the first to address analysis, beginning with analyzing relationships and causation.

TABLE 6-3 Comparison of Common Data Collection Instruments

Instruments	Level of Data				Advantages	Limitations
	Reaction	Learning	Application	Impact		
Questionnaire	✓	✓	✓	✓	• Low cost • Honesty increased • Anonymity optional • Respondent sets pace • Variety of options	• May not collect accurate information • On-job responding conditions uncontrolled • Respondent sets pace • Return rate difficult to control
Survey	✓	✓	✓		• Standardization possible • Quickly processed • Easy to administer	• Predetermined alternatives • Response choices • Reliance on norms may distort individual performance • May not reflect true feelings
Test		✓			• Low purchase cost • Readily scored • Quickly processed • Easily administered • Wide sampling possible • Reliability • Simulation potential • Objective-based	• May be threatening to participants • Possible low relations to job performance • Reliance on norms may distort individual performance • Possible cultural bias

Method	Advantages	Disadvantages
Interview	• Flexible • Opportunity for clarification • Depth possible • Personal contact	• High reactive effects • High cost • Face-to-face threat potential • Labor-intensive • Trained interviewers necessary
Focus Groups	• Flexible • Low cost • Good qualitative responses • Personal contact	• Effectiveness rests with facilitator • Subjective • Sometimes difficult to summarize findings
Observation	• Nonthreatening to participants • Excellent way to measure behavior change	• Possibly disruptive • Reactive effect • Unreliable • Trained observers necessary
Performance Records	• Reliability • Objectivity • Job-based • Ease of review • Minimal reactive effects	• Lack of knowledge of criteria for keeping/discarding records • Information system discrepancies • Indirect nature of data • Need for conversion to usable forms • Records prepared for other purposes • Sometimes expensive to collect

CHAPTER 7

Analyze Relationships, Causation, and Attribution

In many human capital analytics projects, the question is, "What is causing the apparent problem?" Sometimes a particular measure is unacceptable or out of the norm of what is expected. Understanding the cause of deteriorating performance is crucial. Sometimes the impact measures are adequate but could be much better, and the focus is on the barriers that keep them from improving. Various tools help to illuminate answers, ranging from problem solving and analytical tools to qualitative tools. A technique to analyze the relationship between variables, such as correlation and regression analysis, might be in order. Or simple hypothesis testing or factor analysis may be appropriate. A qualitative approach may be necessary. The point is that a particular tool, process, or technique must be implemented to understand the relationship.

Also, one of the standard processes in the human capital analytics model is determining how much of the improvement in impact data can be directly attributed to a particular solution. This chapter describes several isolation methods, ranging from classic experimental versus control group, trend-line analysis and analytical processes, to estimates from a variety of sources. Because this step is always recommended, a default method is needed: expert estimation with error adjustment.

OPENING STORY

Secor Bank is a small bank with branches in several southern states. (This bank is now owned by Regions Bank.) Secor, like many financial institutions, experienced high turnover of its tellers. The position of teller is typically a high-turnover job, but it was extraordinarily high at Secor. The challenge is to understand its cause and find preventive solutions. Exit interviews proved to be of little help because employees indicated they were leaving for reasons unrelated to their jobs at the bank. Frequently mentioned responses included higher pay, more responsibility, a chance to progress in an organization, and so on.

At the time of this study, the teller network comprised about 600 tellers. The analytics team discussed several techniques during project planning, settling on a process called nominal group technique. This approach essentially works as a focus group process with slight adjustments. The team assembled focus groups of employees who were in the target group of "likely to leave," from all teller locations. The team wanted to ask them why their colleagues were leaving the bank, not why they themselves would leave. When facilitated properly, the focus groups were a way to get them to talk about what was bothering them and why they would leave—all in the context of why others were leaving.

Each of the six focus groups contained 12 employees, one group for each of six regions. This approach provided a sample of more than 10 percent of all tellers, which was considered a sufficient number to pinpoint the problem. Participants represented areas where turnover was highest. Input was solicited from participants in a carefully structured format, using third-party facilitators. The data were integrated and weighted so that the most important reasons were clearly identified. This process has the advantages of low cost, high reliability, and unbiased feedback. Data were captured in a two-hour meeting in each regional location. Only two days of external facilitator time was necessary to collect and summarize data for review. The nominal group technique unfolds quickly in 10 easy steps:

1. The process is briefly described, along with a statement of confidentiality. The importance of participant input is underscored, and participants understand what they must do and what it means to the bank.

2. On a piece of paper, participants are asked to list specific reasons why they feel their colleagues have left or why others may leave in the future. It is important for the question to reflect the actions or potential actions of others, although their comments will probably reflect their own views (and that is what is actually needed).

3. In a round-robin format, each person reveals one reason at a time and it is recorded on flip-chart paper. At this point, no attempts are made to integrate the issues, but simply to record the data on paper. It is important to understand the issue and fully describe it on paper. The lists are placed on the walls so that when this step is complete, as many as 50 or 60 items are listed and visible.

4. The next step is to consolidate and integrate the lists. Some of the integration is easy because the items may contain the same words and meaning. For others, it is important to ensure that the meanings for the cause of the turnover are the same before they are consolidated. When integrated, the remaining list may contain 30 or 40 different reasons for turnover.

5. Participants are asked to review all of the items and carefully select the 10 items they consider the most important causes and list them individually on index cards. At first, participants are not concerned about which cause is No. 1, but are instructed to simply list the 10 most important ones on the cards. Participants usually realize that their original list was not complete or accurate, and they will pick up other issues for this list.

6. Participants sort the 10 items by order of importance.

7. In a round-robin format, each participant reveals a cause of turnover, starting from the top. Each participant reveals his or her No. 1 item, and 10 points are recorded on the flip-chart paper next to the item. The next participant reveals the No. 1 issue and so on until the entire group offers their top cause for turnover. Next, the No. 2 reason is identified, and nine points are recorded on the flip-chart paper next to the item. This process continues until all cards have been revealed and points recorded.

8. The numbers next to each item are totaled. The item with the most points becomes the No. 1 cause of turnover. The item with the second highest points becomes the No. 2 cause of turnover, and so on. The top 15 causes are then captured from the group and reported as the weighted average cause of turnover from that group.

9. This process was completed for all six regional groups to ensure adequate representation of those likely to leave. Trends emerged quickly from one group to another.

10. The raw scores are then combined to integrate the results of the six regional focus groups.

From this analysis, the 10 most important reasons for turnover in the bank branches were identified.

1. Lack of opportunity for advancement

2. Lack of opportunity to learn new skills and new product knowledge

3. Inadequate pay level

4. Not enough responsibility and empowerment

5. Lack of recognition and appreciation of work

6. Lack of teamwork in the branch

7. Lack of preparation for customer service problems

8. Unfair and unsupportive supervisor

9. Too much stress at peak times

10. Not enough flexibility in work schedules

Recognizing that not all the causes of turnover could be addressed immediately, the bank's management set out to work on the top five reasons while it considered a variety of options. Eventually, a skill-based pay system was created. The program was designed to expand the scope of the jobs, with increases in pay for acquiring skills, and to provide a clear path for advancement and improvement. Jobs were redesigned from narrowly focused teller duties to an expanded job with a new title: The tellers all became Banking Representative I, II, or III.[1]

This case illustrates the power of focus groups to identify the cause of the problem, or in this case, several causes. The benefit of this approach is that it is better than trying to analyze classic data from records or using exit interviews. This insightful process digs to the heart of the problem. It is not overly analytical and illustrates that you can still keep processes simple. It also arrives at the causes, using a qualitative approach.

CORRELATION AND CAUSATION

A basic understanding of data analysis makes it possible for even the novice practitioner to understand evaluations. This chapter is not intended to build significant skills. The material covers a few basic concepts and provides enough insight so that elementary analyses can be performed. The simple and most useful statistical methods are presented, while more sophisticated techniques are described in other publications.[2]

The presentation of one part of the subject of statistics often leads to other possibilities. Many variables can influence the statistical techniques that should be used and the type of analysis to pursue. Any analysis involving all of the concepts in this chapter should be reviewed by someone familiar with statistical methods.

Measures of Association

Many human capital analytics projects involve a need to know if a relationship exists between two or more groups of data. These groups of data may be referred to as variables. This relationship can help predict performance based on program results or prerequisite criteria. The following example illustrates this point.

An automobile manufacturer recruits candidates to work on the assembly line. Employees selected for this job must complete an initial training program. At the end of the program, a test is administered, covering all the procedures necessary to perform the job effectively. The test scores at the end of the program are compared to the production efficiency of their work after training. The efficiency relates to the time to complete tasks. A direct relationship between the end-of-the-program scores and after-the-program performance would not only assist in the validation of the test but also provide a predictor of performance without the expense of a follow-up. Table 7-1 shows the program scores (listed in random order) and production efficiency for this example.

The goal, then, is to determine whether a relationship exists between two variables and also the extent of that relationship. This relationship is called correlation, and the degree of that relationship is measured by a correlation coefficient.

A basic approach to examining data for a possible relationship is to plot the two variables on a diagram and visually determine the likelihood of the correlation. Figure 7-1 shows a plot, called a scatter diagram, of the two variables from Table 7-1. End-of-program test scores are plotted on the horizontal, or x, axis. The production efficiency is plotted on the vertical, or y, axis. The diagram shows that the higher the test score, the higher the production efficiency rate of the employee, revealing a good possibility of correlation between the two.

A relationship between two variables can be expressed in the form of an algebraic equation. The process of determining the relationship or the equation for the relationship between variables is known as curve fitting. In the example in Figure 7-1, a straight line approximates the relationship. In this linear relationship, the line through the data is called a trend line. This trend line can be extended to show approximately where data will be located past the data points on the graph.

TABLE 7-1   Performance of Automobile Assembly Employees

Program Test Scores (%)	Production Efficiency
75	105
68	95
88	116
92	119
78	111
82	113
74	100
90	120
95	125
100% = Perfect Score	100 = Standard Score

FIGURE 7-1   Scatter Diagram of Two Variables

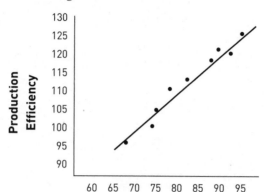

Program Test Scores

CALCULATING THE CORRELATION

The method of determining the equation of a relationship is called the method of least squares. When the equation of the relationship is known, test scores can be plugged in to the equation, and the corresponding values for production efficiency can be calculated. The specific formulas for determining the equations are beyond the scope of this book. Many resources appropriate for providing information on these calculations are available.[3]

Among the several different types of correlation coefficients, the particular coefficient to use depends on the type of data, how the data are arranged, and the relationship between the two variables. Most of the data used in evaluation will be numerical from test scores and performance measurements. For this type of data, the correlation coefficient used is the Pearson product-moment correlation coefficient. This coefficient applies only in cases of a linear relationship (i.e., a straight-line relationship with no curve in the trend line of the graphical plot of the data). Fortunately, in many cases a linear relationship exists, particularly with performance data. Consult one of the additional references for additional information on the other correlation coefficients and when they should be used.

The correlation coefficient varies between −1 and +1: the minus denotes negative correlation, and the plus denotes positive correlation. A perfect negative correlation results in the coefficient of −1; no correlation between the two variables results in a coefficient of 0; and perfect positive correlation provides a coefficient of +1. Figure 7-2 illustrates these extreme situations graphically.

FIGURE 7-2 Extreme Examples of Correlation Coefficients

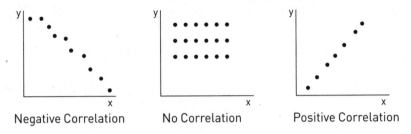

Negative Correlation   No Correlation   Positive Correlation

The range between these two extreme values represents the degree of correlation. As a rough guide, Table 7-2 shows ranges of possible correlations and their rough interpretations. These interpretations are only approximate, and the actual interpretation of a specific correlation value depends on the confidence placed on that value.

Software packages or scientific calculators preprogram correlation coefficient formulas on function keys. It may be helpful to illustrate the calculation, using the two variables of program test scores and efficiency. The coefficient for this set of data is $+.97$, which represents almost perfect

TABLE 7-2 Ranges of Correlation Coefficients and Their Approximate Interpretations

Correlation Value	General Description
-1.0	Perfect negative correlation
$-.8$ to -1.0	Very high degree of negative correlation
$-.6$ to $-.8$	High degree of negative correlation
$-.4$ to $-.6$	Medium degree of negative correlation
$-.2$ to $-.4$	Low degree of negative correlation
$+.2$ to $-.2$	Probably no correlation
$+.2$ to $+.4$	Low degree of positive correlation
$+.4$ to $+.6$	Medium degree of positive correlation
$+.6$ to $+.8$	High degree of positive correlation
$+.8$ to $+1.0$	Very high degree of positive correlation
$+1.0$	Perfect positive correlation

positive correlation. Correlation does not necessarily mean causation. Many other variables could cause the difference. Just because two measures seem to change in concert with each other doesn't necessarily mean that one causes the other. Unfortunately, too often when a correlation is developed, causation is assumed. It is correct to assume causation in most cases, particularly when a hypothesis is developed. For example, a highly engaged sales representative should lead to increased sales. So sales force engagement should influence actual sales. If these two numbers show a correlation and nothing else seems to be influencing during the same time frames, then it is highly likely that the engagement caused the increase in sales. However, without testing the hypothesis of the causation, this conclusion may not result.

Unfortunately, much literature about correlation does not cover this issue and leaves it up to others to do so. For example, in the book, *Applied Regression Modeling*, the author states this comment five times throughout: "The regression modeling techniques described in this book can really only be used to quantify associations between variables and to identify whether a change in one variable is associated with a change in another variable, not to establish whether the change in one variable 'causes' another to change."[4] The book goes on to discuss the causality in the context of regression, instructing readers to see other references.[5] This statement is disappointing, particularly for such a popular book used in a course at statistics.com.

Another important contribution to this field is *Big Data: A Revolution That Would Transform the Way We Live, Work, and Think*.[6] The authors suggest that causation is not especially important, and that with enough data, hypothesis testing is unnecessary as well. They suggest running all of the data on all of the variables to see which one has the strongest correlation. And while it is not really causation, it would be safe to say that the variables with the strongest correlation suggest the possibility of causality. The authors suggest it takes too much time to set up the hypothesis only to have it rejected, so why not move on to another possibility, running all the numbers. At the same time, the authors state that most of the existing data are messy and must be cleaned up considerably for the analysis, which can take weeks, if not months. So, using all of the data may not be the most efficient way. Instead, using sample data and hypothesis testing may be the logical way to proceed.

The position taken in this book is that causation must be addressed. It comes from the hypothesis, which makes the process much more efficient.

This approach is confirmed by perhaps one of the leading experts in analytics, Thomas Davenport.[7]

In this chapter we discuss four analytical approaches to address causation. The first is hypothesis testing, which is covered in a document on the ROI Institute's website. The second is the comparison of groups using the classic experimental versus control group method. The third is the trend-line analysis, and the fourth is the forecasting analysis. In reality, these approaches are possible in many situations and make the process credible. If they cannot be used, qualitative processes may be used. The chapter contains a full array of qualitative approaches to determine the causation, such as the example in the opening story. This determination may include the best judgment from a group of people using their assessments as to the cause, which are often presented as estimates. It is also interesting to note that the developer for correlation analysis, Francis Galton, is perhaps best known for showing that estimates from a group are highly accurate.[8] Also, it may be helpful to use other references about causation, particularly for correlation and regression analysis.

EXPERIMENTAL VERSUS CONTROL GROUPS

The most accurate approach for isolating the impact of a solution is the use of an experimental group that is involved in the solution and a control group that is not. The two groups should be as similar in composition as possible and, if feasible, participants for each group should be randomly assigned. When aspects are achievable and the groups are subjected to the same environmental influences, any difference in performance between the two groups can be attributed to the solution.

As illustrated in Figure 7-3, the control group and experimental group do not necessarily require premeasurements. Measurements can be taken during and after solution implementation, with the difference in performance between the two groups indicating the amount of improvement directly related to the solution.

Figure 7-4 shows an experimental and control group comparison. Both groups are experiencing about 40 hours of overtime per week, too much for these two nursing units. An overtime reduction solution involving nurse managers was implemented with the experimental group. The control group was not involved. The criteria used to select the two groups

FIGURE 7-3   Use of Control Groups

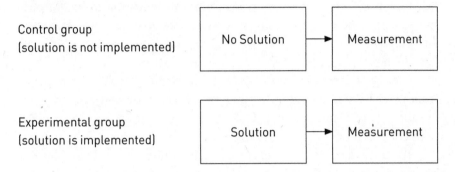

Control group
(solution is not implemented)

Experimental group
(solution is implemented)

FIGURE 7-4   Experimental versus Control Group for Overtime Reduction

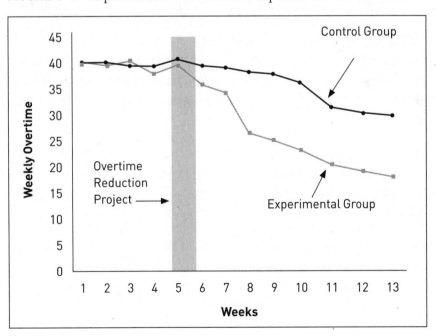

included current performance on overtime, staffing levels, type of care, and sick time use. The control group experienced a reduction from 40 hours to 28 hours. The experimental group moved from 40 hours to 18 hours. The improvement connected to the overtime reduction solution is 10 (28–18) hours per week.

The use of control groups may create the impression that the analytics team is creating a laboratory setting, which can raise concern for some executives and administrators. To avoid this perception, some organizations conduct a pilot using participants as the experimental group. A similarly constituted nonparticipant comparison group is selected but does not receive any communication about the solution. The terms *pilot* and *comparison group* are a little less threatening to executives than *experimental group* and *control group*.

The control group approach can be difficult to apply in practice. The first major problem is the group selection. From a theoretical perspective, having identical control and experimental groups is next to impossible. Dozens of factors affect performance, some individual and others contextual. On a practical basis, it is best to select the four to six variables with the greatest influence on performance. Essentially, the selection process involves the 80/20 rule or the Pareto principle.

The 80/20 rule suggests selecting the factors that might account for 80 percent of the difference. The Pareto principle requires working from the most important factors to cover perhaps four or five issues that capture the vast majority of the factors having influence.

Another issue is that the control group process is unsuitable in many situations. For some solutions, withholding the program from one particular group while implementing it with another may not be appropriate. Particularly when critical solutions are needed immediately, management is typically not willing to withhold a solution from one area to see how it works in another. However, in practice, many opportunities arise for a natural control group to develop, even in situations where a solution is implemented throughout an organization. If it takes several months for the solution to encompass everyone in the organization, enough time may be available for a parallel comparison between the initial group and the last group to be affected. In these cases, ensuring that the groups are matched as closely as possible is critical. Such naturally occurring control groups can often be identified in the case of major enterprise-wide program implementations. The challenge is to address this possibility early enough to influence the implementation schedule to ensure that similar groups are used in the comparison.

Contamination develops when participants in the experimental group communicate with members of the control group. Sometimes, the reverse situation occurs, where members of the control group model the behavior of the experimental group. In either case, the experiment becomes contaminated as the influence of the solution is carried over to the control group. This hazard can be minimized by ensuring that the control and experimental groups are at different locations, are on different shifts, or occupy different floors of the same building. When these precautions are not possible, it should be explained to both groups that one group will be involved in the solution now and the other will be involved later. Appealing to participants' sense of responsibility and asking them not to share information with others may help prevent contamination.

Another consideration is the passage of time. The longer a control versus experimental group comparison operates, the greater the likelihood that other influences will affect the results; more variables will enter into the situation, contaminating the results. On the other end of the scale, enough time must pass to allow a clear pattern to emerge distinguishing the two groups. Thus, the timing of control group comparisons must strike a delicate balance between waiting long enough for performance differences to show, but not so long that the results become contaminated.

Still another problem occurs when the different groups function under different environmental influences. This occurrence is usually the case when groups are at different locations. Sometimes the selection of the groups can prevent this problem. Another tactic is to use more groups than necessary and discard those groups that show significant environmental differences.

A final issue is that the use of control and experimental groups may appear too research oriented for most business organizations. For example, management may not want to take the time to experiment before proceeding with a program, in addition to the selective withholding problem discussed earlier. These concerns can cause some solution managers to reject the use of control groups.

Because the use of control groups is an effective approach for isolating impact, it should be considered when a major ROI impact study is planned. In these situations, isolating the solution impact with a high level of accuracy is essential, and the primary advantage of the control group process is accuracy.

TREND-LINE ANALYSIS

Another useful technique for approximating the impact of a solution is trend-line analysis. In this approach, a trend line is drawn to approximate the future performance of a measure, using previous performance as a base. When the solution is fully implemented, actual performance is compared with the trend-line projection. Any improvement in performance beyond what the trend line predicted can be reasonably attributed to solution implementation. Although this process is not precise, it can provide a reasonable estimate of the solution's impact.

Figure 7-5 shows a trend-line analysis from the shipping department of a book distribution company. The percentage reflects the level of actual shipments compared with scheduled shipments. Data reflect conditions before and after a human capital solution implementation in July. As shown in the figure, an upward trend for the data began prior to solution implementation. Although the solution apparently had an effect on shipment productivity, the trend line shows that some improvement would have occurred anyway, based on the trend that had previously been established. Solution leaders may have been tempted to measure the improvement by comparing the six-month average for shipments prior to the solution (87.3%) to the average of months 5 and 6, after the solution is implemented (97.1%), which would yield a 9.8 percent difference. However, a more accurate comparison is the months 5 and 6 average after the solution versus the trend line (94.3%), a difference of 2.8 percent. Using this more conservative measure increases the accuracy and credibility of the process in terms of isolating the impact of the solution.

To use this technique, two conditions must be met:

- It can be assumed that the trend that developed prior to the solution would have continued if the solution had not been implemented to alter it (i.e., had the solution not been implemented, this trend would have continued on the same path). The process owner(s) should be able to provide input to confirm

FIGURE 7-5 Trend-Line Analysis

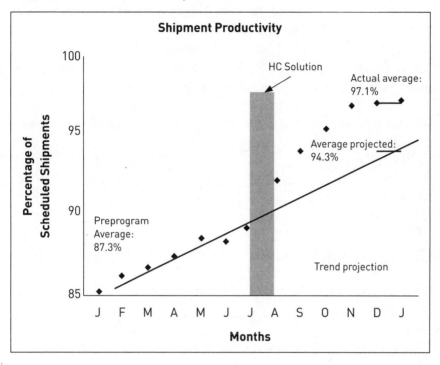

this assumption. If the assumption does not hold, trend-line analysis cannot be used. If the assumption is a valid one, the second condition is considered.

- No other new variables or influences entered the process during solution implementation. The key word here is *new*; the understanding is that the trend has been established from the influences already in place, and no additional influences have entered the process beyond the solution. If this is not the case, another method will have to be used. Otherwise, the trend-line analysis presents a reasonable estimate of the impact of this solution.

Presolution data must be available in order for this technique to be used, and the data should show a reasonable degree of stability. If the variance of the data is high, the stability of the trend line is in question. If the stability cannot be assessed from a direct plot of the data, more detailed statistical analyses can be used to determine whether the data are stable enough to allow a projection. The trend line can be projected directly from historical data using a simple formula that is available in many calculators and software packages, such as Microsoft Excel.

A primary disadvantage of the trend line is that it is not always accurate. This approach assumes that the events that influenced the performance variable prior to solution implementation are still in place, except for the effects of the implementation (i.e., the trends established prior to the solution will continue in the same relative direction). Also, it assumes that no new influences entered the situation during the course of the solution.

The primary advantage is that a trend line is simple and inexpensive. If historical data are available, a trend line can quickly be drawn and the differences estimated. Even though not exact, it does provide a quick general assessment of solution impact.

FORECASTING METHODS

More analytical than trend-line analysis is the use of forecasting methods that predict a change in performance variables. This approach represents a mathematical interpretation of the trend-line analysis when other variables enter the situation at the time of implementation. The actual value of the measure is compared with the forecast value, and the difference reflects the contribution of the solution.

An example will help illustrate the effect of the forecasting: One healthcare organization was focusing on decreasing length of stay. In July, a new solution changed several procedures that made the diagnosis, treatment, and healing process faster, with various ways to recognize improvement quickly and make decisions and adjustments accordingly. All of these procedures were aimed at reducing the average length of stay. Figure 7-6 shows the length of stay prior to the change in medical procedures. The actual data show a significant downward improvement during the 10 months after the program was implemented. However, two important changes occurred about the same time as the new solution was implemented. A major provider reissued a maximum length of stay that it would reimburse for illnesses. This influence has a tendency to cause organizations to focus more intensely on getting patients discharged as quickly as possible. At the same time, the severity of the influx of patients had slightly decreased. The types

FIGURE 7-6 Forecasting Example

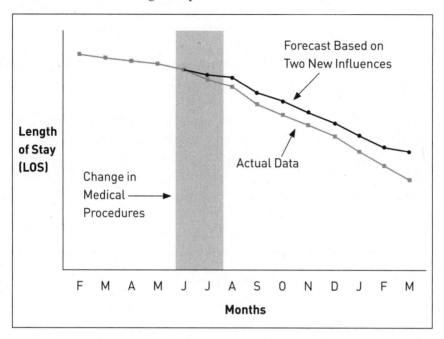

of illnesses dramatically affected the length of stay. Analysts in the business process improvement department developed a forecast showing the effects of the provider reimbursement process and the change in the illnesses of the patients upon admission. They were able to develop multiple variable analyses to forecast the length of stay, as shown in the figure. The data from March show the difference in the forecasted value and the actual value. That difference represents the impact of the new medical procedures, because they were not included in the forecasted value.

A major disadvantage to this approach emerges when several variables enter the process. The complexity multiplies, and the use of sophisticated statistical packages designed for multiple variable analyses is necessary. Even with this assistance, however, a good fit of the data to the model may not be possible. Unfortunately, some organizations have not developed mathematical relationships for output variables as a function of one or more inputs, and without them the forecasting method is difficult to use.

ESTIMATES

The most common method of isolating the effects of a solution is to use estimates from a group of individuals. This qualitative method is not preferred; it is practical in many situations and it can enhance the credibility of the analysis if adequate precautions are taken. First the analytics team must ensure that the estimates are provided by the most reliable source, which is often the participant, not a higher-level manager or executive removed from the process. The individual who provides this information must understand the different factors and, particularly, the influence of the solution on those factors. Essentially, four categories of input can be used. The participants directly involved in the solution are the first source considered. Managers are another possible source. Customers provide credible estimates in particular situations, and external experts may provide insight into causes for improvement. These sources are described in greater detail next.

Participants' Estimate of Impact

An easily implemented method of isolating the impact of a solution is to obtain information directly from participants during solution implementation. The usefulness of this approach rests on the assumption that participants are capable of determining or estimating how much of the performance improvement is related to the solution implementation. Because their actions have led to the improvement, participants may provide highly accurate data. Although an estimate, the value they supply is likely to carry considerable weight with management because they know that the participants are at the center of the change or improvement. The estimate is obtained by defining the improvement and then by asking participants a series of questions.

1. What is the link between these factors and the improvement?

2. What other factors have contributed to this improvement in performance?

3. What percentage of this improvement can be attributed to the implementation of this project?

4. How much confidence do you have in this estimate, expressed as a percentage? (0% no confidence, 100% complete confidence)

5. What other individuals or groups could provide a reliable estimate of this percentage to determine the amount of improvement contributed by this project?

Table 7-3 illustrates this approach with an example of one participant's estimation in a solution designed to reduce errors. Participants who do not provide answers to the questions are excluded from the analysis. Erroneous, incomplete, and extreme information should also be discarded before the analysis. To obtain a conservative estimate, the confidence percentage can be factored into each of the values. The confidence percentage is a reflection of the error in the estimate. Thus, an 80 percent confidence level equates to a potential error range of plus or minus 20 percent. In this approach, the estimate is multiplied by the level of confidence using the lower side of the range. In the example, the participant allocates 60 percent of the improvement to the solution and has a level of confidence in the estimate of 80 percent.

The confidence percentage is multiplied by the estimate to produce a usable solution value of 48 percent. This adjusted percentage is then multiplied by the actual amount of the improvement (postsolution minus presolution value) to isolate the portion attributed to the solution. For example, if errors declined 10 per week, 4.8 of the reduced errors would be attributed to the solution. The adjusted improvement is now ready for conversion to monetary value and, ultimately, use in the ROI calculation.

TABLE 7-3   Example of a Participant's Estimation

Factor Causing Improvement	Percentage of Improvement Caused	Confidence (%)	Adusted Percentage of Improvement
Project	60	80	48
Process changes	15	70	10.5
Environmental changes	5	60	3
Compensation changes	20	80	16
Other	—	—	—
Total	100		

Although the reported contribution is an estimate, this approach offers considerable accuracy and credibility. Five adjustments are effectively applied to the participant estimate to produce a conservative value:

1. Participants who do not provide usable data are assumed to have observed no improvements.

2. Extreme data values and incomplete, unrealistic, or unsupported claims are omitted from the analysis, although they may be included in the "other benefits" category.

3. For short-term solutions, it is assumed that no benefits are realized from the solution after the first year of full implementation. For long-term solutions, several years may pass after solution implementation before benefits are realized.

4. The amount of improvement is adjusted by the portion directly related to the solution, expressed as a percentage.

5. The improvement value is multiplied by the confidence level, expressed as a percentage, to reduce the amount of the improvement in order to reflect the potential error.

As an enhancement of this method, the level of management above the participants may be asked to review and concur with each participant's estimate.

In using participants' estimates to measure impact, several assumptions are made:

1. The solution encompasses a variety of different activities, practices, and tasks all focused on improving the performance of one or more business measures.

2. One or more business measures were identified prior to the solution and have been monitored since the implementation process. Data monitoring has revealed an improvement in the business measure.

3. It is important to associate the solution with a specific amount of performance improvement and determine the monetary impact of

the improvement. This information forms the basis for calculating the actual ROI.

Given these assumptions, the participants can specify the results linked to the solution and provide data necessary to develop the ROI. Gathering these data can be accomplished using a focus group, an interview, or a questionnaire.

MANAGERS' ESTIMATE OF IMPACT

In lieu of, or in addition to, participant estimates, the participants' manager may be asked to provide input concerning the solution's role in improving performance. In some settings, the managers may be more familiar with the other factors influencing performance and therefore may be better equipped to provide estimates of impact. The questions to ask managers, after identifying the improvement ascribed to the solution, are similar to those asked of the participants.

Managers' estimates should be analyzed in the same manner as the participant estimates, and they may also be adjusted by the confidence percentage. When participants' and managers' estimates have both been collected, the decision of which estimate to use becomes an issue. If a compelling reason indicates that one estimate is more credible than the other, then that estimate should be used. The most conservative approach is to use the lowest value and include an appropriate explanation. Another option is to recognize that each estimate source has a unique perspective and that an average of the two may be appropriate, with equal weight placed on each input. It is recommended that input be obtained from both participants and their managers.

In some cases, upper management may provide an estimate of the percentage of improvement attributable to a solution. After considering other factors that could contribute to the improvement, such as technology, procedures, and process changes, they apply a subjective factor to represent the portion of the results that should be attributed to the solution. Despite its subjective nature, this input by upper management is usually accepted by the individuals who provide or approve funding for the solution. Sometimes, their comfort level with the processes used is the most important consideration.

Customer Input on Solution Impact

An approach that is useful in some narrowly focused solution situations is to solicit input on the impact of a solution directly from customers. Customers are asked why they chose a particular product or service or are asked to explain how their reaction to the product or service has been influenced by individuals or systems involved in the solution. This technique often focuses directly on what the solution is designed to improve. For example, after the implementation of a customer service solution involving an electric utility, market research data showed that the level of customer dissatisfaction with response time was 5 percent lower compared with the rate before the solution implementation. Because response time was reduced by the solution and no other factor was found to contribute to the reduction, the 5 percent improvement in customer satisfaction was attributed to the solution.

Routine customer surveys provide an excellent opportunity to collect input directly from customers concerning their reactions to new or improved products, services, processes, or procedures. Pre- and postsolution data can pinpoint the improvements spurred by a new solution.

Customer input should be elicited using current data collection methods; the creation of new surveys or feedback mechanisms is to be avoided. This measurement process should not add to the data collection systems in use. Customer input may constitute the most powerful and convincing data if those data are complete, accurate, and valid.

Internal or External Expert Input

External or internal experts can sometimes estimate the portion of results that can be attributed to a solution. With this technique, experts must be carefully selected based on their knowledge of the process, solution, and situation. For example, an expert in quality might be able to provide estimates of how much change in a quality measure can be attributed to a quality solution and how much can be attributed to other factors.

This approach has its drawbacks, however. It can yield inaccurate data unless the solution and the setting in which the estimate is made are quite similar to the program with which the expert is familiar. Also, this approach may lack credibility if the estimates come from external sources and do not involve those close to the process.

As one advantage of this process, its reliability is often a reflection of the reputation of the expert or independent consultant. It is a quick and easy form of input from a reputable expert or consultant. Sometimes top management has more confidence in such external experts than in its own staff.

QUESTIONNAIRES AND SURVEYS

Questionnaires and surveys represent another group of qualitative approaches. Questionnaires come in all sizes, from brief reaction forms to detailed instruments. Questionnaires can be used to obtain all types of data, ranging from subjective information about employees' feelings, to business impact data. They are convenient for exploring the cause of problems. Here is an example that illustrates the power of a questionnaire: An office product firm was concerned about the lack of sales and market share growth. A questionnaire was sent to the sales team asking their perspective of what was inhibiting sales growth, the current level of customer loyalty, the strength of their competition, the challenges the organization was facing, and the outlook for the next year. In addition, the questionnaire prompted employees to provide specific suggestions for improving sales, customer loyalty, and market share. This powerful questionnaire generated tremendous insight into the cause of the problem (e.g., lack of sales and market share growth).

Some organizations are using a data collection process that taps the input of part or all of the employees through the use of brief surveys. The particular problem is identified and is presented to the group through a quick and informal survey method. In one example, an upscale retail chain was experiencing an excessive turnover rate. Using eePulse, a technology that supports fast surveys and quick reads of employee energy, employees were asked five simple questions to identify problems that could be leading to turnover. The data were immediately fed back to the group, and additional questions were assembled.

The next week they were asked to react to additional questions. The results were then communicated to the group, along with proposed solutions. The solutions were rated the next week. Eventually this process continued until the best solutions were identified and action plans were put in place. It provided an excellent way to tap the creative spirit of the group, the collaborative approach of the entire team, and use brief surveys in the process.

INTERVIEWS

Another helpful qualitative method to uncover a cause is the interview, although it is not used as frequently as questionnaires or surveys. The analytics project team, or an outside third party, can conduct interviews. Interviews can provide data that are not available in performance records or are difficult to obtain through written responses. Employees may be reluctant to provide input on a questionnaire, but will volunteer the information to a skillful interviewer who uses probing techniques to uncover changes in perceptions and attitudes.

Two basic types of interviews are structured and unstructured. Much like a questionnaire, the structured interview presents specific questions with little room to deviate. The unstructured interview is more flexible and can include probing for additional information. As important data are uncovered, a skilled interviewer can ask a few general questions that can lead to more detailed information.

One of the most utilized processes to uncover the causes of problems is the exit interview, taken just before or after an employee leaves the organization. Exit interviews can be face-to-face interviews, a questionnaire, a brief survey, or even a focus group. An anonymous questionnaire, administered confidentially, usually gets the best results for the costs.

Although exiting employees would seem to be the best source of data to determine why employees are leaving, exit interviews are notoriously inaccurate and unreliable; however, they need not be. When properly designed and implemented, they can provide excellent data to develop retention solutions. Three key issues represent challenges to conducting exit interviews:

- **The response rates may be low.** Departing employees do not feel obligated to provide data. The last thing they may want to do is help the organization after they have decided to leave.

- **The data may be incomplete or inaccurate.** Even when employees respond to the questions, their responses may not be complete or accurate. Because they are no longer attached to the organization, they may be unwilling to devote much time to this issue. Consequently, their responses are short, incomplete, and sporadic.

- **Data may be purposely biased.** For fear of retaliation or negative references, the employee may provide misleading input. An employee may indicate that working conditions were fine, but that he or she received an offer that could not be refused, when that might not be the case.

Two major disadvantages of the interview are that it is time-consuming and offers little sense of anonymity. Also, interviewers must be trained to ensure that the process is consistent across respondents. The primary advantage is that the interview process ensures that a question is answered and that the interviewer understands the responses. Also, the interview allows for probing to uncover more details.

FOCUS GROUPS

Another qualitative approach is the focus group, a small group discussion conducted by an experienced facilitator, can also be used to uncover the cause of a problem. It is designed to solicit qualitative judgments on a planned topic or issue. An extension of the interview, focus groups are particularly helpful when in-depth feedback and probing are required. Group members are all required to provide their input, as individual input builds on group input.

A focus group strategy has several advantages. The basic premise is that when judgments are subjective, several individual judgments are better than one. Thus, the group process in which participants often motivate one another is an effective method for generating new ideas and hypotheses. It is inexpensive and can be quickly planned and conducted. Its flexibility makes it possible to explore a variety of issues.

As discussed earlier, perhaps one of the most useful and productive tools to determine the causes of turnover is a focus group process called the nominal group technique. With this process, a group of employees are asked to provide information on why their colleagues behave a particular way. The key issue is to focus on the reasons why others would exhibit specific behaviors and not why they, themselves, would. This repositions the data collection from a potentially threatening environment to a nonthreatening environment. The recommended audience is a representative sample of the target groups experiencing the behaviors. The group size of each sample should be 8 to 12. A small number of samples would be appropriate for large target groups. The opening story involves an example of this technique. One approach is to sample until trends and patterns begin to emerge. For example, in a target group with a thousand employees doing the same job, 5 to 10 samples would probably be sufficient. The key issue is to examine the results to confirm a pattern. Although the group process is inexpensive compared to some techniques, the issue may represent a balance of economics versus accuracy.

BRAINSTORMING

While brainstorming is perhaps the most widely recognized technique to encourage creative thinking; it has become an important qualitative tool for articulating the causes of organizational problems. The process facilitation is similar to that for a focus group and those design issues and guidelines also apply to the brainstorming session. The goal is to generate as many ideas as possible with no restrictions. The groups are best kept small, usually in range of 6 to 12 participants. The group should focus on the actual problem.

The individuals invited to participate should be those who best understand the problem and are in a position to know the causes and corresponding potential solutions. The group should have a complete understanding of the problems, issues, and challenges. Providing information in advance will help the individuals develop ideas prior to the meeting.

The ground rules for the process are fairly straightforward:

- Individuals are encouraged to offer as many ideas as possible.

- The ideas are not criticized by anyone, regardless of how they may be perceived.

- All ideas are recorded.

- All participants should have ample time to share their ideas.

- Freewheeling is encouraged, even if the ideas seem to be off the wall.

When input ceases to be productive, a variety of techniques are available to stimulate additional creativity and ideas. Three are especially helpful:

1. The participation is rotated through the group to enable one individual to build off the ideas of another. This approach also provides ample time for reflection from those who are not directly participating.

2. Using the concept of idea building, individuals are encouraged to add to or expand on previous ideas or to offer similar or even alternate issues as ideas.

3. Quiet periods can help people reflect and think through the problem, sifting through the data mentally and generating additional ideas. This period could last up to half an hour before it becomes pointless.

The data can be summarized in a variety of ways. Eliminating items, combining items, and reaching consensus on items are key steps in the process.

CAUSE-AND-EFFECT MODEL

The cause-and-effect model is useful for repetitive issues. This process can be used to create what is sometimes called the fishbone diagram because of its appearance, as shown in Figure 7-7. The process follows

FIGURE 7-7 Example of a Fishbone Diagram

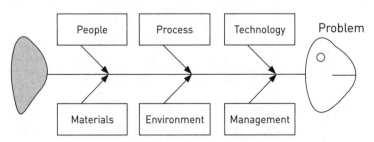

the focus group and brainstorming formats, except the major categories of causes are identified first, with minor causes added. The minor cause categories, which can be considerable, are provided by the group using idea-generating processes. Here, the focus is more specific and the group must be knowledgeable about the problem so that they can offer minor causes of the problem. The steps are simple:

1. The groups are selected based on their capability to provide insight into the causes of the problem.

2. The groups are provided instructions and their role in the process is outlined.

3. The major cause categories are either identified or offered. They are offered if previous information indicates the specific cause (from exit interviews or other data collection methods).

4. After some discussion, the most likely causes are circled. This decision occurs only after each item is critically evaluated and the group has reached a consensus as to which causes are most relevant. This process is more focused and therefore is more likely to help the group find the real cause of a problem.

5. With the major cause categories clearly identified and entered on the diagram, the group members are asked to indicate the minor causes related to each major cause category. These items can be listed as minor causes, or sometimes just the "why" for the particular major cause category.

6. The fishbone diagram is then completed, showing the major and minor causes for the problem.

OTHER TOOLS

A variety of other tools are available, primarily from the quality and performance improvement process, which can be used to analyze the cause of the problem. Listed here are five that might be helpful:

1. **Force field analysis** is a visual tool for analyzing the different elements that resist change (restraining forces) and those elements

that wish for change (facilitating forces). This useful technique can help drive improvement and retention by developing plans to overcome the restraining forces and make maximum use of the facilitating forces.

2. **Mind mapping** is an unstructured cause-and-effect analysis tool primarily designed for taking notes and solving problems. The problem is written on the center of a piece of paper and members of the group offer their suggestions or ideas as to the causes. These causes are drawn from the center as legs or lines. Branches are added to a line as additional causes or subcauses are generated. This approach is similar to the cause-and-effect process, but might be more helpful with those individuals familiar with the mind-mapping process.

3. **Affinity diagrams** are used to collect input from groups and organize it according to the natural relationships between items. This technique has a conceptual and logical simplicity that allows for a clear view of the largest and most complex problems. Basically, it is a way to structure and classify vague ideas. Consequently, it is helpful when there is a need to focus on a complex, multifaceted problem, such as turnover.

4. **Relationship diagrams** are used when building a map of the logical, sequential links among items is helpful, showing interconnectedness and relationships to a central problem, such as turnover. It facilitates the solution of problems when causes interact by dividing a problem into its basic components and isolating the relationships. The basic logic behind this tool is the same as that behind the cause-and-effect diagram.

5. **Tree-shaped diagrams** systematically outline the complete spectrum, paths, and tests that must be carried out in order to achieve a particular goal, such as business alignment. The use of this tool changes some generalities into details by isolating the intermediate conditions that must be satisfied. The diagram leads to identification of the more appropriate procedures and methods to solve the problem.

These and other techniques may be helpful for analyzing causes and relationships between causes. The important point is to use a tool that works best for the organization in a specific setting.

SELECT THE TECHNIQUE

With all these techniques available to isolate the impact of a solution, selecting the most appropriate ones for a specific solution can be difficult. Some techniques are simple and inexpensive; others are time-consuming and costly. In choosing among them, the following factors should be considered:

- Feasibility of the technique

- Accuracy associated with the technique

- Credibility of the technique with the target audience

- Specific cost to implement the technique

- Amount of disruption in normal work activities resulting from the technique's implementation

- Participant, staff, and management time required for the technique

The use of multiple techniques or multiple sources of data input should be considered because two sources are usually better than one. When multiple sources are used, a conservative method should be used to combine the inputs. The reason is that a conservative approach builds acceptance. The target audience should always be provided with an explanation of the process and the subjective factors involved. Multiple sources allow an organization to experiment with different strategies and build confidence in the use of a particular technique. For example, if management is concerned about the accuracy of participants' estimates, the combination of a control group arrangement and participant estimates could be useful for checking the accuracy of the estimation process.

FINAL THOUGHTS

In this chapter, correlation and causation are introduced. Causation is absolutely critical in any human capital analytics project. Many experts ignore the issue and assume that the correlation is causation. The actual cause of a particular problem or situation can be discovered using both quantitative and qualitative analysis. Hypothesis testing is introduced as a concept to address causation. Also, the classic experimental versus control group process can be applied in many situations and was explored along with trend analysis and forecasting. Then a variety of qualitative techniques were covered, including estimates, questionnaires, interviews, focus groups, brainstorming, cause-and-effect diagrams, and others. The important point is the cause of a problem must be uncovered so that the solution can be clearly identified. Also, in every solution implementation, the effects of that solution must be isolated. It is always possible.

CHAPTER 8

Select the Solution and
Set the Objectives

In many human capital analytics projects, the challenge lies in choosing the appropriate solution that is properly aligned to the business. Usually, several solutions are possibilities, so securing a proper match is critical. This step also involves setting objectives at least at four levels—reaction, learning, application, and impact—and in some cases a fifth level, ROI. This chapter explains how to select solutions from various scenarios, modify a particular solution to deliver the value needed, and develop specific objectives for all five levels.

OPENING STORY

Neighborhood Insurance has conducted an annual agents conference for many years. The conference requires about three days off the job and is not mandatory, but agents are encouraged to participate. Each agent is provided a marketing budget, out of which the conference travel expenses are taken. Otherwise, agents can use the money on other marketing activities. The conference focuses on new products, changes in current products, and new sales strategies and tools. It is considered by executives at least to be a valuable event. The senior executives have been concerned that 40 percent of agents do not attend. Apparently, these agents do not see enough value in the conference to spend the marketing money to attend. The CEO is working with the meeting and events staff to explore two issues:

1. Is this the proper solution to drive the business? If so, what is the ROI in this conference?

2. How can ROI results be used to drive attendance in the future?

The director of meetings and events, working with the analytics team, saw this issue as an opportunity to confirm the appropriateness of the solution. Through a series of meetings and actions, she revisited the reasons for the conference in an attempt to align this solution to the business and develop clear objectives for business measures. The review involved meetings with key executives and managers who are involved in and support the conference. The review allowed the team to reflect on the business purpose of the conference, clarifying the specific actions needed by the agents and adjusting the conference learning agenda.

As part of this review, she developed specific objectives for reaction, learning, application, and impact levels. These objectives, approved by the executives, provided focus and direction to designers, developers, speakers, facilitators, agents, and sponsors. The result of the review was a revised version of the conference that properly aligns it with business measures. Executives were convinced that the revised conference will drive the value needed. If it does drive the value anticipated, the results of the new solution (revised conference) will be used to convince the agents who are not attending that they should be there in the future. The good news is that the conference did just that.[1]

COMBINING DATA FROM DIFFERENT SOURCES

Chapter 7 explored various approaches to determining the causes of a problem. Multiple methods are often used, so it is necessary to combine the data in a meaningful way in order to identify and address the primary causes. For example, some organizations review their annual feedback survey results to determine causes of turnover. Or they may review exit interview data or conduct focus groups to explore specific reasons why employees are leaving. Also, the demographic data may be helpful to uncover trends. The challenge is to combine and organize the data in a meaningful way and allow the organization to choose appropriate solutions. The approach of choice depends on the consistency of the data from various sources. Because turnover is a critical topic in many organizations and it's an easy concept to understand, several examples in the next few sections focus on turnover.

Ideally, all of the data sources point to the same causes of the problem, and the task is to combine the data so they illustrate their priority. In some situations, considering the most important causes may be as simple as reviewing the strength of the data. For example, if the likely causes are measured on a scale (a 5-point scale, for example), it is much easier to identify the most important causes (the highest ranked items). However, this scenario is unlikely, because some data sources are more credible than others, some input is more reliable than others, and input scales are sometimes different. The challenge lies in addressing the inconsistencies. Four basic approaches should be considered when managing inconsistent and conflicting data from different sources.

1. Take the mathematical average.

2. Consider the strongest data first.

3. Consider the credibility of the method.

4. Use expert input to make the decision.

DETERMINING THE SIGNIFICANCE OF THE CAUSE

After all the data have been combined, the next step is to judge the significance of the cause, determining how much the impact measure is being influenced by a particular issue or could be prevented by addressing that particular issue. Determining the significance of the cause leads to developing the potential payoff for addressing a particular cause. Four methods are appropriate to tackle this issue.

1. Examine relative rankings of the data.

2. Ask participants to provide input.

3. Use the experiences of others.

4. Use the input of experts.

It is important to bring all of those who are familiar with and affected by the problem together to decide on the best solutions. The group must understand the underlying assumptions and clarify any issues in an entirely open manner before coming to an agreement about which solutions should be used to address the turnover problem.

MATCHING SOLUTIONS TO NEEDS

The most difficult part of the process is to match the best solution or solutions to the needs or causes of the problem. This task is as much an art as it is a science. Several principles should be followed during this process to ensure that the solution addresses all the needs or causes.

A CAUSE CANNOT AUTOMATICALLY BE TRANSLATED INTO A SOLUTION

Not every cause has an obvious solution. For example, if managers are not providing positive feedback or creating a supportive work environment, it does not necessarily mean that they need a learning solution. Too often a learning solution is identified when, in fact, other solutions may be more appropriate. You must know enough about the cause to identify the right solution. In other words, if managers are not providing positive feedback or creating a supportive environment, is it because they do not know how to do it (a learning issue)? Is it not required (a policy issue), or is it because role modeling does not occur for that type of behavior (a coaching issue)?

SOME SOLUTIONS ARE OBVIOUS

Some causes point directly to a solution. If employees need more flexibility in scheduling their work hours, flexible scheduling is the obvious solution. If employees need the flexibility to work at home, telecommuting is an appropriate solution. Although design issues are important, the solutions become obvious in these situations.

Solutions Can Come in Different Sizes

Solutions come with a full range of possibilities and represent a broad scope of investment needs and levels of complexity. For example, if employees have expressed a need for better child care, the solution could range from identifying recommended child-care facilities to operating an on-site center completely funded by the organization. It is helpful to understand what would be considered an acceptable solution to prevent turnover, versus not addressing the issue at all.

The Design of the Solution Is Critical

Because a wide variety of solutions may be available, the actual design of the solution is often just as important as finding it. For example, if employees indicate that they want their salary connected directly to their performance, management can fulfill this need in dozens of ways; however, some designs may be counterproductive and perhaps create more problems, whereas others can motivate and uplift. The design should be considered in relationship to the cause of the problem to ensure that any concerns are addressed. More analysis may be required to find what would actually correct a problem.

Some Solutions Take a Long Time

Although some issues respond to a short-term fix, such as flexible working schedules, others take a long time to rectify. For example, if employees leave because of the public image of the organization (bad press, recent negative events, tarnished image, etc.), it could take a long time to repair the situation. It has to start from the top of the organization. This concept must be recognized early, and it may take a long time to build trust and credibility with all of the employees.

Solutions Should Be Tackled for the Highest Priority Items First

This principle seems obvious, but it requires further discussion. Those issues causing most of the problem demand the most attention, perhaps even the most investment.

Designing a solution following these principles will identify the appropriate mix of solutions. The results of these steps are easily presented as a matrix diagram, described next.

USING A MATRIX DIAGRAM

A matrix diagram is a way to organize a large amount of information. It can be used to arrange the information so that elements are logically connected and presented in a graphic form. A matrix also shows the importance of each connecting point in a relationship and presents the relationships that exist among these variables. The matrix diagram can be "L" shaped, with one row across the top and one column down the side of the page, or it can be "T" shaped, in which two columns containing two types of data are compared with a third.

In Figure 8-1, a T-shaped matrix diagram presents a plan to reduce turnover in four job groups. The job groups with the most turnover in this large banking organization are listed at the top of the matrix. Six causes of turnover are identified along the middle of the diagram, with each matched to a job group. Listed at the bottom are the solutions that are matched to the particular causes. For example, "Implement Pay for Skills" is aimed primarily at the branch teller group and focuses on both the concern about inadequate pay and the lack of career advancement. As an alternative, words can be used in place of a dot to indicate the relative priority, strength, or importance of a particular cause, solution, or job group. Matrix diagrams provide an excellent way of summarizing information about a problem cause and relating it to job groups, regions, or other breakdowns. In addition, as shown in Figure 8.1, it can also be used to relate cause to solutions.

SELECTING SOLUTIONS FOR MAXIMUM PAYOFF

The next step is to make sure that the focus is only on those solutions with maximum payoff. Two major issues can affect that payoff: the cost of the solution and the monetary benefit from the implementation. To achieve maximum payoff, costs should be considered. The smaller the cost, the greater the potential payoff (ROI will be covered in detail in the next four chapters). From the benefits side, the greater the benefits, the greater the potential payoff. Several issues must be considered.

FIGURE 8-1   Matrix Diagram: A Plan to Reduce Turnover

	Inadequate Pay	Inadequate Supervision	Lack of Job Autonomy	Job Stress	Career Advancement	Ineffective Communication
Teller	•	•			•	•
Customer Service Representative		•		•		•
Branch Managers			•			•
Loan Officers		•				•
Job Groups / **Causes** / **Solutions**						
Adjust Base Pay	•					
Revise Incentives	•					
Train Immediate Manager		•				
Revise Job Responsibilities			•			
Increase Staffing				•		
Implement Pay for Skills	•				•	
Improve Communication						•

SHORT-TERM VERSUS LONG-TERM COSTS

Some solutions, such as building a day-care center, will be expensive to implement on a short-term basis. The initial cost of this solution might be prohibitive. Other solutions, such as an incentive plan, may have little up-front cost but a tremendous long-term expense—one that may exceed the actual payoff. Compensation plans are usually long-term and require careful consideration before implementing. The short-term versus long-term cost implication must always be considered.

CONSIDER FORECASTING ROI

A forecast can be developed showing the expected monetary benefits compared to the projected cost of the solution. The solutions with the highest forecasted ROI value become the best prospects for implementation.

Time Needed for Implementation

Some solutions are implemented quickly, while others take a long time. It may mean that long-term solutions should be implemented in conjunction with short-term fixes. In other words, the organization should recognize that both quick fixes and long-term changes are in store. This approach shows employees that the organization is taking steps now and also building for the future, which results in enhanced commitment and loyalty.

Avoid Mismatches

The impact of a mismatched problem and solution can be significant. For example, having to discontinue an employee incentive plan can affect job satisfaction. Mismatches can cause three major problems:

1. Funds are wasted because money is spent on a solution that did not correct the problem and drained the organization's resources.

2. Inappropriate solutions have a negative impact. For example, if learning is implemented as a solution when no deficiency in knowledge and skills actually exists, the impact can be adverse. The participants being trained (e.g., supervisors or managers) may resent the training because they have been coerced into participating in a solution that has no value for them or forced to work on skills they already possess.

3. When time, effort, and money are spent on a mismatched solution, an opportunity to implement the correct solution has been missed. An unmet need still exists and the cause is still there, resulting in damage to the organization while resources have been wasted on other solutions.

The message: Avoid mismatches at all costs!

Tackling Multiple Solutions

The answer to whether an organization should tackle a problem with more than one solution at a time is not clear-cut. To a certain extent, the answer depends on the relative priority of the causes. Clearly, too many solutions undertaken at the same time can reduce the potential effectiveness of each one and result in confusion and waste.

It is essential to examine the top priorities to determine which solutions are feasible, the time needed for implementation, and the level of others' involvement. These factors may mean taking on three or four (five, at the most) solutions. Avoid the quick fix, especially if the issue calls for a longer-term solution. Most turnover problems are not solved through quick fixes and are usually issues that have evolved over time (either internally or externally). As a result, they will take time to correct.

Consider the level of involvement and support needed for the solution. Most employees must be involved in the solution in some way, requiring time away from routine duties or time to keep track of what is being developed. The level of support from managers is also important. They need to be on board with solutions and their implementation. How much they can (or are willing to) support is significant.

Finally, available resources play a key role in whether multiple solutions can be implemented. For most organizations, the costs of the solutions can be substantial, and taking on too many solutions may drain available resources. The result may even have an impact on the earnings of the organization, potentially creating another serious problem.

Verifying the Match

After identifying possible solutions, one must verify that a match exists between the need and the solution. It is often helpful to return to the source of input (focus groups, employees, etc.) to affirm that the solution meets the needs. This approach is not applicable for every solution, because employees may be biased. However, their input may provide insight into progress made or indicate whether a solution is on target or off base. When input was obtained from interviews or focus groups, it may be easier to return to these groups to check whether a solution is addressing the cause of the problem. The important point is to find a way to discover whether a mismatch exists.

Upon initial implementation of the solution, obtain feedback to ensure that the solution is a fit and is working based on the early objectives. Early feedback can prompt adjustments that need to be made or, in worst-case scenarios, suggest abandonment of the solution altogether.

Seeking feedback represents another opportunity to involve a group of experts.

In addition, communicate the early results quickly. Letting the target group know that a solution has been implemented and that the results are positive (or developing, or need improvement) provides an opportunity to collect feedback from them. Employees need to see that action is being taken, progress is developing, and, more important, that the organization is responsive.

LEVELS OF OBJECTIVES FOR SOLUTIONS

Solutions are driven by objectives. Regardless of the solution, objectives (ranging from qualitative to quantitative) define precisely what will occur as a solution is implemented. These objectives are so critical that they need special attention in their development and use.

REACTION OBJECTIVES

For any solution to succeed, various stakeholders must react favorably, or at least not negatively, toward the solution. Ideally, the stakeholders should be satisfied with the solution and see its value, creating a win-win relationship for all stakeholders. Figure 8-2 shows typical areas for specific reaction objectives. This information must be obtained routinely during the solution so that feedback can be used to make adjustments, keep the solution on track, and perhaps even redesign certain parts.

FIGURE 8-2   Typical Areas for Reaction Objectives

• Usefulness of solution materials	• Motivational effect of solution
• Relevance of solution content	• Perceived support for the solution
• Importance of solution to success	• Intent to use content of solution
• Perceived value of solution	• Intent to recommend solution to others
• Solution necessity	• Amount of new information
• Solution appropriateness	• Overall satisfaction with the solution

Developing reaction objectives should be straightforward and relatively easy. The objectives reflect immediate and long-term satisfaction and explore issues important to solution success. They also form the basis for evaluating the chain of impact. In addition, they emphasize planned action, when feasible and useful.

LEARNING OBJECTIVES

Every solution involves at least one learning objective and usually more. With major skill-building solution, the learning component is incredibly important. In other situations, such as the implementation of a new policy, the learning component is minor but necessary. Learning objectives ensure that the various stakeholders learn what they need to know to make the solution successful. Figure 8-3 shows typical learning objectives. Learning objectives are critical to measuring learning because they communicate the expected outcomes of learning and define the desired competence or performance necessary for solution success.

Learning objectives provide a focus for participants, indicating what they must learn and do, sometimes with precision. Developing learning objectives is straightforward.

FIGURE 8-3 Typical Learning Objectives

After completing the learning session, participants will be able to:
- Identify the six features of the new ethics policy
- Demonstrate the use of each software routine in the standard time
- Use problem-solving skills when faced with a problem
- Know whether they are eligible for the early retirement program
- Score 75 or better on the new-product quiz
- Demonstrate success with all five customer interaction skills
- Explain the value of diversity in a work group
- Document and submit suggestions and ideas for award consideration
- Score at least 9 out of 10 on a sexual harassment policy quiz
- Identify five new technology trends explained at the conference
- Name the six pillars of the division's new strategy
- Successfully complete the leadership simulation

APPLICATION AND IMPLEMENTATION OBJECTIVES

As the solution is implemented, the application and implementation objectives clearly define what is expected, often to the specific level of performance. Application objectives are similar to learning objectives but reflect actual use on the job. They also involve specific milestones, indicating when part or all of the process is implemented. Figure 8-4 presents typical application objectives.

Application objectives are critical because they describe the expected outcomes in the intermediate area between the learning of new tasks and procedures and the impact that the learning will deliver. Application and implementation objectives describe how things should be or the state of the workplace after the solution is implemented. They provide a basis for the

FIGURE 8-4 Typical Application Objectives

When the solution is implemented . . .

- At least 99.1 percent of software users will be following the correct sequences after three weeks of use.
- Within one year, 10 percent of employees will submit documented suggestions for saving costs.
- The average 360-degree leadership assessment score will improve from 3.4 to 4.1 on a 5-point scale.
- 95 percent of high-potential employees will complete individual development plans within two years.
- Employees will routinely use problem-solving skills.
- Sexual harassment activity will cease within three months after the zero-tolerance policy is implemented.
- 80 percent of employees will use one or more of the three cost-containment features of the healthcare plan.
- 50 percent of conference attendees follow up with at least one contact from the conference.
- Pharmaceutical sales reps have communicated adverse effects of a specific prescription drug to all physicians in their territories.
- Managers initiate three workout projects.
- Sales and customer service representatives use all five interaction skills with at least half the customers.

---

evaluation of on-the-job changes and performance. They emphasize what has occurred on the job as a result of the solution by addressing these key questions:

- What new or improved *knowledge* was applied to the job?

- What new or improved *skill* was applied to the job?

- What is the *frequency of skill* application?

- What new *tasks* will be performed?

- What new *steps* will be implemented?

- What new *action items* will be implemented?

- What new *procedures* will be implemented or changed?

- What new *guidelines* will be implemented or changed?

- What new *processes* will be implemented or changed?

Application objectives are almost always included to some degree in programs or projects, but are not always as specific as they could be or need to be. To be effective, they must clearly define the expected environment in the workplace following successful program implementation.

BUSINESS IMPACT OBJECTIVES

Human capital solutions should drive one or more business impact measures. Impact objectives represent key business measures that should improve as the application and implementation objectives are achieved. Figure 8-5 shows typical business impact objectives. Business impact objectives are critical to measuring business performance because they define the ultimate expected outcomes of the solution. Above all, they emphasize bottom-line results that key client groups expect and demand.

ROI OBJECTIVES

The fifth level of objectives for programs is the acceptable return on investment (ROI), the monetary impact. These objectives define the expected payoff from the solution and compare the input resources (the cost of the solution) to the value of the ultimate outcome (the monetary benefits). An ROI objective is typically expressed as an acceptable percentage that

FIGURE 8-5 Typical Business Impact Objectives

After completion of this solution, the following conditions should be met:

- Grievances will be reduced from three per month to no more than two per month at the Golden Eagle tire plant.
- The average number of new accounts opened at Great Western Bank increased from 300 to 350 per month.
- Tardiness at the Newbury foundry will decrease by 20 percent within the next calendar year.
- Overtime is reduced by 20 percent for front-of-house managers at Tasty Time restaurants in the third quarter of this year.
- Employee complaints are reduced from an average of three per month to an average of one per month at Guarantee Insurance headquarters.
- The average number of product defects will decrease from 214 per month to 153 per month at all Amalgamated Rubber extruding plants in the Midwest region.
- The companywide job satisfaction index will rise by 2 percentage points during the next calendar year.
- Sales expenses for all titles at Proof Publishing Company will decrease by 10 percent in the fourth quarter.
- Pharmaceuticals Inc. brand awareness among physicians will show a 10 percent increase during the next two years.

---

compares the annual monetary benefits minus the cost, divided by the actual cost, and multiplied by 100. A 0 percent ROI indicates a break-even solution. A 50 percent ROI indicates that the cost of the solution is recaptured and an additional 50 percent "earnings" (50 cents for every dollar invested) is achieved.

For some solutions, the ROI objective is larger than what might be expected from the ROI of other expenditures, such as the purchase of a new company, a new building, or major equipment. However, the two are related, and the calculation is the same for both.

For many organizations, the ROI objective for a solution is set slightly higher than the ROI expected from other "routine investments" because of the relative newness of applying the ROI concept to these types of solutions. For example, if the expected ROI from the purchase of a new company is 20 percent, the ROI from a new team leader development program might be in the 25 percent range. The important point is that the ROI objective should be established up front and in coordination with the sponsor.

THE IMPORTANCE OF SPECIFIC OBJECTIVES

Developing specific objectives at different levels for solutions provides important benefits. First, they provide direction to the participants directly involved in making the solution work to help keep them on track. Objectives define exactly what is expected at different time frames and show the ultimate outcomes of the solution. Objectives provide guidance for the facilitators so that they understand the ultimate goal and impact of the solution. They also provide information and motivation for the solution designers and developers as they see the implementation and impact outcomes. In most programs, multiple stakeholders are involved and will influence the results. Specific objectives provide goals and motivation for the stakeholders so that they see the gains that should be achieved. Objectives provide important information to help the key sponsor groups clearly understand how the landscape will look when the solution is successful. Finally, from an evaluation perspective, objectives provide a basis for measuring the success of the solution.

FINAL THOUGHTS

This brief chapter tackles the critical issue of selecting the solution to the cause of the problem—a critical step. If the cause is not fully understood, the solution will not be appropriate. If the solution addresses the cause in an ineffective way, the results will be less than optimal. In addition, taking on too many solutions can create significant problems in the organization, diminishing the overall effort of the human capital analytics team. Several concepts are crucial: understanding the real causes, the relative priority of various causes, appropriateness of solutions to those causes, and timeliness of high-priority, high-payoff solutions. Next, objectives were detailed, with guidance on developing them for each level. The output of this chapter is objectives, which provide a focus for designers, developers, and facilitators, as well as participants and users who must make the solution successful.

CHAPTER 9

Calculate Monetary Benefits, Costs, and ROI

Human capital analytics offers HR teams an important opportunity to show value by converting data to money, and in turn gaining appreciation, particularly from executives and operating managers. Some measures, such as quality, time, and productivity, are easily converted to money. Others, such as company image, reputation, job satisfaction, engagement, stress, and teamwork, prove more difficult. And sometimes, "show me the money" isn't the right approach, especially when certain benefits should be reported as intangibles. This chapter explores the techniques, challenges, and opportunities for converting data to money.

In almost any project, the cost of the project becomes an important issue. When a solution is implemented, the cost of the solution is needed for the ultimate accountability, ROI. In these situations, all the cost should be tracked using both direct and indirect cost categories. A typical human capital analytics project has a budget that will usually involve direct cost. When presenting cost data to management, it is helpful to include indirect cost such as the time of people involved in the project. When a solution is implemented, a fully loaded cost of the solution builds credibility with top executives. This chapter explores the cost standards necessary for a credible analysis. The challenge is to be consistent with which cost categories to use and to ensure that all costs are included.

This chapter concludes with the process for calculating the ROI and the benefit-cost ratio (BCR).

OPENING STORY

The CEO of Family Mutual Insurance was a socially responsible executive. On a trip to Canada, he saw a report on the evening news about how a company had allowed some of its employees work at home, which had saved tons of carbon from being released into the environment. With that thought, he embarked on a project to allow certain groups of employees work at home. The project analyses were conducted using the V Model described earlier, and it appeared that it would be quite successful. With their growth, more buildings would be needed to house the employees, and with real estate costs increasing, this appeared to be the answer. Operations executives thought that several measures could be connected to a solution.

Two jobs were selected for this possibility: claims processor and claims examiners were offered the opportunity to work from home on a voluntary basis. In total almost 350 employees volunteered to work at home. They had to meet certain requirements and follow guidelines, and in doing so they would have a particular room in their house modified to be an office at home. In essence, they could accomplish the same work at home as they could working at the office.

Because this program was expensive, with huge ramifications as a departure from current policy, the CEO and other executives wanted to see the financial ROI. They wanted to understand the benefits of the program from the company's perspective, the employee's perspective, and the environment's perspective. The employees working at home became the experimental group. A carefully matched group not working at home became the control group. Table 9-1 shows the comparisons for the two groups.

Table 9-2 shows the monetary benefits from the solution, based on improvement in office expenses, turnover, and productivity. If a measure cannot be converted to money credibly with a reasonable effort, it is left as an intangible. Several intangibles emerged in this study. Employees felt that working at home gave them more flexibility and improved their job satisfaction with less stress. Quality of work life dramatically increased for the

TABLE 9-1   Impact Data Improvements

Business Performance	Work-at-Home Group	Comparison Group	Change	Number of Participants
Daily Claims Processed	35.4	33.2	2.2	234
Daily Claims Examined	22.6	20.7	1.9	77
Office Expense Per Person	$12,500	$17,000	$4,500	311
Annualized Turnover (Processors and Examiners)	9.1%	22.3%	13.2%	311

employees. This solution prevented 1,478 tons of carbon emissions from going into the environment each year.

Table 9-3 shows the total cost for the solution. All direct and indirect costs are included to be conservative in the analysis. This solution led to a significant impact and ROI analysis, delivering an ROI of 299 percent. It was truly a win-win project that received recognition from the Society of Human Resource Management, as well as other groups.[1]

This story illustrates the power of conducting an impact and ROI study where impact measures are converted to money and the costs are calculated. Many human capital analytics projects will lead to a solution and when those solutions are implemented, the executives may require (or would like to see) this level of analyses, to Level 4 for impact and Level 5 for ROI. These analyses are particularly important for solutions that are strategic, critical, and expensive and are connected to major issues in the organization.

THE ROI PROCESS MODEL

The next challenge for many analytics project leaders is to collect a variety of data along a chain of impact that shows the solution's value. Figure 9-1

TABLE 9-2 Converting Data to Money

Productivity Improvement

Cost (value) of processing one claim = $10

Cost (value) of examining one disputed claim = $12

Daily improvement = 2.2 claims processed per day

Daily improvement = 1.9 claims examined per day

Annual value = 234 participants × 220 work days × 2.2 × $10 = $1,132,560

Annual value = 77 participants × 220 work days × 1.9 × $12 = $386,232

Office Expense Reduction

Office expenses in company office per person = $17,000 annually

Office expenses at home office per person = $12,500 first year; $3,600 second year

Net improvement = $4,500, first year

Total annual value = 311 participants × $4,500 = $1,399,500

Turnover Reduction

Value of one turnover statistic = $25,400

Annual improvement related to program = 41 turnovers (prevented), first year

Annual value = $25,400 × 41 = $1,041,400

TABLE 9-3 Project Costs

Initial Analysis and Assessment	$ 21,000
Forecasting Impact and ROI	$ 10,000
Solution Development	$ 35,800
IT Support and Maintenance	$ 238,000
Administration and Coordination	$ 213,000
Materials (400 @ $50)	$ 20,000
Facilities and Refreshments (21 meetings)	$ 12,600
Salaries Plus Benefits for Employee and Manager Meetings	$ 418,280
Evaluation, Monitoring, and Reporting	$ 23,000
Total First-Year Costs	**$991,680**

FIGURE 9-1 The ROI Process Model

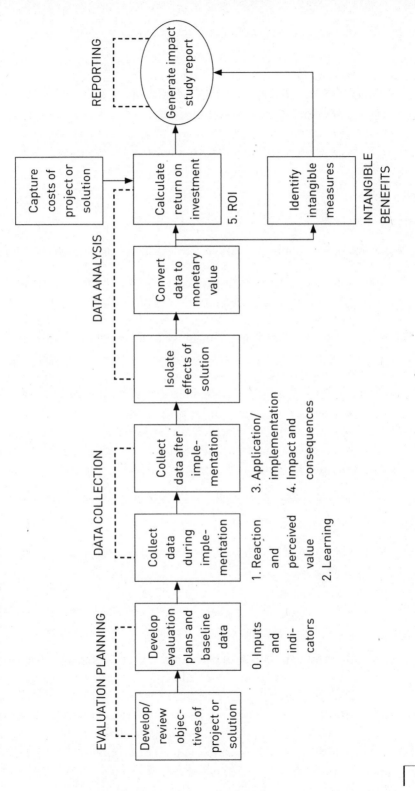

displays the sequential steps that lead to data categorized by the five levels of results. This figure shows the ROI Methodology, a step-by-step process beginning with the objectives and concluding with reporting of data. The model assumes that proper analysis is conducted to define needs. This chapter focuses on converting data to money, capturing the costs, and calculating ROI.

KEY STEPS IN CONVERTING DATA TO MONEY

Converting data to monetary value involves five steps for each data item:

1. **Focus on a unit of measure.** First, a unit of measure must be defined. For output data, the unit of measure is the item produced (one item assembled), service provided (one package shipped), or sale completed. Time measures could include the time to complete a project, cycle time, or customer response time, and the unit is usually expressed in minutes, hours, days, and so on. Quality is another common measure, with a unit defined as one error, reject, defect, or reworked item. Soft data measures vary, with a unit of improvement expressed in terms of absence, turnover, or a change in the customer satisfaction index. Specific examples of units of measure are:

    - One student enrolled
    - One patient served
    - One loan approved
    - One FTE employee
    - One reworked item
    - One grievance
    - One voluntary turnover
    - One hour of downtime

    - One hour of cycle time
    - One hour of employee time
    - One customer complaint
    - One person removed from welfare
    - One unplanned absence
    - One less day of incarceration

2. **Determine the value of each unit.** Now, the challenge: placing a value (V) on the unit identified in the first step. For measures of productivity, quality, cost, and time, the process is relatively easy. Most organizations maintain records or reports that can pinpoint the cost of one unit of production or one defect. Soft data are more difficult to convert to money. For example, the monetary

value of one customer complaint or a one-point change in an employee's attitude may be difficult to determine. This chapter provides an array of approaches for making this conversion. When more than one value is available, the most credible or lowest value is generally used in the calculation.

3. **Calculate the change in performance data.** The change in output data is calculated after the effects of the project have been isolated from other influences. This change (Δ) represents the performance improvement directly attributable to the project, represented as the Level 4 impact measure. The value may represent the performance improvement for an individual, a team, a group of participants, or several groups of participants.

4. **Determine the annual amount of change.** The value is annualized to develop a value for the total change in the performance data for one year (ΔP). Using annual figures is a standard approach for organizations seeking to capture the benefits of a particular solution, even though the benefits may not remain constant throughout the year. For a conservative, short-term solution, first-year benefits are used even when the project produces benefits beyond one year.

5. **Calculate the annual value of the improvement.** The total value of improvement is calculated by multiplying the annual performance change (ΔP) by the unit value (V) for the complete group in question. For example, if one group of participants is involved in the project being evaluated, the total value will include the total improvement for all participants providing data in the group. This value for annual project benefits is then compared with the costs of the project to calculate the BCR and ROI, or payback period.

An example from a labor-management cooperation solution at a manufacturing plant describes the five-step process of converting data to monetary values. This solution was developed and implemented after the initial needs assessment and analysis revealed that a lack of teamwork was causing excessive labor grievances. The grievances were managed using a four-stage

TABLE 9-4   Converting Labor Grievance Data to Monetary Values

Setting: Labor-management cooperation project in a manufacturing plant
Step 1: Define the unit of measure. The unit is defined as one grievance reaching stage two in the four-stage grievance resolution process.
Step 2: Determine the value (V) of each unit. According to internal experts (i.e., the labor relations staff), the cost of an average grievance was estimated at $6,500, when time and direct costs are considered (V = $6,500).
Step 3: Calculate the change (Δ) in performance data. Six months after the project was completed, total grievances per month reaching stage two had declined by 10. Seven of the 10 reductions were related to the project, as determined by first-level supervisors (see the discussion in Chapter 7 about isolating project impact).
Step 4: Determine an annual amount of the change (ΔP). Using the six-month value of seven grievances per month yields an annual improvement value of 84 (ΔP = 84).
Step 5: Calculate the annual value of the improvement.   Annual value $= \Delta P \times V$ $= 84 \times \$6,500$ $= \$546,000$

process. The number of grievances resolved at stage two was selected as an output measure. Table 9-4 shows the steps for assigning a monetary value to the data, resulting in a total project impact of $546,000.

STANDARD MONETARY VALUES

Most hard data items (output, quality, cost, and time) have standard values. A standard value is a monetary value assigned to a unit of measurement that is accepted by key stakeholders. Standard values have been developed because these are often the measures that matter to the organization. They reflect problems, and their conversion to monetary value shows their impact on the operational and financial well-being of the organization.

For the past two decades, quality programs have typically focused only on the cost of quality. Organizations have been obsessed with placing a value on mistakes or the payoff from avoiding these mistakes. This assigned value—the standard cost of an item—is one of the critical outgrowths of the quality management movement. In addition, a variety of process improvement programs such as reengineering, reinventing the corporation, transformation, and continuous process improvements have included a component in which the cost of a particular measure is determined. Finally, the development of a variety of cost-control, cost-containment, and cost-management systems, such as activity-based costing, have forced organizations to place costs on activities and, in some cases, relate those costs directly to the revenues or profits of the organization. The following discussion describes how measures of output, quality, and time can be converted to standard values.

Converting Output Data to Money

The value of the increased output can usually be determined from the organization's accounting or operating records. For organizations operating on a profit basis, this value is typically the marginal profit contribution of an additional unit of production or service provided. An example is a team within a major appliance manufacturing firm that was able to boost the production of small refrigerators after a comprehensive work cell redesign project; the unit of improvement is the profit margin associated with one refrigerator. For organizations that are performance driven rather than profit driven, this value is usually reflected in the savings realized when an additional unit of output is realized for the same input. For example, in the visa section of a government office, one additional visa application may be processed at no additional cost; an increase in output translates into a cost savings equal to the unit cost of processing a visa application.

The formulas used to calculate this contribution depend on the type of organization and the nature of its record keeping. Most organizations have standard values readily available for performance monitoring and goal setting. Managers often use marginal cost statements and sensitivity analyses to pinpoint values associated with changes in output. If the data are not available, the project team must initiate or coordinate the development of appropriate values.

The benefit of converting output data to money using standard values is that these calculations are already available for the most important data items. Perhaps no area has as much experience with standard values as the sales and marketing area. Table 9-5 shows a sampling of the sales and marketing measures that are routinely calculated and reported as standard values.

TABLE 9-5 Examples of Standard Values from Sales and Marketing

Metric	Definition	Conversion Notes
Sales	The sale of the product or service recorded in a variety of different ways: by product, by time period, by customer	The data must be converted to monetary value by applying the profit margin for a particular sales category.
Profit margin (%)	Price minus Cost Cost for the product, customer, and time period	Factored to convert sales to monetary value added to the organization
Unit margin	Unit price less unit cost	Shows the value of incremental sales
Channel margin	Channel profits as a percentage of channel selling price	Used to show the value of sales through a particular marketing channel
Retention rate	The ratio of customers retained to the number of customers at risk of leaving	The value is the saving of money necessary to acquire a replacement customer.
Churn rate	Ratio of customers leaving to the number who are at risk of leaving	The value is the saving of money necessary to acquire a new customer.
Customer profit	The difference between the revenues earned and the cost associated with the customer relationship during the specified period	The monetary value added is the profit obtained from customers, which all goes toward the bottom line.
Customer value lifetime	The present value of the future cash flows attributed to the customer relationship	Bottom line; as customer value increases, it adds directly to the profits; as a customer is added, the incremental value is the customer lifetime average

Metric	Definition	Conversion Notes
Cannibalization rate	The percentage of new product sales taken from existing product lines	This metric is to be minimized, because it represents an adverse effect on existing product, with the value added being the loss of profits due to the sales loss.
Workload	Hours required to service clients and prospects	This metric includes the salaries, commissions, and benefits from the time the sales staff spend on workload.
Inventories	The total amount of product or brand available for sale in a particular channel	Because inventories are valued at the cost of carrying the inventory, costs involve space, handling, and the time value of money; insufficient inventory is the cost of expediting the new inventory or the loss of sales because of the inventory outage.
Market share	Sales revenue as a percentage of total market sales	Actual sales are converted to money through the profit margins, which provides a measure of competitiveness.
Loyalty	The length of time the customer stays with the organization, the willingness to pay a premium, and the willingness to search	Calculated as the additional profit from the sale or the profit on the premium

Calculating the Cost of Quality

Quality and the cost of quality are important issues in most manufacturing and service organizations; therefore, the human capital analytics team may have to place a value on the improvement of certain quality measures. For some quality measures, the task is easy. For example, if quality is measured in terms of the defect rate, the value of the improvement is the cost to repair or replace the product. The most obvious cost of poor quality is the amount of scrap or waste generated by mistakes. Defective products, spoiled raw materials, and discarded paperwork are all the result of poor quality. Scrap and waste translate directly into a monetary value. In a production environment, for example, the cost of a defective product is the total cost incurred up to the point at which the mistake is identified, minus the salvage value. In the service environment, the cost of a defective service is the cost incurred up to the point at which the deficiency is identified, plus the cost to correct the problem, plus the cost to make the customer happy, plus the loss of customer loyalty.

Employee mistakes and errors can be expensive. The costliest form of rework occurs when a product or service is delivered to a customer and must be returned for repair or correction. The cost of rework includes both labor and direct costs. In some organizations, rework costs can constitute as much as 25–35 percent of operating expenses.

Quality costs can be grouped into seven major categories:

1. *Internal failure* represents costs associated with problems detected prior to product shipment or service delivery. Typically such costs include reworking and retesting.

2. *Penalty costs* are fines or penalties incurred as a result of unacceptable quality.

3. *External failure* refers to problems detected after product shipment or service delivery. Typical items here are technical support, complaint investigation, remedial upgrades, and fixes.

4. *Appraisal costs* are the expenses involved in determining the condition of a particular product or service. Typical costs involve testing and related activities, such as product quality audits.

5. *Prevention costs* involve efforts undertaken to avoid unacceptable products or service quality. These efforts include service quality administration, inspections, process studies, and improvements.

6. *Customer dissatisfaction* is perhaps the costliest element of inadequate quality. In some cases, serious mistakes result in lost business. Customer dissatisfaction is difficult to quantify, and arriving at a monetary value may be impossible using direct methods. The judgment and expertise of sales, marketing, or quality managers are usually the best resources to draw upon in measuring the impact of dissatisfaction. More and more quality experts are measuring customer and client dissatisfaction with the use of market surveys.

7. *Legal costs* are applicable when quality problems result in litigation.

As with output data, the good news is that a tremendous number of quality measures have been converted to standard values. Some of these measures are:

- Downtime—equipment
- Downtime—system
- Delay
- Fines
- Uncollected sales
- Defects
- Rework
- Processing errors
- Customer complaints
- Accidents
- Grievances
- Waste

CONVERTING EMPLOYEE TIME USING COMPENSATION

Reducing the workforce or saving employee time is a common objective for solutions. In a team environment, a solution may enable the team to complete tasks in less time or with fewer people. A major project could lead to a reduction of several hundred employees. On an individual basis, a technology project may be designed to help professional, sales, and managerial employees save time in performing daily tasks. The value of the time saved is an important measure, and determining a monetary value for it is relatively easy.

The most obvious time savings stem from reduced labor costs for performing a given amount of work. The monetary savings are found by multiplying the hours saved by the labor cost per hour. For example, a time-saving process in one organization, participants estimated, saved an average of 74 minutes per day, worth $31.25 per day or $7,500 per year, based on the average salary plus benefits for a typical participant.

The average wage, with a percentage added for employee benefits, will suffice for most calculations. However, employee time may be worth more. For example, additional costs for maintaining an employee (office space, furniture, telephones, utilities, computers, administrative support, and other overhead expenses) could be included in calculating the average labor cost. Thus, the wage rate used in the calculation can escalate quickly. In a large-scale employee reduction effort, calculating the costs of additional employees may be more appropriate for showing the value. However, for most projects, the conservative approach of using salary plus employee benefits is recommended.

Beyond reducing the labor cost per hour, time savings can produce benefits such as improved service, avoidance of penalties for late projects, and additional profit opportunities. These values can be estimated using other methods discussed in this chapter.

A word of caution is needed concerning time savings. Savings are realized only when the amount of time saved translates into a cost reduction or a profit contribution. Even if a project produces savings in manager time, monetary value is not realized unless the manager puts the time saved to productive use. Having managers estimate the percentage of time saved that is devoted to productive work may be helpful, if it is followed up with a request for examples of how the extra time was used. If a team-based project sparks a new process that eliminates several hours of work each day, the actual savings will be based on the corresponding reduction in staff or overtime pay. Therefore, an important preliminary step in figuring time savings is determining whether the expected savings will be genuine.

FINDING STANDARD VALUES

Standard values are available for all types of data. Virtually every major department will develop standard values that are monitored for that area.

Typical functions in a major organization where standard values are tracked include:

- Sales and marketing
- Customer service and support
- Procurement
- Logistics
- Compliance
- Research and development
- Engineering
- IT
- Safety and health
- HR

Thanks to enterprise-wide systems software, standard values are commonly integrated and made available for access by a variety of people. In some cases, access may need to be addressed to ensure that the data can be obtained by those who require them.

WHEN STANDARD VALUES ARE NOT AVAILABLE

When standard values are not available, several alternative strategies for converting data to monetary values are available. Some are appropriate for a specific type of data or data category, while others may be used with virtually any type of data. The challenge is to select the strategy that best suits the situation.

USING HISTORICAL DATA FROM RECORDS

Historical records often indicate the value of a measure and the cost (or value) of a unit of improvement. This strategy relies on identifying the appropriate records and tabulating the proper cost components for the item in question. The opening story provided an example of this approach.

For example, a large construction firm initiated a project to improve safety. The project improved several safety-related performance measures, ranging from amounts spent in response to government fines to total worker's compensation costs. From the company's records for one year of data, the average cost for each safety measure was determined. This value included the direct costs of medical payments, insurance payments and premiums, investigation services, and lost-time payments to employees, as well as payments for legal expenses, fines, and other direct services. The amount of time used to investigate, resolve, and correct the issues was also factored in. This time involved not only the health and safety staff, but other personnel as well. In addition, the costs of lost productivity, disruption of services, morale, and dissatisfaction were estimated to obtain a full cost. The corresponding costs for each item were then developed.

This example suggests the challenges inherent in maintaining systems and databases to enable the value for a particular data item to be identified. It also raises several concerns about using historical costs as a technique to convert data to money.

TIME

Sorting through databases, cost statements, financial records, and activity reports takes a tremendous amount of time, time that may not be available for the project. It is important to keep this part of the process in perspective.

AVAILABILITY

In some cases, data are not available to show all of the costs for a particular item. In addition to the direct costs associated with a measure, an equal number of indirect or invisible costs may be present that cannot be obtained easily.

ACCESS

Compounding the problems of time and availability is access. Monetary values may be needed from a system or record set that is under someone else's control. In a typical implementation, the project leader may not have full access to cost data. Cost data are more sensitive than other types of data and are often protected for a number of reasons, including competitive advantage. Therefore, access can be difficult and sometimes is even prohibited unless an absolute need to know can be demonstrated.

ACCURACY

Finally, the need for accuracy in this analysis should not be overlooked. A measure provided in current records may appear to be based on accurate data, but may in fact be an illusion. When data are calculated, estimations are involved, access to certain systems is denied, and different assumptions are made (all of which can be compounded by different definitions of systems, data, and measures). Because of these limitations, the calculated values should be viewed as suspect unless means are available to ensure that they are accurate.

Calculating monetary value using historical data should be approached with caution and only when these two conditions exist:

1. The sponsor has approved the use of additional time, effort, and money to develop a monetary value from the current records and reports.

2. The measure is simple and can be found by searching only a few records.

Otherwise, an alternative method is preferred.

USING INPUT FROM EXPERTS

When it is necessary to convert data items for which historical cost data are not available, input from experts on the process might be a consideration. Internal experts can provide the cost (or value) of one unit of improvement in a measure. Individuals with knowledge of the situation and the confidence of management must be willing to provide estimates as well as the assumptions behind the estimates. Internal experts may be found in the department in which the data originated, such as sales, marketing, payroll, labor relations, or any number of other functions. Most experts have their own methodologies for developing these values. So when their input is required, it is important to explain the full scope of what is needed and to provide as many specifics as possible.

If internal experts have a strong bias regarding the measure or are not available, external experts are sought. External experts should be selected based on their experience with the unit of measure. Fortunately, many experts are available who work directly with important measures, such as employee attitudes, customer satisfaction, turnover, absenteeism, and grievances. They are often willing to provide estimates of the cost (or value) of these intangibles.

External experts, including consultants, professionals, or suppliers in a particular area, can also be found in obvious places. For example, the costs of accidents can be estimated by the worker's compensation carrier, or the cost of a grievance may be estimated by the labor attorney defending the company in grievance transactions. The process of locating an external expert is similar to the external database search, which is described later.

The credibility of the expert, whether internal or external, is a critical issue if the monetary value placed on a measure is to be valid. Foremost among the factors behind an expert's credibility is the individual's experience with the process or measure at hand. Ideally, he or she should work with this measure routinely. Also, the person must be unbiased. Experts should be neutral in connection with the measure's value and should have no personal or professional interest in it.

In addition, the credentials of external experts' published works, degrees, and other honors or awards are important in validating their expertise. Many of these people are tapped often, and their track records can and should be checked. If their estimate has been validated in more detailed studies and was found to be consistent, it can serve as a confirmation of their qualifications in providing such data.

Using Values from External Databases

For some measures, the use of cost (or value) estimates based on the work and research of others may be appropriate. This technique makes use of external databases that contain studies and research projects focusing on the cost of data items. Fortunately, many databases include cost studies of data items related to projects, and most are accessible on the Internet. Data are available on the costs of turnover, absenteeism, grievances, accidents, and even customer satisfaction. The difficulty lies in finding a database with studies or research germane to the particular project. Ideally, the data should originate from a similar setting in the same industry, but that is not always possible. Sometimes, data on industries or organizations in general are sufficient, with adjustments possibly required to suit the project at hand.

Linking with Other Measures

When standard values, records, experts, and external studies are not available, a feasible alternative might be to find a relationship between the measure in question and some other measure that can be easily converted to a monetary value. It involves identifying existing relationships that show a strong correlation between one measure and another with a standard value.

A classic relationship is the correlation between job satisfaction and employee turnover. Suppose that in a project designed to improve job satisfaction, a value is needed to reflect changes in the job satisfaction index. A predetermined relationship showing the correlation between increases in job satisfaction and reductions in turnover can directly link the two measures. Using standard data or external studies, the cost of turnover can easily be determined as described earlier. Therefore, a change in job satisfaction can be immediately converted to a monetary value, or at least an approximate value. The conversion is not always exact because of the potential for error and other factors, but the estimate is sufficient for converting the data to monetary values.

Finding a correlation between a customer satisfaction measure and another measure that can easily be converted to a monetary value is sometimes possible. A strong correlation often exists between customer satisfaction and revenue. Connecting these two variables allows the monetary value of customer satisfaction to be estimated.

In some situations, a chain of relationships may establish a connection between two or more variables. A measure that may be difficult to convert to a monetary value is linked to other measures that, in turn, are linked to measures to which values can be assigned. Ultimately, these measures are traced to a monetary value typically based on profits. Figure 9-2 shows the linkage of health risk to unplanned absenteeism, which is linked to gross productivity, defined as revenue per employee. As the model shows, an improvement in employee health status leads to less absenteeism, which in turn drives an increase in revenue per employee. Applying the profit margin to the revenue results in the monetary contribution. These links between measures offer a promising methodology for applying monetary values to hard-to-quantify measures.

Using Estimates from Participants

In some cases, participants or users in a process or solution should estimate the value of improvement. This technique is appropriate when participants are capable of providing estimates of the cost (or value) of the unit of measure. With this approach, participants should be provided with clear instructions along with examples of the type of information needed. The advantage of this approach is that the individuals who are most closely connected to the improvement are often able to provide the most reliable estimates of its value. When estimates are used to convert measures to monetary values, adjustments are made to reduce the error in those estimates.

Using Estimates from the Management Team

In some situations, participants may be incapable of placing a value on the improvement. Their work may be so far removed from the ultimate value of

FIGURE 9-2 The Linkage Between Health Status of Employees and Gross Productivity

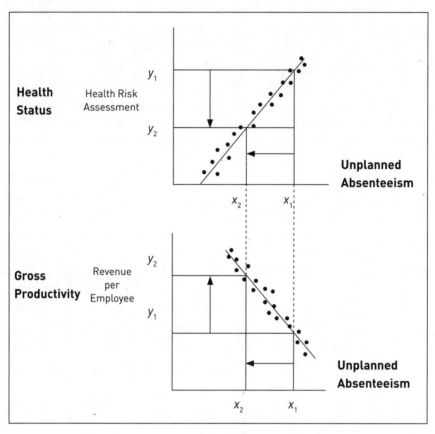

the process that they cannot provide reliable estimates. In these cases, the team leaders, supervisors, or managers of participants may be able to supply those estimates. Thus, they may be asked to provide a value for a unit of improvement linked to the project.

In other situations, managers are asked to review and approve participants' estimates and confirm, adjust, or reject those values. For example, a solution involves customer service representatives and was designed to reduce customer complaints. The solution did result in a reduction in complaints, but the value of a single customer complaint had to be identified to determine the value of the improvement. Although customer service representatives had knowledge of certain issues surrounding customer complaints, their scope was limited, so their managers were asked to provide a value. These managers had a broader perspective of the impact of a customer complaint.

Senior management can often provide estimates of the value of data. In this approach, senior managers concerned with a measure are asked to place a value on it based on their perception of its worth. This approach is used when calculating the value is difficult or when other sources of estimation are unavailable or unreliable.

TECHNIQUE SELECTION AND FINALIZING VALUE

With so many techniques available, the challenge is selecting one or more strategies appropriate for the situation and available resources. Developing a table or list of values or techniques for the situation may be helpful. The guidelines that follow may aid in selecting a technique and finalizing the values.

CHOOSE A TECHNIQUE APPROPRIATE FOR THE TYPE OF DATA

Some strategies are designed specifically for hard data, whereas others are more appropriate for soft data. Thus, the type of data often dictates the strategy. Standard values are developed for most hard data items, and company records and cost statements are used in the process. Soft data often involve the use of external databases, links with other measures, and estimates. Experts are used to convert both types of data to monetary values.

MOVE FROM MOST ACCURATE TO LEAST ACCURATE

The techniques in this chapter are presented in order of accuracy. Standard values are always most accurate and, therefore, the most credible. But, as mentioned earlier, they are not always readily available. When standard values are not available, the following sequence of operational techniques should be tried:

- Historical costs from company records
- Internal and external experts

- Links with other measures

- External databases

- Estimates

Each technique should be considered in turn based on its feasibility and applicability to the situation. The technique associated with the highest accuracy is always preferred if the situation allows.

Consider Source Availability

Sometimes the availability of a particular source of data determines the method selection. For example, experts may be readily accessible. Some standard values are easy to find; others are more difficult. In other situations, the convenience of a technique is a major factor in the selection. The Internet, for example, has made external database searches more convenient.

As with other processes, keeping the time investment for this effort to a minimum is important. Some techniques can be implemented in much less time than others. Devoting too much time to the conversion process may dampen otherwise enthusiastic attitudes about the use of the methodology, plus drive up the costs of the evaluation.

Use the Source with the Broadest Perspective on the Issue

In all situations, the most credible data source must be used. The individual providing estimates must be knowledgeable of the processes and the issues surrounding the valuation of the data. For example, consider the estimation of the cost of a grievance in a manufacturing plant. Although a supervisor may have insight into what caused a particular grievance, he or she may have a limited perspective. A high-level manager may be able to grasp the overall impact of the grievance and how it will affect other areas. Thus, a high-level manager would be a more credible source in this situation.

Use Multiple Techniques When Feasible

The availability of more than one technique for obtaining values for the data is often beneficial. When appropriate, multiple sources should be used to provide a basis for comparison or for additional perspectives. The data must be integrated using a convenient decision rule, such as the lowest value. The conservative approach of using the lowest value is guiding principle, but it only applies when the sources have equal or similar credibility.

Converting data to monetary values has its challenges. Once the particular method has been selected and applied, several adjustments or tests are necessary to ensure the use of the most credible and appropriate value with the least amount of resources.

APPLY THE CREDIBILITY TEST

The discussion of techniques in this chapter assumes that each data item collected and linked to a solution can be converted to a monetary value. Highly subjective data, however, such as changes in employee attitudes or a reduction in the number of employee conflicts, are difficult to convert. Although estimates can be developed using one or more strategies, some estimates may lack credibility with the target audience, which can render their use in analysis questionable.

The issue of credibility in combination with resources is a logical way to decide whether to convert data to monetary values or leave them intangible. Essentially, in the absence of standard values, many other ways are available to capture the data or convert them to monetary values. However, the question to be answered is: Can it be done with minimum resources? Some of the techniques mentioned in this chapter such as searching records or searching the Internet cannot be performed with minimal use of resources. However, an estimate obtained from a group or from a few individuals is available with minimal use of resources. Then we move to the next question: Will the executive who is interested in the solution buy in to the monetary value assigned to the measure with minimum explanation? If so, then it is credible enough to be included in the analysis; if not, then move it to the intangibles. The intangible benefits of a solution are also important.

CONSIDER THE POSSIBILITY OF MANAGEMENT ADJUSTMENT

In organizations where soft data are common and values are derived using imprecise methods, senior managers and administrators are sometimes offered the opportunity to review and approve the data. Because of the subjective nature of this process, management may factor (reduce) the data to make the final results more credible. In one example, senior managers at

Litton Industries adjusted the value for the benefits derived from implementing self-directed teams.

CONSIDER THE SHORT-TERM/LONG-TERM ISSUE

When data are converted to monetary values, usually one year's worth of data is included in the analysis; this guiding principle states that for short-term solutions, only the first year's benefits are used. The issue of whether a solution is short-term or long-term depends on the time it takes to complete the project. If one group participating in the solution and working through the process takes months to complete it, then it is probably not short-term. Some solutions literally take years to implement even for one particular group. In general, it is appropriate to consider a project short-term when one individual takes one month or less to learn what needs to be done to make the project successful. When the lag between solution implementation and the consequences is relatively brief, considering it a short-term solution is appropriate. When a solution is long-term, no time limit for data inclusion is used, but the time value should be set before the solution evaluation is undertaken. Input on the time value should be secured from all stakeholders, including the sponsor, champion, implementer, designer, and evaluator. After some discussion, the estimates of the time factor should be conservative and perhaps reviewed by finance and accounting. When a project is a long-term solution, forecasting will need to be used to estimate multiple years of value. No sponsor will wait several years to see how a solution turns out.

CONSIDER AN ADJUSTMENT FOR THE TIME VALUE OF MONEY

Because investment in a solution is made in one time period and the return is realized at a later time, some organizations adjust solution benefits to reflect the time value of money using discounted-cash-flow techniques. The actual monetary benefits of the solution are adjusted for the time period. The amount of adjustment, however, is usually small compared with the typical benefits of solutions.

Although this time value may not be an issue for every solution, it should be considered for each solution implementation, and some standard discount rate should be used. Consider the following example of how time value is calculated. Assume that a project costs $100,000, and it is expected to take two years for the full value of the estimate to be realized. In other words, this long-term solution spans two years. Using a discount rate of 6 percent, the cost for the solution for the first year would be $100,000 × 106 percent = $106,000. For the second year it is $106,000 × 106 percent, or $112,360. Thus, the solution cost has been adjusted for a two-year value with a 6 percent discount rate. This approach assumes that the solution sponsor could have invested the money in some other solution and obtained at least a 6 percent return on that investment.

CAPTURING FULLY LOADED COSTS

Because a conservative approach is used to calculate the ROI, costs should be fully loaded, which is one of the guiding principles. With this approach, all costs (direct and indirect) that can be identified and linked to a particular project are included. The philosophy is simple: for the denominator, "when in doubt, put it in" (i.e., if you have any question as to whether a cost should be included, include it, even if the cost guidelines for the organization do not require it). When an ROI is calculated and reported to target audiences, the process should withstand even the closest scrutiny, when necessary, to ensure its credibility. The only way to meet this test is to include all costs. Of course, from a realistic viewpoint, if the controller or chief financial officer insists on not using certain costs, then leaving them out or reporting them in an alternative way is suggested.

Costs Reported Without Benefits

Because costs can easily be collected, they are presented to management in many ingenious ways, such as in terms of the total cost of the project, cost per day, and cost per participant. Although these figures may be helpful for efficiency comparisons, presenting them without identifying the corresponding benefits may be problematic. When most executives review project costs, a logical question is raised: What benefit was received from the project? This management reaction is typical, particularly when costs are perceived to be high.

Sources of Costs

It is sometimes helpful to first consider the sources of project costs. Four major categories of sources are illustrated in Table 9-6. The charges and

TABLE 9-6 Sources of Human Capital Analytics Project Costs

Source of Costs	Cost Reporting Issues
Project team fees and expenses	• Costs are usually accurate • Variable expenses are usually underestimated
Vendor/suppliers fees and expenses	• Costs are usually accurate • Variable expenses are usually underestimated
Client expenses, direct and indirect	• Direct expenses are usually not fully loaded • Indirect expenses are rarely included in costs • Sometimes understated
Equipment, services, and other expenses	• May lack accountability

expenses from the project team represent the major segment of costs and are usually transferred directly to the client for payment. These costs are often placed in subcategories under fees and expenses. A second major cost category relates to the vendors or suppliers who assist with the project. A variety of expenses, such as consulting or advisory fees, may fall in this category. A third major cost category includes those expenses, both direct and indirect, borne by the client organization. In many projects, these costs are not identified but nevertheless are part of the costs of the project. The final cost category involves expenses not covered in the other three categories. These include payments for equipment and services needed for the project. Finance and accounting records should track and reflect the costs from these different sources, and the process presented in this chapter can also help track these costs.

PRORATED VERSUS DIRECT COSTS

Usually all costs related to a project are captured and expensed to that project. However, some costs are prorated over a longer period. Equipment purchases, software development and acquisitions, and the construction of facilities are all significant costs with a useful life that may extend beyond the project. Consequently, a portion of these costs should be prorated to the project. Under a conservative approach, the expected life of the project is fixed. Some organizations will assume a period of one year of operation for a simple project. Others may consider three to five years appropriate. If a question is raised about the specific time period to be used in this calculation, the finance and accounting staff should be consulted, or appropriate guidelines should be developed and followed.

EMPLOYEE BENEFITS FACTOR

Employee time is valuable, and when time is required for a project, the costs for that time must be fully loaded, representing total compensation, including employee benefits. This number is usually well-known in the organization and is used in other costing formulas. It represents the cost of all employee benefits expressed as a percentage of payroll. In some organizations, this value is as high as 50 to 60 percent. In others, it may be as low as 25 to 30 percent. The average in the United States is 38 percent.[2]

SPECIFIC COSTS TO INCLUDE

Table 9-7 shows the recommended cost categories for a fully loaded, conservative approach to estimating solution costs. Consistency in capturing all these costs is essential, and standardization adds credibility. Each category is described in this section.

INITIAL ANALYSIS AND ASSESSMENT COSTS

One of the most underestimated items is the cost of conducting the initial analysis and assessment that leads to the need for the solution. In a comprehensive solution, this category involves data collection, problem solving, assessment, and analysis. In some solutions, this cost is near zero because the solution is implemented without an initial assessment of need. However, as more solution sponsors place attention on needs assessment and analysis in the future, this item will become a significant cost.

SOLUTION DEVELOPMENT COSTS

Also significant are the costs of designing and developing the solution. These costs include time spent in both the design and development and

TABLE 9-7 Project Cost Categories

Cost Item	Prorated	Expensed
Initial analysis and assessment	✓	
Development of solutions	✓	
Acquisition of solutions	✓	
Implementation and application		
Salaries/benefits for project team time		✓
Salaries/benefits for coordination time		✓
Salaries/benefits for participant time		✓
Project materials		✓
Hardware/software	✓	
Travel/lodging/meals		✓
Use of facilities		✓
Capital expenditures	✓	
Maintenance and monitoring		✓
Administrative support and overhead	✓	
Evaluation and reporting		✓

the purchase of supplies, technology, and other materials directly related to the solution. As with needs assessment costs, design and development costs are usually charged to the solution. However, if the solution can be used in other solutions, the major expenditures can be prorated.

ACQUISITION COSTS

In lieu of development costs, some project leaders use acquisition costs connected to the purchasing of solutions from other sources to use directly or in a modified format. The costs for these solutions include the purchase price, support materials, and licensing agreements. Some solutions have both acquisition costs and solution development costs. Acquisition costs can be prorated if the acquired solutions can be used in other projects.

IMPLEMENTATION COSTS

The largest cost segment in a solution is associated with implementation and delivery. The time (salaries and benefits), travel, and other expenses of those involved in the solution in any way should be included. These costs can be estimated using average or midpoint salary values for corresponding job classifications. When a solution is targeted for an ROI calculation, participants can provide their salaries directly in a confidential manner. Solution materials, such as field journals, instructions, reference guides, case studies, surveys, and participant workbooks, should be included in the implementation costs, along with license fees, user fees, and royalty payments. Supporting hardware, software, and tools should also be included.

The cost for the use of facilities needed for the solution should be included. External meeting costs would include the direct charge for the conference center, hotel, or motel. If the meetings are conducted in-house, the conference room represents a cost for the organization, and the cost should be estimated and incorporated—even if it is uncommon to include facilities costs in other cost reporting. If a facility or building is constructed or purchased for the solution, it is included as a capital expenditure, but is prorated. The same is true for the purchase of major hardware and software when they are considered capital expenditures.

MAINTENANCE AND MONITORING COSTS

Maintenance and monitoring involve routine expenses necessary to maintain and operate the solution. These ongoing expenses allow the new solution to continue. They may involve staff members and additional expenses, and they may be significant for some solutions.

SUPPORT AND OVERHEAD COSTS

The cost of support and overhead includes the additional costs not directly charged to the solution—any solution cost not considered in the previous categories. Typical items are the cost of administrative/clerical support, telecommunication expenses, office expenses, salaries of client managers, and other fixed costs. Usually, this cost is provided in the form of an estimate allocated in some convenient way.

EVALUATION AND REPORTING COSTS

The total evaluation cost completes the fully loaded costs. Activities under evaluation costs include developing the evaluation strategy, designing instruments, collecting data, analyzing data, preparing a report, and communicating the results. Cost categories include time, materials, purchased instruments, surveys, and any consulting fees.

CALCULATING ROI

The term *return on investment for projects and programs* is occasionally misused, sometimes intentionally. In this misuse, a broad definition for ROI is given that includes any benefit from the project. ROI becomes a vague concept in which even subjective data linked to a program are included. In this book, the return on investment is defined more precisely and represents an actual value determined by comparing project costs to benefits. The two most common measures are the benefit-cost ratio (BCR) and the ROI formula. Both are presented along with other approaches to calculate the return or payback.

The formulas presented in this chapter use annualized values so that the first-year impact of the investment can be calculated for short-term projects. Using annualized values is becoming an accepted practice for developing the ROI in many organizations. This approach is a conservative way to develop the ROI, because many short-term projects have added value in the second or third year. For long-term projects, longer time frames should be used. For example, in an ROI analysis of a solution involving major software purchases, a five-year time frame was used.

When selecting the approach to measure ROI, the formula used and the assumptions made in arriving at the decision to use this formula should be communicated to the target audience. This disclosure helps prevent misunderstandings and confusion surrounding how the ROI value was developed. Although several approaches are described in this chapter, two stand out as preferred methods: the benefit-cost ratio and the basic ROI formula.

Benefit-Cost Ratio

One of the original methods for evaluating projects was the benefit-cost ratio. This method compares the benefits of the project with the costs, using a simple ratio. In formula form:

$$BCR = \frac{\text{Project benefits}}{\text{Project costs}}$$

In simple terms, the BCR compares the annual economic benefits of the project with the costs of the project. A BCR of 1 means that the benefits equal the costs. A BCR of 2, usually written as 2:1, indicates that for each $1 spent on the project, $2 were returned in benefits.

The following example illustrates the use of the BCR. A behavior modification project designed for managers and supervisors was implemented at an electric and gas utility. In a follow-up evaluation, action planning and business performance monitoring were used to capture the benefits. The first-year payoff for the program was $1,077,750. The total, fully loaded implementation costs were $215,500. Thus, the ratio was:

$$\frac{\$1,077,750}{\$215,000} = 5.01 : 1$$

For every $1 invested in the project, $5 in benefits were returned.

ROI FORMULA

Perhaps the most appropriate formula for evaluating project investments is net program benefits divided by costs. This traditional financial ROI calculation is directly related to the BCR. The ROI ratio is usually expressed as a percentage where the fractional values are multiplied by 100. In formula form:

$$\frac{\text{Net project benefits}}{\text{Project costs}}$$

Net project benefits are project benefits minus costs. Another way to calculate ROI is to subtract 1 from the BCR and multiply by 100 to get the ROI percentage. For example, a BCR of 2.45 is the same as an ROI value of 145 percent (1.45 × 100%). This formula is essentially the same as the ROI for capital investments. For example, when a firm builds a new plant, the ROI is developed by dividing annual earnings by the investment. The annual earnings are comparable to net benefits (annual benefits minus the cost). The investment is comparable to the fully loaded project costs.

An ROI of 50 percent means that the costs were recovered and an additional 50 percent of the costs were returned. An ROI of 150 percent indicates that the costs have been recovered and an additional 1.5 times the costs are returned.

An example illustrates the ROI calculation: Public- and private-sector groups concerned about literacy have developed a variety of projects to address the issue. Magnavox Electronics Systems Company was involved in one literacy project that focused on language and math skills for entry-level electrical and mechanical assemblers. The results of the project were impressive. Productivity and quality alone yielded an annual value of $321,600.

The total, fully loaded costs for the project were just $38,233. Thus, the return on investment was:

$$\frac{\$321,600 - \$38,233}{\$38,233} \times 100 = 741\%$$

For each dollar invested, Magnavox received $7.41 in return after the costs of the consulting project were recovered.

Investments in plants, equipment, subsidiaries, or other major items are not usually evaluated using the benefit-cost method. Using the ROI formula to calculate the return on project investments essentially places these investments on a level playing field with other investments whose valuation uses the same formula and similar concepts. The ROI calculation is easily understood by key management and financial executives who regularly work with investments and their ROIs.

BENEFITS OF ROI ANALYSIS

The methodology presented in this book has been used consistently and routinely by thousands of organizations in the past decade. In some fields and industries, it has been more prominent than in others. Much has been learned about the success of this methodology and what it can bring to the organizations using it.

VALIDATING THE HYPOTHESIS

In reality, most projects are undertaken to deliver value. As described in this chapter, the definition of value may on occasion be unclear, or may not be what a project's various sponsors, organizers, and stakeholder's desire. Consequently, value shifts may often occur. When the values are finally determined, the value proposition is detailed. The ROI Methodology will forecast the value in advance, and if the value has been delivered, it verifies the value proposition agreed to by the appropriate parties.

IMPROVING PROCESSES

ROI Methodology is a process improvement tool by design and by practice. It collects data to evaluate how things are or are not working. When things are not where they should be, as when projects are not proceeding as effectively as expected, data are available to indicate what must be changed to make the project more effective. When things are working well, data are available to show what else could be done to make them better. Thus, this process improvement system is designed to provide feedback to make changes. As a project is conducted, the results are collected and feedback is provided to the various stakeholders for specific actions for improvement. These changes drive the project to better results, which are then measured while the process continues. This continuous feedback cycle is critical to process improvement and is inherent in the ROI Methodology.

ENHANCING THE IMAGE, BUILDING RESPECT

Many functions, and even entire professions, are criticized for being unable to deliver what is expected, and as a result, their public image suffers. The ROI Methodology is one way to help build the respect a function or profession needs.

The ROI Methodology can make a difference in any function, not just those under fire. Many HR executives have used ROI to show their projects' and programs' value, perhaps changing the perception of a project from one based on activity to one that credibly adds value. This methodology makes a connection to the bottom line and shows the value delivered to stakeholders. It removes issues about value and a supposed lack of contribution to the organization. Consequently, this methodology is an important part of the process of changing the image within the function of the organization and building needed respect.

IMPROVING SUPPORT

Securing support for projects is critical, particularly at the middle manager level. Many projects enjoy the support of the top-level managers who allocated the resources to make the projects viable. Unfortunately, some middle-level managers may not support certain projects because they do not see the value the projects deliver in terms the managers appreciate and understand. Having a methodology that shows how a project or program is connected to the manager's business goals and objectives can change this support level. When middle managers understand that a project is helping them meet specific performance indicators or departmental goals, they will usually support the process, or will at least resist it less. In this way, the ROI Methodology may actually improve manager support.

Justifying or Enhancing Budgets

Some organizations have used the ROI Methodology to support proposed budgets. Because the ROI shows the monetary value expected or achieved from specific projects, the data can often be leveraged into budget requests. When a particular function is budgeted, the amount budgeted is often in direct proportion to the value that the function adds. If little or no credible data support the contribution, the budgets are often trimmed—or at least not enhanced. Organizations have reported significant budget increases for an entire function based on ROI projects pursued during the previous year. Bringing accountability to this level is one of the best ways to secure future funding.

Building a Partnership with Key Executives

Almost every function attempts to partner with operating executives and key managers in the organization. Unfortunately, some managers may not want to be partners. They may not want to waste time and effort on a relationship that does not help them succeed. They want to partner only with groups and individuals who can add value and help them in meaningful ways. Showing the projects' results will enhance the likelihood of building these partnerships, with the results providing the initial impetus for making the partnerships work.

FINAL THOUGHTS

Showing value in monetary terms requires just that—money. Sometimes an HCA project is to convert data to money, such as converting employee turnover to money. At other times, business impact data that have improved as a result of a solution must be converted to monetary values. For example, when a program leads to a reduction in accidents, the measure of accidents would be converted to money. Standard values make the data conversion process easier, but easy is not always an option; therefore, other techniques must sometimes be used. However, if a measure cannot be converted with minimum resources or with no assurance of credibility, the improvement in the measure should be reported as an intangible benefit.

Costs are important and should be fully loaded in the human capital analytics projects and in measuring the success of solutions. From a practical standpoint, some costs may be optional and depend on the organization's guidelines and philosophy. However, because of the scrutiny that analytics projects typically receive, all costs should be included, even if this effort goes beyond the requirements of the organization's policy for solutions. After the benefits are collected and converted to monetary values and the solution costs are tabulated, the ROI calculation itself is easy. Plugging the values into the appropriate formula is the final step. Now that the process has been fully laid out, the next chapter details how to forecast the value of a project, including its ROI.

Forecast, Predict, Test, and Optimize

I n today's economy, models have to be tested, forecasts have to be accurate, and a solution has to be optimized to deliver the most value. Often, these issues have to be addressed in advance of the implementation of the model or solution. This chapter focuses on looking into the future to predict or forecast outcomes in advance.

In some cases, it may be helpful to predict which prospective employees will have accidents, be absent, perform better, or will stay with the organization. Inside the organization, a forecast is needed to predict which employees will remain with the organization, achieve high performance, or create new ideas. In terms of proposed new solutions, the pressure from executives today is to forecast the value of the solution in advance of implementation. The need to know in advance has been amplified since the global recession that began in 2008.

Even when a solution is implemented, follow-up is needed to see how well it is working. A follow-up analysis will include data needed to make changes. If it is unsuccessful, the changes will usually make it successful. If it is already successful, the changes will make it even more successful. This process is optimizing the impact of the solution by making adjustments in the solution early in the cycle. These critical steps and processes are necessary to forecast, predict, test, and optimize.

OPENING STORY

Retail Merchandise Company has 420 large stores selling household items, electronics, and jewelry. It is an old company that previously operated through a catalog process but is now trying to change its model to increase sales. One important adjustment is to have more interaction between the sales associates and the customers in the store. Previously, the associate waited until the customer selected the item and processed it through the store's automated system. The item then came out on a conveyer belt for the customer to purchase, minimizing associate-customer interaction.

This newer approach, envisioned by the top executives, encourages routine interaction with the customers to help guide them to purchasing decisions. The thought was that they would influence sales and would be able to upsell to a higher-priced item. The hypothesis: Use of these customer interaction skills would drive increased sales as recorded with weekly sales per associate. Because of the potential for this solution, executives asked for an ROI forecast.

The difficult issue is that forecasting involves estimating impact of a solution that has not been implemented, so the best experts were assembled. The human capital analytics team contacted "experts" (as shown in Table 10-1) who provided an estimate of sales increases in three months that would be attributed to the proposed solution. Each expert was provided with a description of the solution, the skills, and the need. The estimate is a "best guess" based on their experience and perspective.

The critical issue was the credibility of the experts. Quickly, the team could begin to see potential bias in the sales associates because they perceived this solution as extra work. They could see bias in the supplier of the solution who would obviously have a high forecast. They also could see a conservative approach from the finance staff who were disconnected from the actual work. The marketing team often discounts a solution that does not involve promotion or advertising. The most critical data sets were the data from the executives asking for this solution, who suggested sales would increase by 15 percent. Analysts, who explored the need for this program in more detail, were also credible. Their benchmarking data, where the same solution is benchmarked with other organizations, was also considered

TABLE 10-1   Expert Input for the Forecast

"Expert" Input for Estimate	Sales Increase Estimate (Δ)	Forecasted ROI
Sales Associates	0%	−100%
Department Managers	5%	−30%
Store Managers	10%	33%
Senior Executives (Sponsors)	15%	110%
Analyst (Needs Assessment)	12%	95%
Vendors (Suppliers)	25%	350%
Marketing Analysts	4%	−40%
Finance Staff	2%	−80%
Benchmarking Data	9%	22%

credible. So the approach taken with the team is to take an average of the credible data and present that as a possibility. Also, each of the items was adjusted for the confidence, which is an error adjustment. The break-even position is calculated as well. The calculation shows the sales increase necessary for a zero ROI, which is complete cost recovery of the solution. All these data were presented to the management team to enable them to make a decision.[1]

This chapter covers the subject of forecasting in much more detail. Forecasting, which has become an important topic, enables the analytics team to calculate the potential impact and ROI of a solution. Even without a predictive model, a forecast shows how this solution will drive value. When a predictive relationship is known in a predictive model, it is a matter of calculating the impact and the ROI. In classic forecasting, that relationship is not known in detail and perhaps a group of experts will suggest what it might be. Forecasting and predicting go hand in hand. Much of the emphasis of this chapter is on forecasting, with considering predicting to be a special case of the forecasting.

WHY FORECAST ROI?

Although ROI calculations based on follow-up data are the most accurate, sometimes it is important to know the forecast before the project is initiated or before final results are tabulated. Certain critical issues drive the need for a forecast before the solution is completed, or even pursued.

EXPENSIVE PROJECTS

In addition to reducing uncertainty, forecasting may be appropriate for costly solutions. In these cases, implementation is not practical until the solution has been analyzed to determine the potential ROI. For example, if the solution involves a significant amount of effort in design, development, and implementation, a client may not want to expend the resources—not even for a pilot test—unless some assurance of a positive ROI can be given. In another example, an expensive equipment purchase may be necessary to launch a process or system. An ROI may be necessary prior to purchase, to ensure that the monetary value of the process outcomes outweighs the cost of equipment and implementation. Although trade-offs may be part of deploying a lower-profile, lower-cost pilot, the presolution ROI is still important and may prompt some clients to stand firm until an ROI forecast is produced.

HIGH RISKS AND UNCERTAINTY

Sponsors want to remove as much uncertainty as possible from the solution and act on the best data available. This concern sometimes pushes forecast of the solution's ROI, even before any resources are expended to design and implement it. Some solutions are high-risk opportunities or solutions. In addition to being expensive, they may represent critical initiatives that can make or break an organization. Or the situation may be one in which failure would be disastrous, with only one chance to get it right. In these cases, the decision maker must have the best data possible, and the best data possible often include a forecast ROI.

For example, one large restaurant chain developed an unfortunate reputation for racial insensitivity and discrimination. The fallout brought many lawsuits and caused a public relations nightmare. The company undertook a major solution to transform the organization—changing its image, attitudes, and actions. Because of the solution's high stakes and critical nature, company executives requested a forecast before pursuing the solution. They needed to know not only whether this major solution would be worthwhile financially, but also what would change, and how the solution would unfold. This assessment required a comprehensive forecast involving various levels of data, up to and including the ROI.

Postsolution Comparison

An important reason for forecasting ROI is to see how well the forecast holds up under the scrutiny of postsolution analysis. Whenever a plan is in place to collect data on a solution's success, comparing actual results to presolution expectations is helpful. In an ideal world, a forecast ROI would have a defined relationship with the actual ROI—or at least one would lead to the other, after adjustments. The forecast is often an inexpensive process because it involves estimates and assumptions. If the forecast becomes a reliable predictor of the postsolution analysis, then the forecast ROI might substitute for the actual ROI, saving money on the use of postsolution analysis.

Compliance

More than ever, organizations are requiring a forecast ROI before they undertake major projects. For example, one organization requires any project with a budget exceeding $500,000 to have a forecast ROI before it grants project approval. Some units of government have enacted legislation that requires project forecasts. With increasing frequency, formal policy and legal structures are reasons to develop ROI forecasts.

Collectively, these reasons lead more organizations to develop ROI forecasts so their sponsors will have an estimate of the projects' expected payoff.

THE TRADE-OFFS OF FORECASTING

The ROI can be developed at different times and with different levels of data. Unfortunately, the ease, convenience, and costs involved in capturing a forecast ROI create trade-offs in accuracy and credibility. As shown in Table 10-2, ROI can be developed during five distinct time intervals of a solution. The relationship between the timing of the ROI and the factors of credibility, accuracy, cost, and difficulty is also shown in the table.

- A **presolution forecast** can be developed using estimates of the impact of the project. This approach lacks credibility and accuracy, but it is the least expensive and least difficult to calculate. Because of the interest in presolution forecasting, this scenario is expanded.

- **Reaction data** can be extended to develop an anticipated impact, including the ROI. In this case, participants anticipate the chain of impact as a project is implemented and drives specific business

TABLE 10-2 Time Intervals When ROI Can Be Developed

ROI with	Data Collection Timing (Relative to Project)	Credibility	Accuracy	Cost to Develop	Difficulty
1. Preproject data	Before project forecast	Not very credible	Not very accurate	Inexpensive	Not Difficult
2. Reaction data	During project forecast				
3. Learning data	During project forecast				
4. Application data	After project forecast				
5. Business impact data	After project	Very credible	Very accurate	Expensive	Very difficult

measures. It is undertaken after the project has begun. Although accuracy and credibility increase from the presolution basis, this approach lacks the credibility and accuracy desired in many situations. However, it is easily accomplished and is a low-cost option.

- In projects containing a substantial learning component, **learning data** can be used to forecast the ROI. This approach is applicable only when formal testing shows a relationship between test scores and subsequent business performance. When this correlation is available (it is usually developed to validate the test), test data can be used to forecast subsequent performance. The performance can then be converted to monetary impact, and the ROI can be developed. This approach has less potential as a forecasting tool.

- When frequency of skills or knowledge use is critical, the **application and implementation** of those skills or knowledge can be converted to a value using a concept called *utility analysis*. This approach is particularly helpful in situations where competencies are being developed and value is placed on improving competencies, but it has limited applications in most projects.

- Finally, the ROI can be developed from **business impact data** converted directly to monetary values and compared to the cost of the program. These calculations are not a forecast, but rather a postsolution evaluation that provides the basis for other ROI calculations in this book. It is the preferred approach, but because of the pressures already mentioned, examining ROI calculations at other times and with other levels is sometimes necessary.

This chapter discusses in detail presolution ROI forecasting and ROI forecasting based on reactions. In less detail, ROI forecasts developed from learning and application data are also discussed.

PREPROJECT ROI FORECASTING

Perhaps one of the most useful ways to convince a sponsor that a project is beneficial is to forecast the ROI for the project. The process is similar to the postsolution analysis, except that the extent of the impact must be estimated along with the project costs.

Basic Model

Figure 10-1 shows the basic model for capturing the data necessary for a presolution forecast, a modified version of the postprogram ROI process model presented in the next chapter. In the presolution forecast, the project outcomes are estimated, rather than being collected after project implementation. Data collection is kept simple, and relies on interviews, focus groups, or surveys of experts. Tapping into benchmarking studies or locating previous studies may also be helpful.

Beginning at the reaction level, anticipated or estimated reactions are captured. Next, the anticipated learning that must occur is developed, followed by the anticipated application and implementation data. Here, the estimates focus on what must be accomplished for the project to be successful. These items may be based on the objectives at each of these levels. Finally, the impact data are estimated by experts. These experts may include subject matter experts, the supplier, or potential participants in the solution. In this model, the levels build on each other. Having data estimated at Levels 1, 2, and 3 enhances the quality of the estimated data at Level 4 (Impact), which is needed for the analysis.

The model shows no need to isolate the effects of a solution as in the postsolution model. The individual providing the data is asked the following question: "How much will the business impact measure change as a result of the solution?" This question ties the change in the measure directly to the solution; thus, isolation is not needed. This approach makes this process easier than the postsolution evaluation model, where isolating solution impact is always required.

Converting data to money is straightforward using a limited number of techniques. Locating a standard value or finding an expert to make the estimate is the logical choice. Records and databases are less likely alternatives for analysis at the forecasting stage. Securing estimates from stakeholders is the technique of last resort.

Estimating the solution's costs should be an easy step because costs can easily be anticipated on the basis of previous or similar solutions, factoring in reasonable assumptions about the solution. To achieve a fully loaded cost profile, include all cost categories.

FIGURE 10-1   Model for Preproject Forecasting

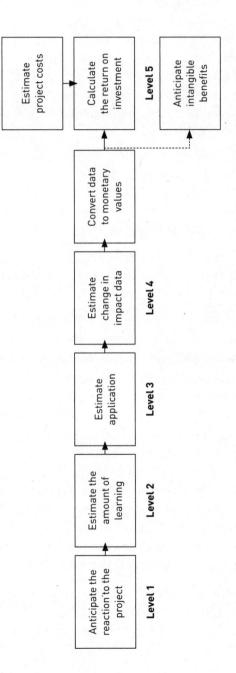

Anticipate the reaction to the project	Estimate the amount of learning	Estimate application	Estimate change in impact data	Convert data to monetary values	Estimate project costs → Calculate the return on investment
Level 1	Level 2	Level 3	Level 4		Level 5
					Anticipate intangible benefits

The anticipated intangibles are merely speculation in forecasting but can be reliable indicators of which measures may be influenced in addition to those included in the ROI calculation. At this point, it is assumed that these measures will not be converted to money.

The formula used to calculate the ROI is the same as that used in the postsolution analysis. The net monetary value from the data conversion is included as the numerator, and the estimated cost of the solution is inserted as the denominator. The projected cost-benefit analysis can be developed along with the ROI for a Level 5 evaluation. The specific steps to develop the forecast are detailed next.

BASIC STEPS TO FORECAST ROI

Eighteen detailed steps are necessary to develop a credible presolution ROI forecast using expert input:

1. **Understand the situation.** Individuals providing input to the forecast and conducting the forecast must have a good understanding of the present situation. This knowledge is typically a requirement for selecting the experts.

2. **Predict the present.** The solution is sometimes initiated because a particular business impact measure is not doing well. However, such measures often lag the present situation; they may be based on data that are several months old. Also, these measures are based on dynamic influences that may change dramatically and quickly. It may be beneficial to estimate where the measure is now, based on assumptions and current trends. Although this aspect appears to be a lot of work, it does not constitute a new responsibility for most of the experts, who are often concerned about the present situation. Market share data, for example, are often several months old. Trending market share data and examining other influences driving market share can help organizations understand the current situation.

3. **Observe warnings.** Closely tied to predicting the present is making sure that warning signs are observed. Red flags signal that something is going against the measure in question, causing

it to go in an undesired direction or otherwise not move as it should. These observations often raise concerns that lead to solutions. These early warnings indicate that things may get worse and must be factored into the situation as forecasts are made.

4. **Describe the new process, solution, program, or solution.** The solution must be completely and clearly described to the experts so they fully understand the mechanics of what is to be implemented. The description should include the solution scope, the individuals involved, time factors, and whatever else is necessary to express the magnitude of the solution and the profile of the solution.

5. **Develop specific objectives.** These objectives should mirror the levels of evaluation and should include reaction objectives, learning objectives, application objectives, and impact objectives. Although these objectives may be difficult to develop, they are part of the up-front analysis described earlier. Objectives provide clear direction toward the solution's end. The cascading levels represent the anticipated chain of impact that will occur as the solution is implemented.

6. **Anticipate what participants will think about the solution.** In this step, the experts are trying to understand participants' reaction: Will they support the solution? How will they support it? What may cause participants to become unsupportive? Their responses are important because a negative reaction can cause a solution to fail.

7. **Estimate what the participants will learn.** To some extent, every solution will involve learning, and the experts will estimate what learning will occur. Using the learning objectives, the experts will define what the participants will learn as they enter the solution, identifying specific knowledge, skills, and information the participants must acquire or enhance during the solution.

8. **Anticipate what participants should accomplish in the solution.** Building on the application objectives, the experts will

identify what will be accomplished as the solution is implemented successfully. This step details specific actions, tasks, and processes that will be taken by the individuals. Steps 6, 7, and 8—based on reaction, learning, and application—provide important information that serves as the basis for the next step, estimating improvement in business impact data.

9. **Estimate the improvement in business impact data.** This step is critical because the data generated are needed for the financial forecast. The experts will provide the estimate in either absolute numbers or percentages of the monetary change in the business impact measure (ΔP). Even though accuracy is important, it is also important to remember that a forecast is no more than an estimate based on the best data available at a given point, which is why the next step is included.

10. **Apply the confidence estimate.** Because the estimate attained in the previous step is not highly accurate, an error adjustment is developed by deriving a confidence estimate. The experts are asked to indicate the confidence they have in the previous data values. The confidence level is expressed as a percentage, with 0 indicating "no confidence" and 100 percent indicating "certainty." This calculation becomes a discount factor in the analysis.

11. **Convert the business impact data to monetary values.** Using one or more methods described earlier, the data are converted to money. If the impact measure is a desired improvement such as productivity, the value represents the gain obtained by having one more unit of measure. If it is a measure that the organization is trying to reduce, such as downtime, mistakes, or complaints, the value is the cost that the organization incurs as a result of one incident. For example, the cost of unwanted employee turnover may be 1.5 times annual pay. This value is noted with the letter V.

12. **Develop the estimated annual impact of each measure.** The estimated annual impact is the first-year improvement directly related to the solution. In formula form, it is expressed as $\Delta I = \Delta P \times V \times 12$ (where ΔI = annual change in monetary value,

ΔP = annual change in performance of the measure, and V = the value of that measure). If the measure is weekly or monthly, it must be converted to an annual amount. For example, if three lost-time accidents will be prevented each month, the annual change in performance is 36.

13. **Factor additional years into the analysis for solutions that will have a significant useful life beyond the first year.** For these solutions, the factor should reflect the diminished benefit of subsequent years. The client or sponsor of the solution should provide some indication of the amount of the reduction and the values developed for the second, third, and successive years. It is important to be conservative by using the smallest numbers possible.

14. **Estimate the fully loaded solution costs.** In this step, use all the cost categories described in Chapter 9, and denote the value as C when including it in the ROI equation. Include all direct and indirect costs in the calculation.

15. **Calculate the forecast ROI.** Using the total projected benefits and the estimated costs in the standard ROI formula. Calculate the forecast ROI as follows:

$$\text{ROI (\%)} = \frac{\Delta I - C}{C} \times 100$$

16. **Use sensitivity analysis to develop several potential ROI values with different levels of improvement (ΔP).** When more than one measure is changing, the analysis may take the form of a spreadsheet showing various output scenarios and the subsequent ROI forecasts. The break-even point will be identified.

17. **Identify potential intangible benefits.** Anticipate intangible benefits using input from those most knowledgeable about the situation on the basis of assumptions from their experience with similar solutions. Remember, the intangible benefits are those benefits not converted to monetary values but possessing value nonetheless.

18. **Communicate the ROI projection and anticipated intangibles with caution.** The target audience must clearly understand that the forecast is based on several assumptions (clearly defined), and that although the values are the best possible estimates, they may include a degree of error.

Following these eighteen steps will enable an individual to forecast the ROI.

SOURCES OF EXPERT INPUT

Several sources of expert input are available for estimating improvement of impact data when the solution is implemented. Ideally, experience with similar solutions in the organization will help form the basis of the estimates the experts make. The experts may include:

- Clients and/or sponsors

- Members of solution team

- Prospective participants

- Subject matter experts

- External experts

- Advocates (who can champion the solution)

- Finance and accounting staff

- Analysts (if involved with the solution)

- Executives and/or managers

- Customers

Collectively, these sources provide an appropriate array of possibilities for helping estimate the value of an improvement. Because errors may develop, ask for a confidence measure when using estimates from any source.

SECURING INPUT

With the experts clearly identified, three major steps must be addressed before developing the ROI. First, data must be collected from the individuals listed as experts. If the number of individuals is small (e.g., one person from each of the expert groups involved), a short interview may suffice. During interviews, it is critical to avoid bias and to ask clear, succinct questions that are not leading. Questions should be framed in a balanced way to capture what may occur as well as what may not. If groups are involved, using focus groups may be suitable. For large numbers, surveys or questionnaires may be appropriate.

When the groups are diverse and scattered, the Delphi technique may be appropriate. This technique, originally developed by the Rand Corporation in the 1950s, has been used in forecasting and decision making in a variety of disciplines. The Delphi technique was originally devised to help experts achieve better forecasts than they might obtain through traditional group meetings by allowing access to the group without in-person contact. Necessary features of a Delphi procedure are anonymity, continuous iteration, controlled feedback to participants, and a physical summary of responses. Anonymity is achieved by means of a questionnaire that allows group members to express their opinions and judgments privately. Between all iterations of the questionnaire, the facilitator informs the participants of the opinions of their anonymous colleagues. Typically this feedback is presented as a simple statistical summary using a mean or median value. The facilitator takes the group judgment as the statistical average in the final round.

In some cases, benchmarking data may be available and can be considered as a source of input for this process. The success of previous studies may provide input essential to the solution as well. It may include an extensive search of databases using a variety of search engines. The important point is to understand, as much as possible, what may occur as a result of the solution.

CONVERSION TO MONEY

The measures forecast by the experts must be converted to monetary values for one, two, three, or more years depending on the nature and scope of the solution. Standard values are available for many of these measures. Considering the importance of these measures, someone has probably placed monetary values on them. If not, experts are often available to convert the data to monetary values. Otherwise, existing records or databases may be appropriate sources. Another option is to ask stakeholders, perhaps some of the experts listed previously, to provide these values for the forecast. This step is the only means of showing the money made from the solution.

ESTIMATE SOLUTION COSTS

Solution cost estimates are based on the most reliable information available, and include the typical categories presented in the chapter. The estimates can be based on previous solutions. Although the costs are unknown, this task is often relatively easy to accomplish because of its similarity to budgeting, a process with usually routine procedures and policies in place. Dividing costs into categories representing the functional processes of the solution provides additional insight into solution costs. Areas often not given enough attention include analysis, assessment, evaluation, and reporting. If these elements are not properly addressed, much of the value of the solution may be missed.

CASE STUDY: FORECASTING ROI FOR A SALES ENABLEMENT SOLUTION

Global Financial Services (GFS) was in the process of implementing contact management software to enable its sales relationship managers to track routine correspondence and communication with customers. A needs assessment and initial analysis determined the solution was needed. The solution would involve further detailing, selecting an appropriate software package, and implementing the software with appropriate job aids, support tools, and training. However, before pursuing the solution and purchasing the software, a forecast ROI was needed. Following the steps previously outlined, it was determined that four business impact measures would be influenced by implementation of this solution:

1. Increase in sales to existing customers

2. Reduction in customer complaints caused by missed deadlines, late responses, and failure to complete transactions

3. Reduction in response time for customer inquiries and requests

4. Increase in the customer satisfaction composite survey index

Several individuals provided input in examining the potential problem. With comprehensive customer contact management software in place, relationship managers should benefit from quick and effective customer communication and have easy access to customer databases. The software should also provide the functionality to develop calendars and to-do lists. Relationship managers should further benefit from features such as built-in contact management, calendar sharing, and the fact that the software is Internet–ready. To determine the extent to which the four measures would change, input was collected from six sources:

1. Internal software developers with expertise in various software applications provided input on expected changes in each of the measures.

2. Marketing analysts supplied information on sales cycles, customer needs, and customer care issues.

3. Relationship managers provided input on expected changes in the variables if the software was used regularly.

4. The analyst who confirmed the initial need for the software provided supplemental data.

5. The sponsor provided input on what could be expected from the solution.

6. The proposed vendor provided input based on previous experience.

When input is based on estimates, the actual results will usually differ significantly. However, GFS was interested in a forecast based on analysis that, although limited, would be strengthened with the best easily available expert opinion. Input was adjusted on the basis of the estimates and other information to assess its credibility. After discussing the availability of data and examining the techniques to convert it to monetary values, the following conclusions were reached:

• The increase in sales could easily be converted to a monetary value as the average margin for sales increase is applied directly.

• The cost of a customer complaint could be based on an internal value currently in use, providing a generally accepted cost.

• Customer response time was not tracked accurately, and the value of this measure was not readily available, making it an intangible benefit.

- No generally accepted value for increasing customer satisfaction was available, so customer satisfaction impact data would be listed as an intangible benefit.

The forecast ROI calculation was developed from combined input based on the variety of estimates. The increase in sales was easily converted to monetary values using the margin rates, and the reduction in customer complaints was easily converted using the discounted value of a customer complaint. The costs for the solution could be estimated based on input from those who briefly examined the situation. The total costs included development costs, materials, software, equipment, facilitators, facilities, and lost time for learning activities, coordination, and evaluation. This fully loaded projected cost, compared to the benefits, yielded a range of expected ROI values. Table 10-3 shows possible scenarios based on payoffs of the two measures as assessed by six experts. The ROI values range from a low of 12 percent to a high of 180 percent. The break-even point could be developed with different scenarios. With these values in hand, the decision to move forward was easy: even the worst-case scenarios were positive and the best case was expected to yield more than 10 times the ROI of the worst. As this example illustrates, the process must be simple and must use the most credible resources available to quickly arrive at estimates.

FORECASTING WITH A PILOT PROGRAM

Because of inaccuracies inherent in a presolution forecast, a better approach is to develop a small-scale pilot solution with the ROI based on post-program data. This process involves the following steps:

1. As in the previous process, develop Level 1, 2, 3, and 4 objectives.

2. Implement the solution on a small-scale sample as a pilot solution, excluding all the bells and whistles. (Simplicity keeps the solution costs low without sacrificing solution integrity.)

3. Fully implement the solution with one or more of the groups who can benefit from the initiative.

4. Develop the ROI using the ROI process model for postsolution analysis as outlined in previous chapters.

TABLE 10-3 Expected ROI Values for Different Outputs

Expert	Potential Sales Increase	Basis	Potential Complaint Reduction		Expected ROI	Credibility Rating (5 = highest; 1 = lowest)
			Monthly	Basis		
Relationship manager	3.5%	Sales opportunity	3	Lower response time	60%	3
District manager	4%	Customer satisfaction	4	Lower response time	90%	4
Marketing analyst	3%	Missed opportunity	5	Quicker response	120%	4
Project sponsor	5%	Customer services	4	Quicker response	77%	4
Vendor	10%	Customer loyalty	12	Higher priority	180%	2
IT analyst	2%	Customer relationship	3	Faster response	12%	2

5. Based on the results of the pilot solution, decide whether to implement the solution throughout the organization. Data can be developed using all six of the measures outlined in this book: reaction, learning, application, impact, ROI, and intangibles.

Evaluating a pilot solution and withholding full implementation until its results can be developed provides less risk than developing an ROI forecast. A large global retailer uses this method to evaluate pilot programs before implementing them throughout its chain of 6,000 U.S. stores. Using pilot groups of 18 to 30 stores called *flights*, the decision to implement a solution throughout the system is based on the six types of postprogram data (reaction, learning, application, impact, ROI, and intangibles).

FORECASTING ROI WITH REACTION DATA

When a reaction evaluation includes the planned applications of a solution, the data can ultimately be used in an ROI forecast. ROI information can be developed with questions concerning how participants plan to implement the solution and what results they expect to achieve. For example, consider a solution proposed by a major pharmaceutical company. The firm was considering installing high-speed DSL lines in the homes of each of its pharmaceutical sales representatives on the premise that this factor would save the reps time that they could then spend with their customers. However, reaction to the proposed solution was not positive. The sales reps said they do most of their online work at night when speed is not such an issue, and even if they did save time, they would be unlikely to add another call to their schedule, or even be able to spend more time with customers. Although the solution's goals had merit, from the standpoint of forecast monetary value, the solution would not add value or improve the original measure.

Data Collection

To forecast ROI at this level, at the beginning of a solution participants are asked to state specifically how they plan to use the solution and what results they expect to achieve. They are asked to convert their planned accomplishments into monetary values and show the basis for developing the values. Participants can adjust their responses with a confidence factor to make the data more credible. Next, estimates are adjusted for confidence level. When tabulating data, participants multiply the confidence levels by annual monetary values to produce a conservative estimate for use in data analysis. For example, if a participant estimated the monetary impact of the solution at $10,000 but was only 50 percent confident in his or her estimate, a $5,000 value would be used in the ROI forecast calculations.

To develop a summary of the expected benefits, discard any data that are incomplete, unusable, extreme, or unrealistic. Then total the individual data items. Finally, as an optional exercise, adjust the total value again by a factor that reflects the unknowns in the process and the possibility that participants will not achieve the results they anticipate. This adjustment factor can be estimated by the solution team. In one organization, the benefits are divided by two to develop a number to use in the calculation. Finally, calculate the forecast ROI using the net benefits from the solution divided by the solution costs.

Case Study: Data Collection in a Safety Performance Solution

This process can best be described using an actual case. Global Engineering and Construction Company (GEC) designs and builds large commercial solutions such as plants, paper mills, and municipal water systems. Safety is always a critical matter at GEC and usually commands much management attention. To improve safety performance, a safety improvement solution was initiated for solution engineers and construction superintendents. The solution involved policy changes, audits, and training. The solution focused on safety leadership, safety planning, safety inspections, safety meetings, accident investigation, safety policies and procedures, safety standards, and workers' compensation. Safety engineers and superintendents (participants) were expected to improve the safety performance of their individual construction solutions. A dozen safety performance measures used in the company were discussed and analyzed at the beginning of the solution. At that time, participants completed a feedback questionnaire that probed specific action items planned as a result of the safety solution and provided estimated monetary values of the planned actions. In addition, participants explained the basis for estimates and placed a confidence level on their estimates. Table 10-4 presents data provided by the participants. Only 19 of the 25 participants supplied data (experience has shown that approximately 50–90 percent of participants will provide usable data on this series

TABLE 10-4 Level 1 Data for ROI Forecast Calculations

Participant No.	Estimated Value	Basis	Confidence Level %	Adjusted $
1	$80,000	Reduction in lost-time accidents	90%	$72,000
2	91,200	OSHA reportable injuries	80%	72,960
3	55,000	Accident reduction	90%	49,500
4	10,000	First aid visits/ visits to doctor	70%	7,000
5	150,000	Reduction in lost-time injuries	95%	142,500
6	Millions	Total accident cost	100%	—
7	74,800	Workers' compensation	80%	59,840
8	7,500	OSHA citations	75%	5,625
9	50,000	Reduction in accidents	75%	37,500
10	36,000	Workers' compensation	80%	28,800
11	150,000	Reduction in total accident costs	90%	135,000
12	22,000	OSHA fines/ citations	70%	15,400
13	140,000	Accident reductions	80%	112,000
14	4 million	Total cost of safety	95%	—
15	65,000	Total workers' compensation	50%	32,500
16	Unlimited	Accidents	100%	—
17	20,000	Visits to doctor	95%	19,000
18	45,000	Injuries	90%	40,500
19	200,000	Lost-time injuries	80%	160,000
				Total $990,125

of questions). The estimated cost of the solution, including participants' salaries for the time devoted to the solution, was $358,900.

The monetary values of the planned improvements were extremely high, reflecting the participants' optimism and enthusiasm at the beginning of an impressive solution from which specific actions were planned. As a first step in the analysis, extreme data items were omitted (one of the guiding principles of the ROI Methodology). Data such as "millions," "unlimited," and "$4 million" were discarded, and each remaining value was multiplied by the confidence value and totaled. This adjustment is one way of reducing highly subjective estimates. The resulting tabulations yielded a total improvement of $990,125 (rounded to $990,000). The projected ROI, which was based on the feedback questionnaire at the beginning of the solution, is:

$$\text{ROI} = \frac{\$990,000 - \$358,900}{\$358,900} \times 100 = 175\%$$

Although these projected values are subjective, the results were generated by solution participants who should be aware of what they could accomplish. A follow-up study would determine the true results delivered by the group.

Use of the Data

Caution is required when using a forecast ROI: The calculations are highly subjective and may not reflect the extent to which participants will achieve results. A variety of influences in the work environment and solution setting can enhance or inhibit the attainment of performance goals. Having high expectations at the beginning of a solution is no guarantee that those expectations will be met. Solution disappointments are documented regularly.

Although the process is subjective and possibly unreliable, it does have some usefulness:

1. If the evaluation must stop at this point, this analysis provides more insight into the value of the solution than data from typical reaction input, which report attitudes and feelings about a solution. Sponsors and managers usually find this information more useful than a report stating that, "40 percent of solution team participants rated the solution above average."

2. These data can form a basis for comparing different solutions of the same type (e.g., safety solutions). If one solution forecast results in an ROI of 300 percent and a similar solution forecast results in a 30 percent ROI, it would appear that one solution may be more effective. The participants in the first solution have more confidence in the planned implementation of the solution.

3. Collecting these types of data focuses increased attention on solution outcomes. Participants will understand that specific action is expected, which produces results for the solution. The data collection helps participants plan the implementation of what they are learning. This issue becomes clear to participants as they anticipate results and convert them to monetary values. Even if the forecast is ignored, the exercise is productive because of the important message it sends to participants.

4. The data can be used to secure support for a follow-up evaluation. A skeptical manager may challenge the data, and this challenge can be converted into support for a follow-up to see whether the forecast holds true. The only way to know whether these results will materialize is to conduct a postsolution evaluation.

5. If a follow-up evaluation of the solution is planned, the postsolution results can be compared to the ROI forecast. Comparisons of forecast and follow-up data are helpful. If a defined relationship between the two is established, the less expensive forecast can be substituted for the more expensive follow-up. Also, when a follow-up evaluation is planned, participants are usually more conservative with their projected estimates.

The use of ROI forecasting with reaction data is increasing, and some organizations have based many of their ROI forecast calculations on this type of data. For example, a large national bank routinely develops ROI forecasts with reaction data. Although they may be subjective, the calculations do add value, particularly if they are part of a comprehensive evaluation system.

FORECASTING ROI WITH LEARNING DATA

Testing for changes in skills and knowledge in a solution or program is a common method for measuring learning. In many situations, participants are required to demonstrate their knowledge or acquired skills during a solution implementation, and their performance is expressed as a numeric value. When this type of test is developed, it must be reliable and valid. Because a test should reflect the content of the solution or program, successful mastery of content should be related to improved job performance. A relationship between test scores and subsequent on-the-job performance should be evident. This relationship, expressed as a correlation coefficient, is a measure of validity for the test.

This situation provides an opportunity for an ROI calculation with learning data using valid test results. When a statistically significant relationship exists between test scores and on-the-job performance (output) and the performance can be converted to monetary values, it is possible to use test scores to estimate the ROI during the solution.

This approach is best applied when significant learning takes place or when the solution focuses almost entirely on developing learning solutions. The absence of validated tests can create problems because the instruments cannot be used to forecast actual performance unless their validity is ensured. Other resources provide more detail on how to conduct a forecast from learning data.

FORECASTING ROI WITH APPLICATION DATA

Although not as credible as desired, a forecast can be made on the basis of the improved competencies or skills of the project implementation team. This process uses the concept of utility analysis, which is best described in the experience of a large European bank that was seeking to develop a leadership program for its executives. Bank managers identified the specific competencies they wanted to develop. Before making the €8 million investment in the program, the senior executive team wanted to know the value it would add. The project team used utility analysis to conduct the forecast.

First, the team assessed the percentage of executives' jobs covered in the leadership competencies. To keep it simple, assume that this aspect involved

40 percent of their job content. This amount was derived from the sample of the management team. Next the average salary was determined—say, €100,000, to keep it simple. Thus, the project could influence 40 percent of €100,000, or €40,000. The managers assessed the team's current level of performance of the competencies using a convenient scale. After reviewing the competencies and the program's objectives, the managers indicated that a 10 percent improvement could be achieved on these competencies by implementing the leadership development program. Thus, the pro-gram had a potential of improving the €40,000 portion of their salary by 10 percent, or €4,000. (In essence, it would add €4,000.) Table 10-5 provides a summary of this process. This value is compared to the proposed participant cost for the leadership program to determine the forecast on an individual basis. If the cost of the program is €3,000, the ROI is 33 percent.

Although this example is simple, it shows the concept of fore-casting based on improving competencies. It could be forecasted, as in the example, or collected at application time, after the competencies have been developed and applied. However, it ignores what the managers or exec-utives will accomplish with the competencies, so it is not as credible as a Level 4 (Impact) ROI. Nevertheless, it has value and is described in more detail in other sources.

TABLE 10-5 Forecasting Using Improved Competencies

Percentage of managers' jobs covered by competencies	40%
Average manager's salary	€100,000
Monetary value of covered competencies (40% × €100,000)	€40,000
Percentage of anticipated improvement in competencies	10%
Added benefit of improved competencies in monetary terms (€40,000 × 10%)	€4,000 per manager
Cost of program per participant	€3,000 per manager
ROI	33%

FORECASTING GUIDELINES

With the four different forecasting time frames outlined in this chapter, it may help to follow a few guidelines known to drive the forecasting possibilities within an organization. These guidelines are based on experience in forecasting in a variety of solutions and programs.[2]

1. **If you must forecast, forecast frequently.** Forecasting is an art *and* a science. Users can build comfort, experience, and history with the process by using it frequently.

2. **Make forecasting an essential part of the evaluation mix.** This chapter began with a list of essential reasons for forecasting. The use of forecasting is increasingly being demanded by many organizations. It can be an effective and useful tool when used properly and in conjunction with other types of evaluation data. Some organizations have targets for the use of forecasting (e.g., if a solution exceeds a certain cost, it will always require a presolution forecast). Others will target a certain number of solutions for a forecast based on reaction data and use those data in the manner described. It is important to plan for the forecast and let it be a part of the evaluation mix, using it regularly.

3. **Forecast different types of data.** Although most of this chapter focuses on how to develop a forecast ROI using the standard ROI formula, forecasting the value of the other types of data is important as well. A usable, helpful forecast will include predictions about reaction and perceived value, the extent of learning, and the extent of application and implementation. These types of data are important in anticipating movements and shifts, based on the solution that is planned. They assist in developing the overall forecast and help the solution team understand the solution's total anticipated impact.

4. **Secure input from those who know the process best.** As forecasts are developed, it is essential to secure input from individuals who understand the dynamics of the workplace and the measures being influenced by the solution. In other words, go to the experts. Their input will increase not only the accuracy

of the forecast, but also the credibility of the results. In other situations, it may be the analysts who are aware of the major influences in the workplace and the dynamics of those changes.

5. **Long-term forecasts will usually be inaccurate.** Forecasting works better when it covers a short time frame. Most short-term scenarios afford a better grasp of the influences that might drive the measures. In the long-term, a variety of new influences, unforeseen now, could enter the process and drastically change the impact measures. If a long-term forecast is needed, it should be updated regularly.

6. **Expect forecasts to be biased.** Forecasts will consist of data coming from those who have an interest in the issue. This partiality is unavoidable. Some will want the forecast to be optimistic; others will have a pessimistic view. Almost all input is biased in one way or another. Every attempt should be made to minimize the bias, adjust for the bias, or adjust for the uncertainty in the process. Still, the audience should recognize the forecast as a biased prediction.

7. **Serious forecasting is hard work.** The value of forecasting often depends on the amount of effort put into the process. High-stakes solutions or programs need a serious approach, collecting all possible data, examining different scenarios, and making the best prediction available. It is in these situations that mathematical tools can be most valuable.

8. **Review the success of forecasting routinely.** As forecasts are made, it is imperative to revisit the forecast with postsolution data to check its accuracy. Such review can aid in the continuous improvement of the processes. Sources could prove to be more or less credible, specific inputs may be more or less biased, or certain analyses may be more appropriate than others. It is important to constantly improve the methods and approaches for forecasting within the organization.

9. **The assumptions are the most serious error in forecasting.** Of all the variables that can enter the process, assumptions offer the

greatest opportunity for error. It is important for the assumptions to be clearly understood and communicated. When multiple inputs are given, each forecaster should use the same set of assumptions, if possible.

10. **Utility is the most important characteristic of forecasting.** The most important use of forecasting is providing information and input for the decision maker. Forecasting is a tool for those attempting to make decisions about solution implementation. It is not a process intended to maximize the output or minimize any particular variable. It is not a process undertaken to dramatically change the way a solution is implemented. It is a process to provide data for decisions.

RELATIONSHIP TO PREDICTING, TESTING, AND OPTIMIZATION

The terms at the heading of this chapter—*forecasting, predicting, testing,* and *optimizing*—are related. Forecasting is presented in detail because it holds much promise and is an important part of the process that links to predicting, testing, and optimization.

PREDICTING IS FORECASTING

Predicting is a particular model that predicts success. Under classic predictive modeling, one or more input variables are predicting an outcome variable. For example, an applicant score on a values survey can predict tenure as the value system of the individual is aligned to the value system of the organization. A predictive model would be developed to show the connection between the two, with the input being the assessment score and the outcome being retention. A causal effect would be determined so that one predicts the other. In this case, the forecast can easily be developed because the guessing or estimation is removed from the process. Mathematically, a relationship is developed and the forecast becomes straightforward. As we invest in this tool for values assessment, we can forecast the retention, improvement (the impact), and the monetary value of increased retention (avoiding the cost of turnover). This modeling could produce a credible ROI forecast if it is a valid predictive model.

In this chapter the forecast is developed, not from a mathematical relationship, but from expertise from different stakeholders. The individuals, who know the situation, context, and solution, estimate the improvement that will be driven by the solution and make adjustments for error and extreme data to ensure credibility. This approach is used in many situations, because valid predictive models are not there. The good news is that more of them are being developed. If they are available, they will make forecasting much easier, following the steps and the processes covered in this chapter.

TESTING

When a predictive model is developed, it is often tested multiple times, under different conditions and scenarios. In the previous example, the value instrument would be repeated again and again to make sure the causal relationship holds up and that it indeed is a predictor and not a coincidence that the two measures have improved. Testing is a critical part of developing a predictive relationship.

OPTIMIZATION

The goal of many human capital solutions is to optimize the effects on outcomes. As the ROI calculation is developed, the questions would be: What adjustments, changes, or other assumptions could be made so that the outcomes are enhanced? What levels of optimization can be achieved? The answers involve three different scenarios:

1. **Adjusting the guiding principles.** The guiding principles, presented earlier, are conservative. Sometimes critics will argue that they are too conservative. Different assumptions can be made, without changing the standards, to see the effects of other scenarios. For example, for a short-term solution, one-year impact data are used. Sometimes, it is debatable whether a solution is long-term or short-term. Multiple years may be entered to show how the ROI changes. This approach helps in understanding what may eventually occur as these standards are adjusted. It is important to report value using the standards, and then report other scenarios, if different assumptions are made.

2. **Consider changing the benefits side.** In an ROI calculation the impact measure is converted to money to produce the benefits for the numerator. Although in a predictive model or estimated forecast, the impact measures are specific, every model has room for improvement. It may be helpful to make adjustments to improve outcome measures to see the different effects they may have on ROI.

3. **Consider changing in the cost side.** The denominator of the ROI calculation is the cost of the solution. The standard is that all costs are included, both direct and indirect. Although some of the indirect costs may be subject to debate, they should be included. One way to optimize the process is to examine ways to lower cost. If costs are lowered, obviously the ROI goes up, so adjusting these cost values shows different variations of the outcome.

Optimization can occur on a forecast to show what may be possible as different assumptions and changes are applied and the ROI is developed. On a postsolution ROI, changes in the inputs can be made. For example, changes in the design, development, and implementation of the solution can be altered to drive improvements. These changes show what can be done (or should be done) to make the results better, particularly when the initial results are disappointing. On a positive note, most solutions deliver positive ROI values, sometimes even high values. Optimization lets us examine what we must change to make ROI even more valuable.

FINAL THOUGHTS

This chapter focuses on forecasting before a solution is implemented and illustrates that forecasts can be developed at different times and with different levels of data, although most human capital analytics solution leaders focus only on impact data. The chapter also explores predicting, testing, and optimizing.

ROI forecasts developed before a solution begins can be useful to the sponsor and are sometimes necessary before solutions can be approved. Forecasts made during solution implementation can be useful to management and participants, and can focus participants' attention on the economic impact of the solution. However, using ROI estimates during the solution may give a false sense of accuracy. As expected, presolution ROI forecasts have the least credibility and accuracy, yet have the advantage of being inexpensive and relatively easy to develop. The reality is that forecasting is an important part of the measurement mix. It should be pursued routinely and used regularly in decision making. Whether a forecast ROI or a postsolution ROI, the results must be reported to stakeholders. The next chapter focuses on reporting and using results of your analytics project.

CHAPTER 11

Report Results and Drive Improvement

The missing piece in some human capital analytics projects is communication of results to the proper audiences and use of those results to drive change, improvement, and optimization. Too often, the project team delivers results to the client and fails to present data to other stakeholders who need to understand the project's implications. Every project should result in some sort of improvement. The analytics team should take the responsibility for ensuring that improvement occurs. Sometimes a project uncovers problems or barriers that inhibit success, and the analytics team must remove these in order to move forward. They must monitor these improvements and changes and report them in the spirit of complete accountability for the project. This chapter presents the different ways to communicate results, identifies various audiences and the rationale for communicating to them, and provides details about appropriate communication content. In addition, it focuses on following through and driving improvement.

OPENING STORY

Hewlett-Packard Corporation (HP), like many global technology firms, is concerned about talent retention—a considerable issue, given its workforce of 330,000 employees. In some areas, HP was facing higher-than-expected talent departure. By the time the departure occurred, it was too late to respond. An earlier intervention perhaps could have kept the employee from leaving. Predicting a potential flight risk ahead of time poses a challenge. Working with a specific group of 300 specialists, HP developed a model to predict the flight risk of an individual based on his or her job, pay raises, job performance ratings, rotational assignments, and salaries. Not included in the predictors was a promotion, unless the promotion resulted in a significant pay increase.

With this model, HP developed a flight risk score, much like a score for credit risk. In theory, this score would enable managers to intervene in the case of a departure risk. In the beginning, HP was concerned about how the model would be used and the fact that it would be controversial. It could easily be abused if not addressed properly. HP worked diligently with the management team, communicating the model and the flight risk score. The company outlined precise procedures for using these data properly, including a report delivery system.

With this approach, only a select few high-level managers may view individual employee scores—and only scores for employees under them. These managers were trained in interpreting flight risk scores and understanding their limitations, ramifications, and confidentiality. In fact, if unauthorized parties got their hands on the report itself, they would find no names or identifying elements for the employees listed there—only cryptic identifiers, which the authorized manager has the key to unscramble and match to real names. All security systems have vulnerabilities, but this one is fairly bulletproof.

For the team of 300 employees, only three managers see these results. A tool displays the flight risk scores in a user-friendly, nontechnical view that delivers supporting contextual information about each score in order to help explain why it is high or low. These managers are trained in advance to understand the flight risk scores in terms of their accompanying explanations—the factors about the employee that contributed to the score—so that these numbers aren't deferred to as a forceful authority or overly trusted in lieu of other considerations.

The results were impressive. Staff attrition rates that were above 20 percent in some regions decreased to 15 percent and continued to trend downward. This success is credited in large part to the impact of flight risk reports and their well-crafted delivery.[1]

This study illustrates the importance of communicating and using data appropriately so that they are not misused and they drive intended improvement and desired success. The alternative is misused data that never help an organization achieve the intended improvement.

THE IMPORTANCE OF COMMUNICATING RESULTS

Communicating results is critical to project success. The results achieved must be conveyed to stakeholders not just at project completion but throughout the duration of the project. Continuous communication maintains the flow of information so that adjustments can be made and all stakeholders are kept up to date on the status of the project.

Mark Twain once said, "Collecting data is like collecting garbage—pretty soon we will have to do something with it." Implementing analytics projects means nothing unless the findings are communicated promptly to the appropriate audiences so that they can take action in response, if necessary. Communication is important for four primary reasons.

1. Communication is necessary to make improvements.

2. Communication is necessary to explain the contribution.

3. Communication is a politically sensitive issue.

4. Different audiences need different information.

SEVEN STEPS FOR COMMUNICATING RESULTS

Communication of project results must be systematic, timely, and well planned, and the process must include seven components in a precise sequence. Each of these seven steps is covered here.

STEP 1: THE NEED FOR COMMUNICATION

Reasons for communicating results vary, depending on the project, the setting, and the unique needs of each target audience; therefore, a list should be tailored to the organization and adjusted as necessary. Some of the most common reasons for communicating results are:

- Securing approval for the project and the allocation of time and money
- Gaining support for the project and its objectives
- Securing agreement on the issues, solutions, and resources
- Enhancing the credibility of the project leader
- Reinforcing the processes used in the project
- Driving action for project improvement
- Preparing participants for the project
- Optimizing results throughout the project and the quality of future feedback
- Showing the complete project results
- Underscoring the importance of measuring results
- Explaining techniques used to measure results
- Motivating project participants to become involved
- Demonstrating accountability for expenditures
- Marketing future projects

This list is merely a sampling of reasons for communicating results. Each organization has specific needs and should receive tailored information.

STEP 2: COMMUNICATION PLAN

Any activity needs careful planning to achieve maximum results. The actual planning of communication ensures that each audience receives the proper information at the right time and that necessary actions are taken. Several considerations should be taken when planning communication.

- What will be communicated?
- When will the data be communicated?

- How will the information be communicated?

- Where will the information be communicated?

- Who will communicate the information?

- Who is the target audience?

- What are the specific actions required or desired?

The communication plan is usually developed when the project is approved. This plan details how specific information is to be developed and communicated to various groups, and what the expected actions are. In addition, this plan details how the overall results will be communicated, the time frame for communication, and the appropriate groups to receive the information. The project leader, key managers, and stakeholders need to agree on the level of detail in the plan.

STEP 3: THE AUDIENCE

The following questions should be asked about each potential audience for communication of project results:

- Are they interested in the project?

- Do they really want to receive the information?

- Has a commitment been made to include them in the communications?

- Is the timing right for this audience?

- Are they familiar with the project?

- How do they prefer to have results communicated?

- Do they know the project leader? The project team?

- Are they likely to find the results threatening?

- Which medium will be most convincing to this group?

For each target audience, three steps are necessary. To the greatest extent possible, the project leader should get to know and understand the target audience. Also, the project leader should find out what information is needed and why. Each group has its own required amount of information; some want detailed information, while others prefer a brief overview. Second, input from others should determine the audience's needs. And finally, project leaders should take into account audience bias. Some audiences immediately support the results, others may oppose them, and still others are neutral. The staff should be empathetic and try to understand the basis for the differing views. Given this understanding, communications can be tailored to each group. This customization is critical when the potential exists for the audience to react negatively to the results.

Target audiences for project results vary in terms of job levels and responsibilities. Determining which groups will receive a particular piece of communication requires careful thought, because problems can arise when a group receives inappropriate information or is overlooked altogether. A sound basis for audience selection is to analyze the reason for the communication, as discussed earlier. Table 11-1 identifies common target audiences and the basis for audience selection. Several audiences stand out as critical.

The project team must receive information about project results. Whether for small projects in which team members receive a project update or for larger projects where a complete team is involved, those who design, develop, facilitate, and implement the project require information on the project's effectiveness. Evaluation data are necessary so adjustments can be made if the project is not as effective as projected.

Step 4: Information Development: The Human Capital Analytics Study

The type of formal evaluation report to be issued depends on the degree of detail. Brief summaries of project results with appropriate charts may be sufficient for some communication efforts. In other situations, particularly those involving major projects requiring extensive funding, a detailed report is crucial. A complete and comprehensive study report is usually necessary. This report can then be used as the basis for more streamlined information aimed at specific audiences and using various media. One possible format for an impact study report for a solution is presented in Table 11-2.

Although an impact study report is an effective, professional way to present ROI data, several cautions are in order. Before this report documents the success of a project involving a large group of employees, credit for success must go completely to participants and their immediate leaders.

TABLE 11-1 Common Target Audiences

Primary Target Audience	Reason for Communication
Client, top executives	To secure approval for the project
Immediate managers, team leaders	To gain support for the project
Participants, team leaders	To secure agreement with the issues
Top executives	To enhance the credibility of the project leader
Immediate managers	To reinforce the processes used in the project
Project team	To drive action for improvement
Team leaders	To prepare participants for the project
Participants	To improve the results and quality of future feedback
Stakeholders	To show the complete results of the project
Client, project team	To underscore the importance of measuring results
Client, project support staff	To explain the techniques used to measure results
Team leaders	To create the desire for a participant to be involved
All employees	To demonstrate accountability for expenditures
Prospective clients	To market future projects

Their performance generated the success. Also, it is important to avoid boasting about results. Grand claims of overwhelming success can quickly turn off an audience and interfere with the delivery of the desired message.

The methodology should be clearly explained, along with the assumptions made in the analysis. The reader should easily see how the values were developed and how specific steps were followed to make the process more conservative, credible, and accurate. Detailed statistical analyses should be placed in an appendix.

TABLE 11-2 Format of a Human Capital Analytics Impact Study

- General information
  - Background
  - Objectives of study
- Methodology for impact study
  - Levels of evaluation
  - ROI process
  - Collecting data
  - Isolating the effects of the project
  - Converting data to monetary values
- Data analysis issues
- Costs
- Results: General information
  - Response profile
  - Success with objectives
- Results: Reaction and perceived value
  - Data sources
  - Data summary
  - Key issues
- Results: Learning and confidence
  - Data sources
  - Data summary
- Results: Application and implementation
  - Data sources
  - Data summary
  - Key issues
- Results: Impact and consequences
  - General comments
  - Linkage with business measures
  - Key issues
  - Results: ROI and its meaning
  - Results: Intangible measures
- Barriers and enablers

- ○ Barriers
- ○ Enablers
- • Conclusions and recommendations
  - ○ Conclusions
  - ○ Recommendations
- • Exhibits

STEP 5: MEDIA SELECTION

Many options are available for the dissemination of project results. In addition to the impact study report, commonly used media are meetings, interim and progress reports, organization publications, and case studies. Table 11-3 lists a variety of options to develop the content and the message.

MEETINGS

If used properly, meetings are fertile ground for the communication of project results. All organizations hold meetings, and some may provide the proper context to convey project results. Along the chain of command, staff meetings are held to review progress, discuss current problems, and distribute information. These meetings can provide an excellent forum for discussing the results achieved in a project that relates to the group's activities. Project results can be sent to executives for use in a staff meeting, or a member of the project team can attend the meeting to make the presentation.

Regular meetings with management groups are a common practice. Typically, discussions focus on items that might be of help to work units. The discussion of a project and its results can be integrated into the regular meeting format. A few organizations have initiated the use of periodic meetings for all key stakeholders, where the project leader reviews progress and discusses next steps. Highlights from interim project results can prove helpful in building interest, commitment, and support for the project.

INTERIM AND PROGRESS REPORTS

A highly visible way to communicate results, although usually limited to large projects, is the use of interim memos and reports. Published or

TABLE 11-3 Options for Communicating Results

	Detailed Reports	Brief Reports	Electronic Reporting	Mass Publications
Meetings				
Executives	Impact study	Executive summary	Website	Announce-ments
Management	Case study (internal)	Slide overview	E-mail	Bulletins
Stakeholders	Case study (external)	One-page summary	Blog	Newsletters
Staff	Major articles	Brochure	Video	Brief articles

disseminated by e-mail on a periodic basis, they are designed to inform management about the status of the project, to communicate interim results of the project, and to spur needed changes and improvements.

A secondary reason for the interim report is to enlist additional support and commitment from the management group and to keep the project intact. This report is produced by the project team and distributed to a select group of stakeholders in the organization. The report may vary considerably in format and scope and may include a schedule of planned steps or activities, a brief summary of reaction evaluations, initial results achieved from the project, and various spotlights recognizing team members or participants. Other topics may also be appropriate. When produced in a professional manner, the interim report can boost management support and commitment.

ROUTINE COMMUNICATION TOOLS

To reach a wide audience, the project leader can use internal, routine publications. Whether a newsletter, magazine, newspaper, or electronic file, these media usually reach all employees or stakeholders. The content can have a significant impact if communicated appropriately. The scope should be limited to general-interest articles, announcements, and interviews.

Results communicated through these types of media must be important enough to arouse general interest. For example, a story with the headline "Safety Project Helps Produce One Million Hours Without a Lost-Time Accident" will catch the attention of readers because it is likely they participated in the project and can appreciate the relevance of the results.

The audience usually must be able to relate to the results in order to take notice.

For many projects, results are not achieved until weeks or even months after the project is complete. Participants need reinforcement from many sources. Communicating results to a general audience may lead to additional pressure to continue the project or introduce similar ones in the future.

Stories about participants involved in a project and the results they have achieved can help create a favorable image. Employees are made aware that the organization is investing time and money to improve performance and prepare for the future. This type of story provides information about a project that employees otherwise may be unfamiliar with, and it sometimes creates a desire in others to participate if given the opportunity.

General-audience communication can bring recognition to project participants, particularly those who excel in some aspect of the project. Public recognition of participants who deliver exceptional performance can enhance their self-esteem and their drive to continue to excel.

E-MAIL AND ELECTRONIC MEDIA

Internal and external Internet pages, companywide intranets, and e-mails are excellent vehicles for releasing results, promoting ideas, and informing employees and other target groups of project results. E-mail, in particular, provides a virtually instantaneous means of communicating results to and soliciting responses from large groups of people. For major projects, some organizations create blogs to present results and elicit reactions, feedback, and suggestions.

PROJECT BROCHURES AND PAMPHLETS

A brochure might be appropriate for a project conducted on a continuing basis or where the audience is large and continuously changing. The brochure should be attractive and present a complete description of the project, with a major section devoted to results obtained with previous participants, if available. Measurable results and reactions from participants, or even direct quotes from individuals, can add spice to an otherwise dull brochure.

CASE STUDIES

Case studies are another effective communication tool. A typical case study describes situational background and the need for a project, presents the techniques and strategies used to develop the study, and highlights key issues in the project.

Step 6: Communicate Results

This step involves executives communicating the information to each audience using the planned media. Two issues need to be addressed here, providing routine feedback and communicating results to senior management.

ROUTINE FEEDBACK ON PROJECT PROGRESS

A primary reason for collecting reaction and learning data is to know whether any adjustments should be made throughout the project. For most projects, data are routinely collected and quickly communicated to a variety of groups. A feedback action plan designed to provide information to several audiences using a variety of media may be an option. These feedback sessions may point out specific needed actions. This process becomes complex and must be managed in a very proactive manner. The following steps are recommended for providing feedback and managing the overall process. Some of the steps and concepts are based on the recommendations of Peter Block in his successful book *Flawless Consulting*:[2]

- **Communicate quickly.** Whether the news is good or bad, it should be passed on to individuals involved in the project as soon as possible. The recommended time for providing feedback is usually a matter of days and certainly no longer than a week or two after the results become known.

- **Simplify the data.** Condense the data into an easily understandable, concise presentation. This situation is not the appropriate place for detailed explanations and analysis.

- **Examine the role of the project team and the client in the feedback process.** The project leader is often the judge, jury, prosecutor, defendant, and/or witness. On the other hand, sometimes the client fills these roles. These respective functions must be examined in terms of reactions to the data and the actions that are called for.

- **Use negative data in a constructive way.** Some of the data will show that things are not going so well, and the fault may rest with the project leader or the client. In this case, the story basically changes from "Let's look at the success we've achieved" to "Now we know which areas to change."

- **Use positive data in a cautious way.** Positive data can be misleading, and if they are communicated too enthusiastically, they may create expectations that exceed what finally materializes. Positive data should be presented in a cautious way almost in a discounting manner.

- **Choose the language of the meeting and the communication carefully.** The language used should be descriptive, focused, specific, short, and simple. Language that is too judgmental, macro, stereotypical, lengthy, or complex should be avoided.

- **Ask the client for reactions to the data.** After all, the client is the number one customer, and it is most important that the client be pleased with the project.

- **Ask the client for recommendations.** The client may have some good suggestions for what needs to be changed to keep a project on track, or to put it back on track should it derail.

- **Use support and confrontation carefully.** These two actions are not mutually exclusive. At times, support and confrontation are both needed for a particular group. The client may need support and yet be confronted for lack of improvement or sponsorship. The project team may be confronted regarding the problem areas that have developed, but may need support as well.

- **React to and act on the data.** The different alternatives and possibilities should be weighed carefully to arrive at the adjustments that will be necessary.

- **Secure agreement from all key stakeholders.** It is essential to ensure that everyone is willing to make any changes that may be necessary.

- **Keep the feedback process short.** Allowing the process to become bogged down in long, drawn-out meetings or lengthy documents is a bad idea. Burdening stakeholders in this way will cause them to avoid the process instead of being willing participants.

Following these steps will help move the project forward and generate useful feedback, often ensuring that adjustments are supported and can be executed.

PRESENTATION OF RESULTS TO SENIOR MANAGEMENT

Perhaps one of the most challenging and stressful types of communication is presenting an impact study to the senior management team, which also serves as the client for a project. The challenge is convincing this highly skeptical and critical group that outstanding results have been achieved (assuming they have) in a reasonable time frame, addressing the salient points, and making sure the managers understand the process. Two potential reactions can create problems. First, if the results are impressive, helping the managers accept the data may be difficult. On the other extreme, if the data are negative, ensuring that managers don't overreact to the results and look for someone to blame is important. Several guidelines can help ensure that this process is planned and executed properly.

Arrange a face-to-face meeting with senior team members to review the results. If they are unfamiliar with the methodology, this meeting is necessary to make sure they understand the process. The good news is that they will probably attend the meeting because they have never seen the type of data developed for this type of project. The bad news is that it takes precious executive time, usually about 30 minutes to one hour, for this presentation. After the meeting with a couple of presentations, an executive summary may suffice. At this point, the senior members will understand the process, so a shortened version may be appropriate. When a particular audience is familiar with the process, a brief version may be developed, including a one- to two-page summary with charts and graphs showing the six types of measures.

The results should not be disseminated before the initial presentation or even during the session, but should be saved until the end of the session, to allow enough time to present the process and collect reactions to it before the target audience sees the results. Present the methodology step by step, showing how the data were collected, when they were collected, who provided them, how the effect of the project was isolated from other influences, and how data were converted to monetary values. The various assumptions, adjustments, and conservative approaches are presented along with the total cost of the project, so that the target audience will begin to buy in to the process of developing the results.

When the results of a solution are actually presented, they are presented one level at a time, starting with Level 1, moving through Level 5, and ending with the intangibles. This format allows the audience to observe the reaction, learning, application and implementation, business impact, and ROI processes. After some discussion of the meaning of the ROI, the intangible measures are presented. Allocate time for each level as appropriate for the audience to help to defuse potential emotional reactions to an extremely positive or negative ROI.

Show the consequences of additional accuracy if accuracy is an issue. The trade-off for more accuracy and validity often is more expense. Address this issue when necessary, agreeing to add more data if they are required. Collect concerns, reactions, and issues involving the process and make adjustments accordingly for the next presentation.

Collectively, these steps will help in the preparation and presentation of one of the most important meetings for the analytics team. Figure 11-1 shows the recommended approach to an important meeting with the sponsor.

STEP 7: REACTIONS TO COMMUNICATION

The best indicator of how effectively the results of a project have been communicated is the level of commitment and support from managers, executives, and sponsors. The allocation of requested resources and voiced commitment from top management are strong evidence of management's positive perception of the results. In addition to this macro-level reaction, a few techniques can also be helpful in measuring the effectiveness of the communication effort.

When results are communicated, target audience reactions can be monitored. These reactions may include nonverbal gestures, oral remarks, written comments, or indirect actions that reveal how the communication was received. Usually, when results are presented in a meeting, the presenter will have some indication of how they were received by the group. Usually, the interest and attitudes of the audience can be quickly evaluated. Comments about the results, formal or informal, should be noted and tabulated.

Project team meetings are an excellent arena for discussing reaction. Comments can come from many sources, depending on the particular target audience. When major project results are communicated, a feedback questionnaire may be administered to the entire audience or a sample of the audience. The questionnaire determines the extent to which the audience understood and/or believed the information presented. Gathering such

FIGURE 11-1   Presenting the Impact Study to Executive Sponsors

Purpose of the Meeting
- Create awareness and under-standing of ROI.
- Build support for the ROI Methodology.
- Communicate results of study.
- Drive improvement from results.
- Cultivate effective use of the ROI Methodology.

Meeting Ground Rules
- Do not distribute the impact study until the end of the meeting.
- Be precise and to the point.
- Avoid jargon and unfamiliar terms.
- Spend less time on the lower levels of evaluation data.
- Present the data with a strategy in mind.

Presentation Sequence
1. Describe the solution and explain why it is being evaluated.
2. Present the methodology process.
3. Present the reaction and learning data.
4. Present the application data.
5. List the barriers to and enablers of success.
6. Address the business impact.
7. Show the costs.
8. Present the ROI.
9. Show the intangibles.
10. Review the credibility of the data.
11. Summarize the conclusions.
12. Present the recommendations.

feedback is practical only when the effectiveness of the communication will have a significant impact on future actions by the project team.

DRIVING IMPROVEMENT

One of the most important reasons for conducting human capital analytics projects and communicating results to different audiences is to drive improvements. With process improvement in mind, Table 11-4 shows typical uses of analytics results as they relate to the different levels of data. Many uses focus on making the solutions better for the future. Others are involved in improving support through reinforcement and commitment for solutions.

Someone or some group must be charged with the responsibility of ensuring that these appropriate actions are taken. Sufficient effort is rarely focused on this area, resulting in a lack of follow-through. Without these changes or improvements, much of the value of the analytics project is lost. For many projects, particularly those of a comprehensive nature, the original project plan for the study includes all the steps throughout the process—communicating results, tracking the improvements that must be made, and making adjustments and changes to the project. Including all the steps ensures appropriate use of data. Communication, tracking, and making adjustments provide the final piece of the puzzle.

TABLE 11-4 Using HCA Data

Use of HCA Results	Appropriate Level of Data				
	1	2	3	4	5
Adjust solution design	✓	✓			
Improve solution delivery	✓	✓			
Influence application and impact			✓	✓	
Reinforcement for application			✓		
Improve management support for project or solution			✓	✓	
Improve stakeholder satisfaction			✓	✓	✓
Recognize and reward participants		✓	✓	✓	
Justify or enhance budget				✓	✓
Develop norms and standards	✓	✓	✓		
Reduce costs		✓	✓	✓	✓
Market projects or solutions	✓		✓	✓	✓
Expand implementation to other areas				✓	✓

FINAL THOUGHTS

Communication of results, the final step in making analytics work, is a crucial step in the overall evaluation process. If this step is executed improperly, the full impact of the results will not be recognized, and the study may amount to a waste of time. This chapter began with general principles and steps for communicating project results that serve as a guide for any significant communication effort. The various target audiences were then discussed, with emphasis on the executive group. A suggested format for a detailed evaluation report was also provided. The chapter presented the most commonly used media for communicating project results, including meetings, client publications, and electronic media. The chapter concluded with a checklist for the use of analytics results. This effort is necessary to drive the improvement.

A final issue regarding human capital analytics is discussed in the next chapter: managing barriers to the analytics practice.

CHAPTER 12

Manage and Sustain the Human Capital Analytics Practice

H uman capital analytics and analytics in general are hot topics. Rarely does one open an HR publication without seeing a reference to it. Broad-topic books on analytics often reference human capital, because it represents the largest expenditure in an organization. Organizations have created an analytics practice with great hopes and expectations. Executives provide funding, support, and interest in the function, expecting the practice to deliver value—enough value to overcome the cost. Otherwise, it becomes a fad, tried and ultimately discarded. To prevent analytics from becoming a mere fad, an organization must integrate the process into the human capital framework. Successful integration requires carefully allocating the appropriate resources, developing capability, delivering results, and using those results to increase interest in and support for the process. This chapter shows what some organizations are doing to build, manage, and sustain the practice to render it a valuable tool.

OPENING STORY

A large telecommunications company (Telcom), like many global technology giants, is concerned about the value of human capital programs.

The company implements hundreds, if not thousands, of HR programs each year, all aimed at attracting the appropriate talent, motivating them to high performance, and retaining them. To evaluate performance in this area, Telcom is measuring the impact and ROI of human capital programs with the ROI Methodology.

This task requires a comprehensive approach to implementation and sustainability that includes allocating appropriate resources and building capability. For example, more than 150 Telcom employees have participated in the ROI Certification™ process to learn how to conduct ROI studies and to build capability internally. Policies, tools, templates, roles, and responsibilities have been developed or updated. Dozens of studies have been conducted and presented to the management team and used to make improvements and drive additional success. A book of case studies is being published to use internally so others can see the power of human capital in the organization. To make this approach a reality, a comprehensive implementation plan was developed to manage and sustain human capital analytics, ensuring that it becomes a continuous, contributing tool.

This story underscores the need to take a planned approach to a comprehensive human capital analytics practice. This process involves addressing many issues to overcome resistance and allocate necessary resources.

THE NEED TO MANAGE AND SUSTAIN THE PRACTICE

Even the best-designed process, model, or technique, or most skilled analytics team is unsuccessful if the program does not achieve effective integration within the organization. Without integration, resistance to human capital analytics often arises. Some of this resistance is based on fear and misunderstanding. Some is real, based on actual barriers and obstacles. Although the analytics model presented in this book is a step-by-step, simple one, it can fail if not integrated properly and fully accepted and supported by those who must make it work. This chapter focuses on some of the most effective means of overcoming resistance to implementation in an organization.

Planning for Success

Some analytics processes, functions, and teams are dysfunctional at this stage. They are busy, sometimes without direction, occasionally without the needed skills, and they are not earning the confidence of the management team. For human capital analytics to work, the team has to be focused and the projects that are selected for analysis must tackle critical issues. The team must complete projects as quickly as possible, with the results positioned for decision making. The results must be presented in a compelling and simplistic way so that executives can clearly understand the process. Ultimately, the highly skilled professional team wins the support, confidence, and respect of the executives. This support and understanding creates more influence and funding. Figure 12-1 contrasts the difference between an analytics practice that will be quickly doomed for failure and one destined for success. The key is to work on the right side of the chart in virtually every category.

Any new process or change meets some resistance, which may be especially great when implementing a program as complex as human capital analytics. To implement the practice and sustain it as an important accountability tool, resistance must be minimized or removed. Successful implementation essentially equates to overcoming resistance. The following three key reasons reveal the importance of developing a detailed plan to overcome resistance.

Resistance Is Always Present

Resistance to change is a constant. It sometimes exists for good reason, but most often it exists for the wrong reasons. The important point is to sort out both kinds of resistance and try to dispel the myths. Resistance can come from inside the team. In some cases, analytics team members resist efforts to make the process more executive friendly. When legitimate barriers are the basis for resistance, minimizing or removing them altogether poses a challenge.

Implementation Is Key

Effective implementation brings success. In other words, the new technique, tool, or process needs to be integrated into the routine framework.

FIGURE 12-1 Human Capital Analytics Practice Success

Unsuccessful Human Capital Analytics Practice	Successful Human Capital Analytics Practice
1. Sparse resources and inadequate funding.	1. Fully funded with ample resources.
2. Skill gaps exist among the team members.	2. Highly skilled team with complementary skill sets.
3. No model or systematic process.	3. Proven approach and process.
4. No clear way for selecting projects for analysis.	4. A systematic way for selecting critical projects for analysis.
5. Disorganized project teams.	5. Great project management skills.
6. Inefficient project teams.	6. Efficient teams with on-time project completion.
7. No consistent way of presenting results to executive team.	7. Great presentations to executives, including live briefings.
8. Projects not always positioned for action.	8. Projects positioned for immediate actions and/or decisions.
9. Few successes.	9. Several major successes each year.
10. Weak and uncertain manager support.	10. Strong support from the management team.
11. Weak and inconsistent executive commitment.	11. Strong and consistent executive commitment.
12. Weak credibility, influence, and respect.	12. Strong credibility, influence, and respect.

Without proper implementation, even the best process will fail. A process that is never removed from the shelf will never be understood, supported, or improved. Providing clear-cut steps for designing a comprehensive implementation will go a long way in overcoming resistance.

CONSISTENCY AND EFFICIENCY ARE NEEDED

With consistency come accuracy, reliability, and accountability. The only way to make sure consistency is achieved is to follow clearly defined processes, procedures, and standards each time an analytics project is undertaken. Cost control and efficiency are significant considerations in any major undertaking, and human capital analytics is no exception. During implementation, tasks must be completed efficiently and effectively. Doing so will help ensure that process costs are kept to a minimum, that time is used economically, and that the process remains affordable.

IMPLEMENTING THE ANALYTICS PRACTICE: OVERCOMING RESISTANCE

Resistance shows up in varied forms: in comments, remarks, actions, or behaviors. Typical comments that indicate open resistance to human capital projects are:

1. It costs too much.

2. It takes too much time.

3. Who is asking for this change?

4. I did not have input on this change.

5. I do not understand this change.

6. What happens when the results are negative?

7. How can we be consistent with this process?

8. The process looks too complicated.

9. Our managers will not support this change.

10. Human capital analytics is too narrowly focused.

11. Human capital analytics is not practical.

Each comment signals an issue that must be resolved or addressed in some way. A few are based on realistic barriers, whereas others are based on myths that must be dispelled. Sometimes resistance reflects underlying concerns. For example, the individuals involved may fear losing control of their processes, and others may feel vulnerable to whatever action may follow if the new process fails. Still others may feel concerned about any change.

Heavy persuasion and evidence of tangible benefits may be needed to convince project team members that it is in their best interest to make the project succeed. Although most clients do want to see project results, they may have concerns about the information they are asked to provide and about whether their personal performance is being judged while the project is undergoing evaluation. Participants may express the same fears listed on page 277.

Addressing this resistance results in a systematic implementation of the methodology. It must become normal business behavior and a routine and standard process built into projects. Figure 12-2 shows actions outlined in this chapter presented as building blocks to overcoming resistance. The remainder of this chapter presents specific strategies and techniques devoted to each of the nine building blocks identified in the figure. These actions apply equally to the human capital analytics project team, the HR team that provides support, and the client organization that is actively involved. No attempt is made to separate them in this presentation.

ASSESSING THE CLIMATE

As a first step toward implementation, some organizations assess the current climate for achieving results. One approach to this assessment is to develop a survey to determine current perspectives of the management team and other stakeholders (for an example, go to www.roiinstitute.net). Another way is to conduct interviews with key stakeholders to determine their willingness to follow through with analytics projects. With an awareness of the current status, project leaders can plan for significant changes and pinpoint particular issues that need support before and during implementation.

FIGURE 12-2 Building Blocks to Overcome Resistance

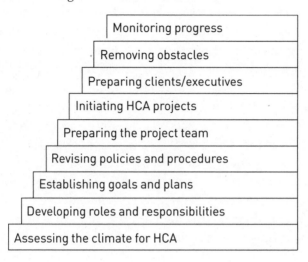

| Monitoring progress |
| Removing obstacles |
| Preparing clients/executives |
| Initiating HCA projects |
| Preparing the project team |
| Revising policies and procedures |
| Establishing goals and plans |
| Developing roles and responsibilities |
| Assessing the climate for HCA |

DEFINING ROLES AND RESPONSIBILITIES

Defining specific roles and responsibilities for different groups and individuals addresses many of the resistance factors and helps pave a smooth path for implementation. Then as an early step in the process, one or more individual(s) should be designated as the internal leader or champion for human capital analytics. As in most change efforts, someone must take responsibility for successful implementation. This leader serves as a champion for human capital analytics and is usually the one who understands the process best and sees vast potential for its contribution. More important, this leader is willing to teach others and will work to sustain sponsorships.

Developing the Analytics Leader

The analytics leader is usually a member of the project team who holds a full-time position in larger project teams or a part-time position in smaller organizations. Client organizations may also have an analytics leader from the client's perspective. The typical job title for a full-time leader is manager/director of human capital analytics. Some organizations assign this responsibility to a team and empower it to lead the effort.

In preparation for this assignment, leaders usually receive special training that builds specific skills and knowledge. The role of the implementation leader is quite broad and serves a variety of specialized duties. In some organizations, that person can take on many roles, ranging from problem solver to communicator to cheerleader. Leading the process is difficult and challenging and requires unique skills. Fortunately, programs exist that teach these skills. For example, one program certifies future analytics project leaders. (For more detail on certification, see www.roiinstitute.net.) This certification is built around specific skill sets linked to successful human capital analytics implementation. It focuses on the critical areas of data collection, causation and attribution, converting data to monetary values, presenting results, and building capability, among others. This process is quite comprehensive but may be necessary to build the skills for taking on this challenging assignment.

ESTABLISHING A TASK FORCE

Making analytics work well may require a task force, usually comprised of a group of individuals from different parts of the project or client team who are willing to develop the human capital analytics practice in the organization. Participation on the task force may be voluntary or mandatory, depending on specific job responsibilities. The task force should represent the cross-section necessary for accomplishing stated goals. Task forces have the additional advantage of bringing more people into the effort and developing more ownership of and support for human capital practices. The task force must be large enough to cover the key areas but not so large that it becomes too cumbersome to function. Six to twelve members is a good size.

ASSIGNING RESPONSIBILITIES

Confusion can arise when individuals are unclear about their assignments within a program. Responsibilities apply to two areas. The first is the responsibility of the entire team for project analysis. Everyone involved must share responsibility for analysis. These responsibilities include providing input on designing instruments, planning specific analytics projects, analyzing data, and interpreting results. Typical responsibilities include the following:

- Ensuring that the initial analysis for the project includes specific business impact measures
- Developing specific objectives for the project
- Keeping participants focused on project objectives
- Communicating rationale and reasons for human capital programs
- Assisting in follow-up activities to capture data
- Providing assistance for data collection, data analysis, and reporting

Although involving each member of the project team in all these activities may not be appropriate, each individual should have at least one responsibility as part of his or her routine job duties. This assignment of responsibility keeps the analytics practice from being disjointed and separated. More important, it brings accountability to those directly involved in project implementation.

Technical support is another issue. Depending on the size of the project team, establishing an individual or a group of technical experts to provide assistance may be helpful. When the group is established, the project team must understand that the experts have been assigned, not for the purpose of relieving the team of its evaluation responsibilities, but to supplement its efforts with technical expertise. These technical experts typically have participated in the certification and training process to build special skills. They may be from IT, where they have access to databases and big data capability. Responsibilities of the technical support group involve six key areas:

1. Designing data collection instruments
2. Providing assistance for developing a human capital analytics strategy
3. Analyzing data, including specialized statistical analyses
4. Interpreting results and making specific recommendations

5. Developing reports to communicate overall results

6. Providing technical support in all phases of analytics projects

The assignment of responsibilities requires attention throughout the analytics process. Although the project team must be assigned specific responsibilities, requiring others to serve in support functions to help with data collection is not unusual. These responsibilities are defined when a particular strategy is developed and approved.

ESTABLISHING GOALS AND PLANS

Establishing goals, targets, and objectives is critical to implementation of any project or program, particularly when several projects are planned. The establishment of goals can include detailed planning documents for the overall process and for individual human capital analytics projects. The next sections discuss establishment of goals and plans.

SELECTING GOALS FOR PROJECTS

Establishing specific projects (or procedures to select projects) is necessary to make progress with analytics. As emphasized throughout this book, not every project should be undertaken. Knowing in advance which project will be pursued helps in planning which measures will be needed and how detailed the project must be at each level of data. The procedure to select projects should be completed early in the process with the full support of the entire project team. If practical and feasible, the targets for the number of projects should also have the approval of key managers, particularly the senior management team.

DEVELOPING A PLAN FOR IMPLEMENTATION

An important part of implementation is establishing a timetable for complete implementation of the analytics project. This document becomes a master plan for completion of the different elements presented earlier. Beginning with forming a team and concluding with delivering completed projects, this schedule is a project plan for transitioning from the present situation to the desired future situation. Items on the schedule include developing specific projects, building staff skills, developing policy, and teaching managers the process. Figure 12-3 shows an example of an

FIGURE 12-3 Implementation Plan for a Large Organization with Many Projects

	J	F	M	A	M	J	J	A	S	O	N	D	J	F	M	A	M	J	J	A
Human capital analytics team formed	▓																			
Responsibilities defined		▓																		
Analytics policy developed			▓	▓																
Goals for projects		▓																		
Staff development					▓		▓													
HCA Project (A)						▓	▓	▓	▓											
HCA Project (B)									▓	▓	▓	▓	▓							
HCA Project (C)											▓	▓	▓	▓	▓					
HCA Project (D)								▓	▓	▓	▓	▓	▓	▓	▓	▓	▓	▓	▓	▓
Support teams trained								▓	▓	▓										
Managers trained on human capital analytics																▓	▓	▓	▓	▓
Support tools developed					▓	▓												▓	▓	
Guidelines developed						▓														

283

implementation plan. The more detailed the document, the more useful it becomes. The project plan is a living, long-range document that should be reviewed frequently and adjusted as necessary. More important, those engaged in human capital analytics practice should always be familiar with the implementation plan.

REVISING POLICIES AND GUIDELINES

Planning includes revising or developing the organization's policy on human capital analytics projects. The policy statement contains information developed specifically for the process. It is developed with input from the project team and key managers or stakeholders. Sometimes policy issues are addressed during internal workshops designed to build analytics skills. The policy statement addresses critical matters that will influence effectiveness. These issues may include adopting the framework presented in this book, requiring objectives at all levels for some or all projects, and defining responsibilities for the project team. Policy statements provide guidance and direction for the staff and others who work closely with human capital analytics.

Policy statements also provide an opportunity to communicate basic requirements and fundamentals of performance and accountability. More than anything else, they serve as learning tools to teach others, especially when they are developed in a collaborative way. If policy statements are created in isolation, staff and management will be denied a sense of ownership, making the statements neither effective nor useful.

Analytics guidelines are important for showing how to use the tools and techniques, guide the design process, provide consistency in the process, ensure that appropriate methods are used, and place the proper emphasis on each of the areas. The guidelines are more technical than policy statements and often include detailed procedures showing how the process is undertaken and developed. They often include specific forms, instruments, and tools necessary to facilitate the process.

PREPARING THE PROJECT TEAM

Project team members may resist the formal structure of an analytics practice. They may see evaluation as an unnecessary intrusion into their responsibilities that absorbs precious time and stifles creative freedom. Several issues must be addressed when preparing the project team for analytics implementation.

INVOLVING THE PROJECT TEAM

The project team should play a part in each key issue or major decision involving implementation. As policy statements are prepared and guidelines developed, team input is essential. Meetings, brainstorming sessions, and task forces involve the team in every phase of developing the framework and supporting documents for human capital analytics.

USING ANALYTICS AS A LEARNING AND IMPROVEMENT TOOL

One reason the project team may resist the analytics process is that projects' effectiveness will be fully exposed, putting the reputation of the team on the line. They may have a fear of failure. To overcome this source of resistance, the human capital analytics practice should be clearly positioned as a tool for learning, not a tool for evaluating project team performance (at least not during the early years of project implementation). Team members will not be interested in developing a process that may reflect unfavorably on their performance.

Team members can learn as much from failures as from successes. If the project is not working, it is best to find out quickly. If a project is ineffective and not producing the desired results, the failure will eventually be known to clients and the management group (if they are not aware of it already). A lack of results will make managers less supportive of immediate and future projects. If the projects' weaknesses are identified and adjustments are quickly made, not only can more effective projects be developed, but the credibility of and respect for project implementation will be enhanced.

TEACHING THE TEAM

The analytics project team and project leader may not have the skills and will need to develop expertise. Human capital analytics is not always a formal part of the team's job. Consequently, the project team leader must learn about analytics and its systematic steps, and the team member must learn to develop specific plans, to collect and analyze data from the evaluation, and to interpret results from data analysis. A one- to two-day workshop can help build the skills and knowledge needed to understand the process and appreciate what it can do for project success and for the client organization. A teach-the-team workshop can serve as a valuable tool in ensuring successful implementation of projects.

INITIATING HUMAN CAPITAL ANALYTICS PROJECTS

The first tangible evidence of the value of using human capital analytics may be seen at the initiation of the first project. The next sections discuss identification of appropriate projects and keeping them on track.

SELECTING THE INITIAL PROJECT

Appropriate projects must be selected for analysis. Only certain types of projects qualify for comprehensive, detailed analysis. Characteristics of projects suitable for analysis are those that (1) involve large groups of participants; (2) are expected to have a long life cycle; (3) will be linked to major operational problems and opportunities upon completion; (4) are important to strategic objectives; (5) are expensive; (6) are time-consuming; (7) have high visibility; and (8) have the interest of management in performing the analytics. Using these or similar criteria, the project leader must select the appropriate projects. Ideally, sponsors should agree with or approve the criteria.

REPORTING PROGRESS

As the projects are developed and implementation gets under way, status meetings should be conducted to report progress and discuss critical issues with appropriate team members. These meetings focus the project team on critical issues, generate the best ideas for addressing problems and barriers, and build a knowledge base for better implementation of future projects. Sometimes an external consultant facilitates these meetings, perhaps an expert in the analytics process. In other cases, the project leader may facilitate. In essence, the meetings serve three major purposes: reporting progress, learning, and planning.

ESTABLISHING DISCUSSION GROUPS

Because human capital analytics can be considered difficult to understand and apply, it might be wise to establish discussion groups to teach the process. These groups can supplement formal workshops and other learning activities and are often flexible in format. An analytics consultant or the project leader usually facilitates these groups. Each session addresses a new topic and includes thorough discussion about how that topic affects the organization. The process can be adjusted for different topics as new group needs arise. Ideally, group discussion participants have an opportunity to apply, explore, or research the topics between sessions. Group assignments, such as reviewing a case study or reading an article, are appropriate between sessions to further the development of knowledge and skills associated with the process.

PREPARING CLIENTS AND THE MANAGEMENT TEAM

Perhaps no group is more important to the use of human capital analytics than the management team that must allocate resources for the project and support its implementation. In addition, the management team often provides input to and assistance for the project. Preparing, training, and developing the management team should be carefully planned and executed.

One effective approach for preparing executives and managers is to conduct a briefing on ROI. Ranging from one hour to half a day, a practical briefing can provide critical information and enhance support for use of human capital analytics. Managers leave these briefings with greater appreciation for the practice and the potential impact of projects, and with a clearer understanding of their roles in them. More important, they often renew their commitment to react to and use the data collected by the analytics team.

A strong, dynamic relationship between the project team and key managers is essential for successful implementation. A productive partnership is needed that requires each party to understand the concerns, problems, and opportunities of the other. The development of such a beneficial relationship is a long-term process that must be thoughtfully planned and initiated by key project team members. The decision to commit resources and support to a project may be based on the effectiveness of this relationship.

REMOVING OBSTACLES

Obstacles will always exist in human capital projects. The obstacles are based on concerns discussed in this chapter, some of which may be valid, others of which may be based on unrealistic fears or misunderstandings.

Dispelling Myths

As part of the implementation, attempts should be made to dispel the myths and remove or minimize barriers or obstacles. Much of the controversy regarding human capital analytics stems from misunderstandings and fears about what the process can and cannot do and how it can or should be implemented in an organization. The following examples demonstrate the extent of the myths that often surround human capital analytics:

- It is too complex for most users.
- It is expensive and consumes too many critical resources.
- If senior management does not require it, there is no need to pursue it.
- It is a passing fad.
- It generates only one type of data.
- It is not future-oriented; it only reflects past performance.
- It is rarely used by organizations.
- HCA cannot be easily replicated.
- It is not a credible process; it is too subjective.
- It cannot be used with soft projects.
- Isolating the influence of other factors is not always possible.
- It is appropriate only for large organizations.
- No standards exist for the human capital analytics.

For more information on these myths, see www.roiinstitute.net.

Delivering Bad News

One of the obstacles perhaps most difficult to overcome is receiving inadequate, insufficient, or disappointing news. Addressing a bad-news situation challenges most project leaders and other stakeholders involved in a project. Table 12-1 presents guidelines to follow when addressing bad news. As the table makes clear, the time to think about bad news is early in the process, but without ever losing sight of the value of the bad news. In essence, bad

TABLE 12-1 How to Address Bad News

When Delivering Bad News:

- Never fail to recognize the power to learn from and improve with a negative study.
- Look for red flags along the way.
- Lower outcome expectations with key stakeholders along the way.
- Look for data everywhere.
- Never alter the standards.
- Remain objective throughout the process.
- Prepare the team for the bad news.
- Consider different scenarios.
- Find out what went wrong.
- Adjust the story line to "Now we have data that show how to make this solution more successful." In an odd way, it puts a positive spin on data that are less than positive.
- Drive improvement.

news means that things can change and need to change, and that the situation can improve. The team and others need to be convinced that good news can be found in a bad-news situation.

USING THE DATA

Too often projects are evaluated and significant data are collected, but nothing is done with the data. Failure to use data is a tremendous obstacle, because once the project has concluded, the team has a tendency to move on to the next project, issue, or other priorities. Data must be used; after all, they were essentially the justification for undertaking the project evaluation in the first place. Failure to use the data may mean that the entire evaluation was a waste.

MONITORING PROGRESS

A final element of the implementation process is monitoring the overall progress made and communicating that progress. Although often overlooked, an effective progress report can help keep the implementation on target and can let others know what human capital analytics is accomplishing for project leaders and the client.

The initial schedule for implementation is based on key events or milestones. Routine progress reports should communicate the status of these events or milestones. Reports are usually developed at six-month intervals but may be more frequent for short-term projects. Two target audiences—the project team and senior managers—must receive progress reports. All project team members should be kept informed of progress, and senior managers should know the extent to which the analytics project is being implemented and how it is working within the organization.

FINAL THOUGHTS

Even the best model or process will die if it is not used and sustained. This chapter explored the implementation of the human capital analytics process and ways to sustain its use. If not approached in a systematic, logical way, the process will not be an integral part of the human capital practice, and project accountability will consequently suffer. This chapter presented the different elements that must be considered and issues that must be addressed to ensure that implementation is smooth and uneventful. Smooth implementation is the most effective means of overcoming resistance to analytics. The result is a complete integration of analytics as a mainstream component of major human capital programs.

Notes

Preface

1. Mundy, J. C. "Why HR Still Isn't a Strategic Partner." *Harvard Business Review* (July 5, 2012).

Chapter 1

1. Springer, C. H., Herlihy, R. E., and Beggs, R. I. *Basic Mathematics: Volume One of the Mathematics for Management Series*. Homewood, IL: Richard D. Irwin, Inc., 1965; Springer, C. H., Herlihy, R. E., and Beggs, R. I. *Advanced Methods and Models: Volume Two of the Mathematics for Management Series*. Homewood, IL: Richard D. Irwin, Inc., 1965; Springer, C. H., Herlihy, R. E., Mall, R. T., and Beggs, R. I. *Statistical Inference: Volume Three of the Mathematics for Management Series*. Homewood, IL: Richard D. Irwin, Inc. 1966; Springer, C. H., Herlihy, R. E., and Beggs, R. I. *Probabilistic Models: Volume Four of the Mathematics for Management Series*. Homewood, IL: Richard D. Irwin, Inc., 1968.
2. Merrihue, W. V., and Katzell, R. A. "ERI—Yardstick of Employee Relations," *Harvard Business Review, 33,* no. 6 (1955), pp. 91–99.
3. Mitchell, C., Ray, R. L., and van Ark, B. "The Conference Board CEO Challenge 2013." www.conference-Board.org/publications.
4. IBM. "Leading Through Connections: Insights from the Global Chief Executive Officer Study." http://www-935.ibm.com/services/us/en/c-suite/ceostudy2012/. Accessed May 2012.
5. Tracey, W. R. *The Human Resources Glossary*, 3rd ed. Boca Raton, FL: St. Lucie Press, 2004.

6. Stewart, T. A., "Taking on the Last Bureaucracy," *Fortune* (January 15, 1996).

7. Durfee, D. *Human Capital Management: The CFO's Perspective.* Boston: CFO Publishing Corp., 2013.

8. Ray, R. L., Mitchell, C., Abel, A. L., and Phillips, P. The State of Human Capital 2012: "False Summit: Why the Human Capital Function Still Has Far to Go." McKinsey & Company and The Conference Board Research Report Number: R-1501-12.RR. 2012.

9. Fitz-enz, J. *The New HR Analytics: Predicting the Economic Value of Your Company's Human Capital Investments.* New York: AMACOM, 2012.

10. Price, T., Nalbantian, H., Levine, B., and Chen, L. "Making the Case for Scaled Management of Human Capital: Valuing Workforce Strategies in Building Services. Human Capital Analytics @ Work Volume 1." The Conference Board. 2014.

11. Davenport, T. H., Harris, J. G., and Morison, R. *Analytics at Work: Smarter Decisions, Better Results.* Boston: Harvard Business School Publishing, 2010.

12. Rucci, A. J., Kirn, S. P., and Quinn, R. T. "The Employee-Customer Profit Chain at Sears." *Harvard Business Review* (January–February 1998), pp. 82–97.

CHAPTER 3

1. A copy of the study, which was published in two journals, is available from the ROI Institute.

2. Phillips, J. J. and P. P., and Smith, K. *Accountability in Human Resource Management*, 2nd ed. Oxfordshire, UK: Routledge, 2015.

CHAPTER 4

1. Phillips, P. P. and Phillips, J. J. *10 Steps to Successful Business Alignment.* Alexandria, VA: ASTD Press, 2012.

CHAPTER 5

1. Phillips, P. P., Phillips, J. J., and Edwards, L. A. *Measuring the Success of Coaching: A Step-by-Step Guide for Measuring Impact and ROI.* Alexandria, VA: ASTD Press, 2012.

CHAPTER 6

1. Rucci, A. J., Kirn, S. P., and Quinn, R. T. "The Employee-Customer Profit Chain at Sears." *Harvard Business Review* (January–February 1998), pp. 82–97.
2. Fowler, F. J. *Survey Research Methods*, 5th ed. Thousand Oaks, CA: Sage Publications, 2013.
3. Litwin, M. S. "How to Measure Survey Reliability and Validity." In Fink, A. *The Survey Kit.* Thousand Oaks, CA: Sage Publications, 1995.
4. Phillips, J. J., Phillips, P. P., and Aaron, B. *Survey Basics: A Complete How-To Guide to Help You.* Alexandria, VA: ASTD Press, 2013.

CHAPTER 7

1. Phillips, J. J. and Edward, L. *Managing Employee Retention.* San Francisco: John Wiley & Sons, Inc., 2009.
2. Anderson, D. R., and Associates. *Statistics for Business and Economics,* 12th ed. Mason, OH: South-Western Publishing, 2013.
3. Miller, T. *Modeling Techniques in Predictive Analytics, Business Problems and Solutions with R.* Upper Saddle River, NJ: Pearson Education, 2014.
4. Pardoe, I. *Applied Regression Modeling,* 2nd ed. Hoboken, NJ: John Wiley & Sons, Inc., 2012.
5. Gelman, A. and Hill, J. *Data Analysis Using Regression and Multilevel/Hierarchical Models.* Cambridge, UK: Cambridge University Press, 2006.
6. Cukier, K. and Schonberger-Mayer, V. *Big Data: A Revolution That Will Transform How We Live, Work, and Think.* New York: Houghton Mifflin Harcourt, 2013.
7. Davenport, T. H. and Kim, J. *Keeping Up with the Quants: Your Guide to Understanding and Using Analytics.* Boston: Harvard Business Review Press, 2013.
8. Surowiecki, J. *The Wisdom of Crowds.* New York: Random House, 2005.

CHAPTER 8

1. For more detail, see Phillips, J. J., Myhill, M. and McDonough, J. *Proving the Value of Meetings and Events* (Birmingham, AL: Meetings Professionals International and The ROI Institute, Inc., 2007).

CHAPTER 9

1. Phillips, J. J. and Phillips, P. P. *Proving the Value of HR: How and Why to Measure ROI,* 2nd ed. Alexandria, VA: SHRM, 2012.
2. U.S. Chamber of Commerce.

CHAPTER 10

1. Phillips, J. J. and Phillips, P. P. *The Consultant's Guide to Results-Driven Business Proposals: How to Write Proposals That Forecast Impact and ROI.* New York: McGraw-Hill, 2010.
2. Phillips, J. J. and Phillips, P. P. *Show Me the Money.* San Francisco: Berrett-Koehler, 2007.

CHAPTER 11

1. Davenport, T. and Siegel, E. *Predictive Analytics: The Power to Predict Who Will Click, Buy, Lie, or Die.* Hoboken, NJ: John Wiley & Sons, Inc., 2013.
2. Block, P. *Flawless Consulting: A Guide to Getting Your Expertise Used.* San Francisco: Pfeiffer, 2011.

Index

About the Authors

Dr. Patti P. Phillips is president and CEO of the ROI Institute, Inc., the leading source of ROI competency building, implementation support, networking, and research. A renowned expert in measurement and evaluation, she helps organizations implement the ROI Methodology in 60 countries around the world. Her work has been featured on CNBC, EuroNews, and in over a dozen business journals.

Phillips serves as principal research fellow for The Conference Board where she coauthored the research reports *Human Capital Analytics @ Work*, vol. 1 (2014) and *Human Capital Analytics: A Primer* (2012). She serves as program director for the Human Capital Analytics Annual Conference and the Human Capital Analytics Council.

Phillips teaches others to implement the ROI Methodology through the ROI Certification process, as a facilitator for ATD's Measuring ROI and Measuring Learning Impact workshops and as professor of practice for The University of Southern Mississippi Gulf Coast Campus PhD in Human Capital Development program. She also serves as adjunct faculty for the UN System Staff College in Turin, Italy, where she teaches the ROI Methodology through their Evaluation and Impact Assessment Workshop and Measurement for Results-Based Management. She serves on numerous doctoral dissertation committees, assisting students as they develop their own research on measurement, evaluation, and ROI.

Phillips's academic accomplishments include a PhD in International Development and a master's degree in Public and Private Management. She is a certified in ROI evaluation and has been awarded the designations of Certified Professional in Learning and Performance and Certified Performance Technologist.

She, along with her husband, Jack Phillips, contributes to a variety of journals and has authored a number of books on the subject of accountability and ROI, including: *Measuring ROI in Environment, Health and Safety* (Wiley, 2014), *Measuring the Success of Organization Development* (ASTD, 2013); *Survey Basics* (ASTD, 2013); *Measuring the Success of Sales Training* (ASTD, 2013); *Measuring ROI in Healthcare* (McGraw-Hill, 2012); *10 Steps to Successful Business Alignment* (ASTD, 2012); *Measuring the Success of Coaching* (ASTD, 2012); *The Bottomline on ROI*, 2nd ed. (HRDQ, 2012); *Measuring Leadership Development: Quantify your Program's Impact and ROI on Organizational Performance* (McGraw-Hill, 2012); *Measuring ROI in Learning and Development: Case Studies from Global Organizations* (ASTD, 2011); *The Green Scorecard: Measuring the ROI in Sustainability Initiatives* (Nicholas Brealey, 2011); *Return on Investment in Meetings and Events: Tools and Techniques to Measure the Success of All Types of Meetings and Events* (Elsevier, 2008); *Show Me the Money: How to Determine ROI in People, Projects, and Programs* (Berrett-Koehler, 2007); *The Value of Learning* (Pfeiffer, 2007); *Return on Investment Basics* (ASTD, 2005); *Proving the Value of HR: How and Why to Measure ROI* (SHRM, 2005); *Make Training Evaluation Work* (ASTD, 2004); *The Bottomline on ROI* (Center for Effective Performance, 2002), which won the 2003 ISPI Award of Excellence; *ROI at Work* (ASTD, 2005); the ASTD In Action casebooks: *Measuring ROI in the Public Sector* (2002), *Retaining Your Best Employees* (2002), and *Measuring Return on Investment*, vol. III (2001); the ASTD Infoline series, including *Planning and Using Evaluation Data* (2003), *Managing Evaluation Shortcuts* (2001), and *Mastering ROI* (1998); and *The Human Resources Scorecard: Measuring Return on Investment* (Butterworth-Heinemann, 2001). Patti Phillips can be reached at patti@roiinstitute.net.

Dr. Jack J. Phillips is a world-renowned expert on accountability, measurement, and evaluation. Phillips provides consulting services for Fortune 500 companies and major global organizations. The author or editor of more than fifty books, he conducts workshops and presents at conferences throughout the world.

Phillips has received several awards for his books and work. On three occasions, *Meeting News* named him one of the 25 Most Powerful People in the Meetings and Events Industry, based on his work on ROI. The Society for Human Resource Management presented him an award for one of his books and honored a Phillips ROI study with its highest award for creativity. The American Society for Training and Development gave him its highest award, Distinguished Contribution to Workplace Learning and Development, for his work on ROI. His work has been featured in the *Wall Street Journal, BusinessWeek,* and *Fortune* magazine. His interviews have been on several networks, including CNN. Phillips serves as president of the International Society for Performance Improvement.

His expertise in measurement and evaluation is based on more than 27 years of corporate experience in the aerospace, textile, metals, construction materials, and banking industries. Phillips has served as training and development manager at two Fortune 500 firms, as senior human resource officer at two firms, as president of a regional bank, and as management professor at a major state university.

This background led Phillips to develop the ROI Methodology—a revolutionary process that provides bottom-line figures and accountability for all types of learning, performance improvement, human resource, technology, and public policy programs.

Phillips regularly consults with clients in manufacturing, service, and government organizations in over 60 countries in North and South America, Europe, Africa, Australia, and Asia.

Phillips and his wife, Dr. Patti P. Phillips, have recently published books such as *Measuring ROI in Environment, Health, and Safety* (Wiley, 2014); *Measuring the Success of Organization Development* (ASTD, 2013); *Survey Basics* (ASTD, 2013); *Measuring the Success of Sales Training* (ASTD, 2013); *Measuring ROI in Healthcare* (McGraw-Hill, 2012); *Measuring the Success of Coaching* (ASTD, 2012); *Measuring Leadership Development: Quantify your Program's Impact and ROI on Organizational Performance* (McGraw-Hill, 2012); *10 Steps to Successful Business Alignment* (ASTD, 2011); *The Green Scorecard: Measuring the Return on Investment in Sustainability Initiatives* (Nicholas Brealey, 2011); and *Project Management ROI* (John Wiley, 2011). They also served as authors and series editors for the *Measurement and Evaluation Series* published by Pfeiffer (2008), which includes a six-book series on the ROI Methodology and a companion book of 14 best-practice case studies. Other books authored by Phillips include *ROI for Technology Projects: Measuring and Delivering Value* (Butterworth-Heinemann, 2008); *Return on Investment in Meetings and Events: Tools and Techniques to Measure the Success of all Types of Meetings and Events* (Butterworth-Heinemann, 2008); *Show Me the Money: How to Determine ROI in People,*

Projects, and Programs (Berrett-Koehler, 2007); *The Value of Learning* (Pfeiffer, 2007); *How to Build a Successful Consulting Practice* (McGraw-Hill, 2006); *Investing in Your Company's Human Capital: Strategies to Avoid Spending Too Much or Too Little* (Amacom, 2005); *Proving the Value of HR: How and Why to Measure ROI* (SHRM, 2005); *The Leadership Scorecard* (Elsevier Butterworth-Heinemann, 2004); *Managing Employee Retention* (Elsevier Butterworth-Heinemann, 2003); *Return on Investment in Training and Performance Improvement Programs*, 2nd ed. (Elsevier Butterworth-Heinemann, 2003); *The Project Management Scorecard*, (Elsevier Butterworth-Heinemann, 2002); *How to Measure Training Results* (McGraw-Hill, 2002); *The Human Resources Scorecard: Measuring the Return on Investment* (Elsevier Butterworth-Heinemann, 2001); *The Consultant's Scorecard* (McGraw-Hill, 2000); and *Performance Analysis and Consulting* (ASTD, 2000). Phillips served as series editor for ASTD's In Action casebook series, an ambitious publishing project featuring 30 titles. He currently serves as series editor for Elsevier Butterworth-Heinemann's Improving Human Performance series.

Phillips has undergraduate degrees in electrical engineering, physics, and mathematics; a master's degree in Decision Sciences from Georgia State University; and a PhD in Human Resource Management from the University of Alabama. He has served on the boards of several private businesses—including two NASDAQ companies—and several nonprofits and associations, including the American Society for Training and Development and the National Management Association. He is chairman of the ROI Institute, Inc., and can be reached at (205) 678-8101, or by e-mail at jack@roiinstitute.net.